4/2000

Farther Along

Farther Along

A Civil Rights Memoir

Marvin Caplan

Louisiana State University Press

Baton Rouge

Designer: Amanda McDonald Scallan
Typeface: Granjon
Typesetter: Coghill Composition
Printer: Edward Brothers, Inc.

Caplan, Marvin Harold, 1919–
    Farther along : a civil rights memoir / Marvin Caplan.
        p. cm.
    Includes index.
    ISBN 0-8071-2352-8 (cloth : alk. paper)
    1. Caplan, Marvin Harold, 1919– . 2. Civil rights workers—
United States—Biography. 3. Civil rights movements—United
States—History—20th century. 4. Afro-Americans—Civil rights—
History—20th century. 5. Washington (D.C.)—Race relations.
6. Civil rights movements—Washington (D.C.)—History—20th century.
I. Title.
E185.98.C37A3 1999
323'.092—dc21
    [b]   98-50883
                                                             CIP

Portions of Chapters 8 and 9 are adapted from articles published in Washington History Magazine of the Historical Society of Washington D. C., volumes 1-1 and 6-1 and are reprinted by permission of the editor. The essay "The Last White Family on the Block' in Chapter 10 was first published in the Atlantic Monthly (July, 1960). A portion of Chapter 17 is reprinted with permission form Congress Bi-Weekly, volume 40, no 2. Copyright © 1973 American Jewish Congress.

Library of Congress Cataloging-in-Publication Data

To
   Arnold Aronson (1912–1998),
   Friend and Mentor of Blessed Memory

   Naomi, Freya, Annique, and Ben,
   In Abiding Love

   and

   Estelle,
   With Whom a New Chapter Has Begun

Farther along, we'll know more about it.
Farther along, we'll understand why.
Cheer up my brother! Live in the sunshine.
We'll understand it all, by and by.

—old song sung in the black churches of Virginia

Contents

Illustrations

Prefatory Note

In the course of my experience in the American civil rights movement—roughly from 1946 till today—I have been aware of the changes in the way we have come to designate dark-complexioned Americans of African descent. I believe "colored" is the oldest designation. After that, "Negro," then "black," and most recently, "African American." In this book I use all of the terms interchangeably, not chronologically. I choose not to suggest any qualitative difference among them.

Farther Along

Prologue

July 1996

*T*HE young African American woman who sat across the table from me in my sunny breakfast room that summer afternoon was the exemplar, it seemed to me, of the gains and aspirations of the civil rights movement as I had known it for five decades.

Born in 1974, in a backwater southern town, she attended public schools that had been desegregated only recently and graduated senior high first in her class and valedictorian. As an undergraduate at Howard University, she made her own commitment to an inclusive society: she helped organize a group of black and Jewish students that sought to confront racial and religious stereotyping, and she traveled with her fellows to South Africa and Israel. A Phi Beta Kappa in her senior year, she was chosen to be a full-time intern at the Leadership Conference on Civil Rights (LCCR), the coalition of 180 national organizations that, since 1950, has led the battles for the enactment and enforcement of federal civil rights legislation. And now, at twenty-two, she had just won a full scholarship to a prestigious southern university law school, a school that only about two generations ago would have refused to admit her because she was black.

For the moment these accomplishments didn't seem to matter. Her sweet brown face, framed in a tapestry of fine black braids, grew sad as we talked. Her major assignment, as an intern, was to write a comprehensive legislative history of the Leadership Conference. So she had come out to the house to interview me, since I had directed the Washington office for eighteen years. Over a pitcher of lemonade, our conversation grew more animated and informal.

But after listening to my account of how far we had come, she was moved, at last, to sigh and offer her own assessment.

"I'm discouraged," she said. "I feel we're slipping back."

Back? I wondered. How far back? Back to a time when her native state had laws imposing racial segregation on everything, from schools to streetcars?

"No. Not legal segregation," she said, with a wan smile. "*Self*-segregation. We don't come together anymore. We don't coalesce." She sensed a new discord. Intolerance was becoming more bold and outspoken. People seemed ready to utter the most dreadful racial epithets. "Chink" was the worst she could bring herself to say by way of example. The mid-century civil rights victories I spoke of so proudly were unraveling. Affirmative action, for instance, was under attack.

She and another LCCR intern, a young white man, had been invited, recently, to discuss affirmative action with a class of undergraduates, all white, at a local university. The two of them were stunned by the hostility they provoked. Affirmative action, the students told them, was "just a handout for the blacks." Black students should be compelled to compete, like everyone else. And look, my young friend went on, at what was happening to welfare. With the slow disintegration of the public welfare system, millions of blacks and other minorities were faced with the specter of hunger and homelessness.

Well? What words of wisdom and consolation did I have for her? I could not try to address her qualms and disappointments directly. Instead, from my vantage point, three and half times her age, I tried to offer perspective.

There's no such thing, I told her, as straight, unbroken progress when it comes to changes in our society. Rather, after each leap forward, we seem to falter and fall back. And sometimes a great advance uncovers new problems, new complexities. The enactment of the major civil rights laws of the sixties and seventies brought rewarding and fulfilling opportunities for millions of able blacks. But their advancement seems to have stripped the urban ghettos of black leaders and role models. The black millions left behind are trapped in lives of hopelessness and despair. And a white majority that fears and despises them is not inclined to help, particularly when a lot of whites feel blacks have already won too many favors.

Oh, it wasn't hard to understand why my young friend was discouraged.

What she needed was an example of how things worked, I said; so let me offer the experience of one black person: that patrician civil rights leader and champion of women's rights, Mary Church Terrell. (Yes, my friend had heard of her.) Not long after the end of the Civil War, young Molly Church, as her friends called her, came to Washington from her home in Memphis to take up a post as a teacher of Greek and Latin in the D.C. public schools. She was gratified to find herself in the open society that seemed to be emerging in the First Reconstruction period after the war. Though African American, she could move freely about in the nation's capital, enjoying the same public pleasures and amenities available to whites.

It was a false dawn. Within a dozen years after war's end, the Southern Democrats, forerunners of the Dixiecrats of my time, were able, by chicanery and violence and with the aid of northern indifference, to regain control of the old states of the Confederacy. Eventually, they gained control of the nation's capital, too.

Mrs. Terrell recalled many years later how she first became aware of what was happening. "In the 1890s," she told an interviewer once, "a colored person could dine anywhere in Washington." That soon changed. She remembered stopping for service at a drugstore on the corner of Ninth and F Streets, which she had often patronized, and being told by the white clerk it was the last time he would serve her. The behavior of a loud Negro man was prompting the store to change its policy. So that door shut. And so did many others. Of the grievous injustices imposed on the District's blacks, one that sorely rankled, because it was so diurnal and demeaning, was to find places of public accommodation—restaurants, hotels, theaters—no longer open to them. And it was not law that prevailed, it was custom, southern custom, imposed by the white southerners who had the city in their grasp. For more than fifty years the nation's capital remained a wretched, segregated, southern town. And then? Why, then, in the upsurge of civil rights activity that followed World War II, Mary Church Terrell, who was in her eighties, led a successful campaign to re-open all places of public accommodation to black citizens. And I could recall a memorable day when a group of us who had worked with her accompanied Mrs. Terrell to a restaurant that only a few months before would not admit her; and there we marked our victory and her ninetieth birthday with a joyful feast of strawberry shortcake and hot tea.

My young friend laughed and shook her head in wonderment.

Oh, I have other stories, I told her, just as incredible. And if I tell them now, I tell them because we must remember how things were, if we're to make them be the way we'd like to have them be. Yes, things today are not good, I told her; but they're better. And if they're to get better still, we cannot give up trying. You may lose hope, I said, but you must not lose heart. You cannot give in to rage or apathy.

But enough speaking in generalities! I'll speak, instead, of the changes I have worked for and witnessed and of the hope—that inescapable word again!—that my young African American friend and her white friends and friends of all the races, religions, and nationalities that enrich this country will be moved to join the unending struggle for a society that, farther along, will come closer to our hearts' desire.

Part I

From Philadelphia to Richmond
1941–1951

1

Here's Where I'm Coming From

The Army of the United States, celebrated in song and story for taking callow youths and making men of them, somehow, in my case, miscalculated. I served in the army during World War II, and instead of making a man, it made a radical out of me. And that, believe me, was not an easy thing to do.

My first twenty years were spent in a section of West Philadelphia, an enclave of snug, row porch houses and little corner stores transected by Lancaster Avenue, a broad commercial thoroughfare. Most of the shopkeepers and homeowners were Jews; Dad was their essential provisioner. His kosher meat market was off the avenue on the corner of two side streets, Forty-second and Brown. We lived behind and over the store, and I grew up helping my parents in the business: delivering orders on foot and bike and, when I turned eighteen, in a Chevy truck that smelled like a chicken coop; fashioning roasts and steaks and chops out of the forequarters of cattle, calves, and lambs; plucking the wing and body feathers, singeing the lice and pinfeathers, and yanking the guts out of the loose, still-warm carcasses of fresh-killed chickens. I hated every working minute.

Only a few years out of high school, I dreaded most the thing that was Dad's dearest wish: to see the sign on our two store windows changed from JOS. CAPLAN to JOS. CAPLAN & SON. And why not? In the Russian shtetl Dad grew up in, Caplans had been kosher butchers for generations. Here in America, he and his three brothers were butchers; so were all their sons. It struck Dad as *narishkayt,* foolishness, for me to want more schooling when I already had a profitable trade. Anyhow, we couldn't afford to have me go to college full-time—the bank failures of the Great Depression had nearly wiped us out. So I went to school at night, after my day's work in the store was done.

My secret dream was to become a writer or, failing that, a high school English teacher. Language and literature were my great passions, especially the German language and German literature—a mad infatuation when you think about it, for Hitler had already begun the extermination of the Jewish people. But what was happening in Germany was, after all, a political matter. In those days, I neither knew nor cared much about politics.

Anyhow, I tended to accept without question the political views of those pillars of propriety, the *Philadelphia Morning Inquirer* by day and the *Evening Bulletin* by night. Although I didn't dislike President Franklin D. Roosevelt as much as they did—after all, my parents voted for him and my mother loved him—I *was* influenced by their characterization of him as an autocrat and an unscrupulous schemer. The word "boondoggle" was often in their editorials. They used it to describe Roosevelt's work, or "make-work," programs—futile, the papers said, since they paid grown men "just to lean on shovels."

The papers were right, too. I could see that with my own eyes. The Spring Garden Street trolley that carried me from home to my night classes at Temple University went directly past the Philadelphia Art Museum, where a WPA landscaping project was under way. And when I looked out of the window on a late summer afternoon, I saw men standing about, *leaning on their shovels.* It vexed me to see Dad's good tax money spent on things like that. Contemptuous, I returned to the book open on my lap. To Goethe, perhaps, or Schiller.

Then Japan bombed Pearl Harbor.

I took a sharply focused view of the war—I saw it as my chance to escape from the butcher business. To my chagrin, they didn't draft me until the second year. About a week before I was scheduled to be inducted, my cousin Dave, home on furlough, dropped in at our store in his sergeant's uniform. Plump, affable, he came to counsel me.

"Marv. Listen. Don't worry. The one thing this army's short on is butchers. Once they know you cut meat, believe me, you can almost write your own ticket. Look at me. Only nine months an' I already made sergeant. I don't hafta fall out for drill or reveille. I don't pull KP. I'm outta the barracks. I got my own room, off the messhall. Uh course I gotta cut up the company's meat and chicken every day. But after that, I'm on my own. An' if I'm hungry, any-time, day or night, I just go in the officers' box and cut myself off a steak or a coupla chops—"

"*Treyf?*"[1] cried my mother. "*Feh!*"

"Aunt Rae," said Dave patiently. "This is the *army*. An even you and Uncle Joe never sold meat like this. Prime. Top-grade steer beef. Marv. Listen. You won't even know there's a war goin' on."

"Listen to him. Listen to him," my mother pleaded.

I did. Down at the induction center when they asked me my civilian occupation, I said: "Truck driver!"

For that, the army sentenced me to eight weeks' basic training in the Tank Destroyer Corps, Camp Hood, Texas.

The day our group of inductees arrived in camp, a second lieutenant was on hand to welcome us. We were fortunate, he said, to be assigned to the Tank Destroyers, an outfit already renowned for its fighting spirit. Our troops were still in North Africa, engaged in the desert phase of the war, and a Tank Destroyer unit was the first to enter Bizerte. What's more, it had sustained 50 percent casualties.

"Sir," a member of our group asked, "is it possible to transfer to another outfit?"

"I'm glad you asked me that, soldier," the lieutenant said. "Yes, it is possible. If you qualify, you can transfer to the paratroops."

A large percentage of our contingent hailed from the Italian neighborhoods of South Philly. The barracks that night was astir with homesick youngsters moaning, "First into Bizerte! Fifty percent casualties! *Mama mia!*"

Things got no better when we fell out for reveille at 7 A.M. and our training got under way. By boot and by jeep, in the summer of '43, under a blazing Texas sun, we Quaker Town rookies jogged and jolted over Hood's bare hills; we crawled on our bellies over the shards of caliche that paved the obstacle course and the rifle range; we subsisted, or so it seemed to me, on salt tablets and tepid water, which we drained out of huge lister bags.

To the Tank Destroyers' bold slogan "Seek! Strike! Destroy!"—emblazoned on our shoulder patches, encircling the head of a black panther with a tank crushed between its jaws—we made emendation. "Sneak," we whimpered to one another, "Peek, Retreat."

One day stands out in what was generally a parched, sweltering blur: the

1. Yiddish: "Non-kosher."

day I was assigned to a detail that was sent out to dig a latrine trench. We began in the cool of the morning, right after breakfast; but soon the sun was up. Digging was new work for me. The only times I'd ever used a shovel was to clean snow off the sidewalks in front of our store. Now, as I labored, I had a revelation. Stripped to the waist, my undershirt knotted around my brow, gasping, my glasses fogged with sweat, I suddenly realized *I was leaning on my shovel.* My God! Of course! There *is* no other way. You cannot dig a ditch without leaning on your shovel. I went back to the barracks with more than an aching back to think about.

New shocks to old assumptions were not far off. I was summoned to another part of the camp for an interview. A captain, who looked more like a Temple University professor than a military man, glanced up from my records and asked, "How would you like to go back to school?"

Sunburnt, blistered, dehydrated, I said I thought I'd like that very much.

"Well. You look like a likely candidate to me. You scored exceptionally high on your AIT.[2] And I see you've had the equivalent of about two and a half years of college at night. But some damn fool sure bollixed up your record. Put you down here as 'Truck Driver.' Let me change that right now: '*Student.*'"

As a student, then, I was shipped to another camp in Texas and given a battery of tests to determine if I could qualify for the Army Specialized Training Program (ASTP). Within a week, a second lieutenant called me in to say I had done well in General Language Ability and German. "We want to assign you to a language program. I think you'll clear." When I looked puzzled, he went on. "You need security clearance for the ASTP. Some of the programs are highly sensitive. But I don't find anything derogatory in our preliminary security check." I swelled with pride. "Some of these GIs, though. We've had to hold up on one soldier today. Brilliant score, too. But our security check shows he subscribes to *In Fact,* one of these left-wing rags. Can you imagine?"

Actually, I could. *In Fact* was a four-page weekly newsletter that a man named George Seldes published to correct what he considered errors and distortions in the daily press. I had run across it in the Temple University library. It had raised doubts in my mind about some daily news accounts I had tended to take for granted. As I read it, I almost wished I could afford a subscription.

I hoped the lieutenant didn't notice my blushes.

---

2. Army Intelligence Test.

Security. It was the watchword of my new career. For security reasons they wouldn't tell us where or what we were to study. And when, in broad daylight, we boarded the train that was to carry us to our new assignment, we were surprised to find the coach lights on and the shades drawn. For reasons of security, we were forbidden to raise those shades. It was exciting to be the object of such secrecy and a bit of a letdown when the train stopped, many hours later, to raise the shades on a spot no more glamorous than a siding in Ann Arbor, Michigan, downhill from the university.

After we stowed our duffel bags in the new dorm that was to be our quarters, and after we reported for orientation, they sprang another surprise on us. All the men in my outfit had qualified for French or German. To our consternation, the company commander informed us that since the French and German programs were full, we would study Japanese.

Japanese! That was daunting enough. What was even more intriguing, if not unsettling, was to discover that we were to be taught by Japanese Americans. From my reading of newspaper editorials I had been persuaded that the Japanese American population was a potential fifth column whose internment was essential for our national security. Now, in our classrooms, we were to come face to face with the presumed enemy.

I found it difficult, however, to feel menaced by any of our teachers. *Who* was the menace? The Issei, the first, or immigrant, generation? But they were either cherubic, bald-headed elderly men or smiling little matrons with plum-shaped faces. The Nisei, then, the second, American-born generation? But they were slangy, snappily dressed youths and gentle, sweet-voiced maidens, with gardenia-petal complexions. Nothing about any of them seemed threatening to me.

An army that supposedly frowned on fraternization with these people now provided opportunities for it. As we chatted with our teachers before or after class, strolled across the quadrangle together, met for ceremonial tea, or sampled our first Japanese meals in their apartments, any suspicions we may have had quickly faded. Bit by bit we learned of the terrible calamity that had befallen them: of homes and farms and businesses sold at a loss or confiscated without compensation, of professions interrupted and college careers abruptly ended, and of the final humiliation of the internment camps.

Our teachers had been released from the camps when they responded to a call for volunteers to instruct us. Maybe the Philadelphia papers would still question their loyalty. But how could they be counted disloyal, I wondered, if to teach us they had to undergo a security check as rigorous as our own? Our teachers taught us Japanese, of course. They taught some of us indignation, as well.

The first sparks of doubt were struck. A number of men in Company D were ready to fan those sparks.

In most World War II novels and movies, the U.S. armed forces are a melting pot. Men of all classes and trades, from every section of the country, are thrown together and surmount their differences in the fellowship of common danger. No doubt that is a true picture of the situation at the battlefront.

But the ASTP was a distillery. It filtered out of the army's great diversity a group whose members were astonishingly alike. Our company ran heavily to men with an interest in language and literature. I was soon one of a circle that shared my enthusiasms: art, poetry, music, words—written and spoken. Above all, the spoken word. Talk was our supreme diversion. It dominated our free time, our common meals, our late-night dorm-room snacks, our weekend picnics in the countryside or the Arboretum with the women we had come to know. And almost every Saturday night there was a beer- and bull-session at the Pretzel Bell, where we sat and drank and talked till early morning.

Not everything said was serious. The best dirty limericks I know I learned in these confabs. But when the talk turned sober, as it often did, to my discomfort it frequently turned to politics.

I am ashamed, today, to confess how politically indifferent I was back then. In Philadelphia, as I was growing up, politics—local, state, national, even international—was something I skimmed over in the daily papers on my way to the arts section and the funnies. At Temple University, I cannot recall ever taking an elective course in social or political science. My political obtuseness seemed to come with the family business. Dad and Mother made up their own minds once every four years and voted for Roosevelt. But when it came to candidates in the state and city contests, they docilely took the choices suggested to them by the Republican boss of our 24th Ward, an obese, gruff local furniture dealer with a name that sounded like something right out of *Pilgrim's Progress:* Workman Driver. The day before elections, Mr. Driver would drop in at the store, buy an eight- or ten-pound rib roast, and tell my parents whom to vote for. The aptness of Lincoln Steffens's sobriquet for Philadelphia—"corrupt and contented"—was something I did not appreciate until long after I had left my home town.

In Ann Arbor, though, I experienced my first political awakening. My imagination was stirred by the postwar plan of some of my new, politically sophisticated friends. It was brief and breathtaking: to set the world to rights. To the consideration of how that was to be done they devoted countless hours. I sat on the sidelines of many hot debates, mute in my ignorance. But soon I was drawn into the discussions. For I found *I* liked to talk, too. In Company D, that bastion of top security, I tasted the first pleasures of subversive thought. I began to read the books that lay about, standard works of American and British Socialists. The Michigan University library subscribed to *In Fact* and *The Nation,* and I began reading them regularly. There was even a copy of *Das Kapital* around, but I was safe from that. I had no head for economics. But what *was* read and said began to change my view of things. Notions of a "classless society," of a government responsive to the needs of the least of its citizens—notions platitudinous and discredited today—gripped my imagination.

And who were my instructors in these heresies? Rumpled GIs like me, all of us reduced by uniform to a common denominator of olive drab. Men as eager and often as troubled about women as I was. Beer reddened their faces as much as intellectual zeal did. But if you look back on them from what they went on to become, why, then, my faculty of friends included the dean of an Ivy League law school, the labor editor of a major California daily, an internationally known scholar of the humanities, a professor of American history who wrote a landmark study of American socialism . . .

When our year in Ann Arbor ended, they split Company D in two. They shipped the bottom half of the outfit overseas, promoted the rest of us from private first class to corporal and sent us to Arlington Hall, a Signal Corps base in Virginia, a few miles outside of Washington. Our assignment was to study military Japanese, in order to decode intercepted radio messages.

The Company D contingent of the Signal Corps was put on night shift, so our days were free. Some of us took advantage of that to wander about and get to know Washington. In my one-year tour of duty there, I grew to love the city. My strong inclination toward the arts drew me often to the newly opened National Gallery, to the Smithsonian museums on the Mall, and to the Phillips Collection, a small but exciting exhibition of Impressionist and contemporary paintings, whose generous owner presented them for public viewing in his own handsome mid-town mansion.

Yet in the end, Washington's greatest attraction for me was Capitol Hill. I approached it with all the fresh-eyed enthusiasm of the convert to a new religion. Still fired up from our Ann Arbor discussions, three or four of my army buddies and I spent hours treading the ornate halls of Congress. Committee meetings, even long, droning ones, drew our rapt attention. Many afternoons found us hunched in the galleries, engrossed in House and Senate floor debates. I had discovered the nerve center of the nation.

Just looking and listening involved me in the legislative process and made me eager to know more. My friends and I sometimes felt as though we were spectators at a drama. Brief episodes sometimes made us feel we were seeing contemporary history unfold before our eyes.

One day, for instance, we found ourselves in the House gallery at roll call and realized we were looking down upon one of the South's most notorious bigots, Congressman John Rankin of Mississippi. It took only a minute or two to watch him stride onto the House floor, call out "Here!," lay a friendly, bony hand on a colleague's shoulder, greet a newcomer, and make judicious proprietary use of one of the gleaming bronze spittoons scattered about the chamber. Yet those few gestures summed up for us the hermetic, good ol' boy white world he lived in, and stirred our hope that some day we would see that world shattered.

Because we were in the D.C. area when President Franklin Roosevelt died, some of us in my circle experienced that epochal, shocking event in almost personal terms. The news first came to us as a break-in announcement on the radio jazz program we were half-listening to, late one afternoon in the Arlington Hall rec room. What stays with me are the intimate terms on which I seemed to relate to what had occurred. The world had lost a great leader. But our nearness to Washington, where we passed the White House almost every day, where a member of our group often regaled us with tidbits of White House gossip he'd picked up from his brother-in-law, who was a member of FDR's staff, made some of us feel as if we had lost a neighbor—one, I should note, I had come to admire and love.

Roosevelt died in Warm Springs, Georgia, on a Thursday. It took all of Friday to carry the body north by train. Quite early Saturday morning, on a bus going into Washington from Arlington Hall, we found ourselves crossing Memorial Bridge alongside a black-draped caisson drawn by six white horses, which three sergeants were bringing into the city from Fort Myer. They were en route to Union Station, someone said, to meet the train from Georgia. And it is this I remember whenever I recall that moment in our history. Not a vast cortege and throngs of weeping thousands at the curb, but thirty or forty of us, hushed as we watched, through the dusty windows of the bus, the strong, galloping steeds tossing their white manes; the empty black caisson flying past us, more evocative of our loss than if it had borne, as it soon would, a formal, flag-covered casket.

By that time we Company D'ers were nearing the end of our Arlington

Hall assignment. I could wish nothing better for myself than that someday, somehow I would return and live and work in the nation's capital.

We were still in Washington when the atom bombs were dropped on Hiroshima and Nagasaki. The reaction of those of us in the Japanese program was mixed: we rejoiced that the war was over; we were appalled at its conclusion. For the bombs fell on cities we felt we knew; on people no longer faceless, whose language we could speak, however haltingly; on the friends and kinfolk of teachers we had come to respect and cherish. So our joy was tempered.

The bombs shortened the war. A group of us was soon en route to an embarkation point on the West Coast, to be outfitted and sent overseas as part of the Army of Occupation.

In Chicago, we were transferred to another train, a string of ramshackle coaches called the Champion. It took us three days and two nights to make the trip, jammed together in a hot, airless car, on mohair seats as rough as coarse-grade sandpaper. Restless, I began to tour the train. The coaches I walked through were exactly like the one I'd left.

But then I opened a door and stepped back in time, into a coach out of an old Hollywood western. Its seats were straight-backed, unpainted wooden benches. It was heated against the prairie winter we were pounding through by its own ancient iron wood-burning stove. And it was occupied by Negro soldiers. Conversation stopped as soon as I came in. Startled, we stared at one another in silence. Then I turned and retreated to my seat. For the first time it dawned on me that there were black men in service, too.

I saw the black troops once again, when we had a three-hour layover in St. Louis because of engine trouble. Members of the group I was with were issued passes and told we could leave the train. Two of my seatmates and I went forth to sample St. Louis food and beer. We encountered the black soldiers on the plaza in front of the station, lined up for drill.

"Poor bastards," one of my companions remarked. "They'll never turn 'em loose in this Jim Crow town."

A Jim Crow town? That was something new to me. Philadelphia, for all its faults, was relatively free of racial segregation, or so I thought. From kindergarten to twelfth grade, I had gone to school with blacks and had even become friends with one or two. But that afternoon I was reminded—as I needed to be—of how little I knew of what had happened to black classmates after graduation and of how deeply race divided us.

My newfound mates and I wandered off into the city, found an agreeable bar, took a tour of the downtown that was cut short because of the blustery weather, and came back near boarding time. The black soldiers were still out on the open plaza, bundled up in winter greatcoats, wheeling smartly to the commands a black sergeant barked at them.

When the trip resumed, I toured the aisles again, but I did not venture back to the Negro soldiers' car. Still, I was aware of it; and knowing it was there and why it was there left me troubled.

I made it to California, but not to Japan. By then, I was army surplus. General Douglas MacArthur, in his wisdom, decided he had too many translator-interpreters. The war's abrupt end had cut down on the number of casualties among soldiers with our skills. So they sent us home.

Some theologians say you can form a child for life in four or five years. The army shaped or reshaped me in less than three. I was so altered in social and political orientation, so changed in aspiration, I felt I didn't fit in anywhere. Not in the kosher butcher business, for sure; not in the Philadelphia public school system, where I once hoped to be; not even back in Temple University.

As I hovered there, lost, not knowing which way to jump, a remarkable thing happened. Harry Bernstein stopped by the store. One of my Company D buddies, a southern iconoclast with a new vision of the South, a former Pretzel Bell debater, a co-discoverer of the political process in Washington, he was en route to Greensboro, North Carolina, for his discharge. Still in uniform, for he had finagled a quick trip to Japan for himself, he came by to say, *"Ohayo!"*[3] and to ask me a question.

His father was about to back him in a new publishing venture: he was going to edit a monthly magazine for the Jewish community in Virginia.

Would I like to join him?

3. Japanese: "Good morning!"

2

An Ofay in the Capital
of the Confederacy

In Richmond, Virginia, one afternoon, when I was still new to the city, I boarded a streetcar and took the first empty seat I saw, about halfway up the aisle.

As soon as I sat down, the woman in the window seat jumped up. She brushed by me and headed for the rear of the car.

Startled, I looked back. All the seats behind me were taken. The woman, a colored woman of middle age, as I now saw, was standing in the aisle between two rows of grave black faces all staring in my direction. Then I realized what had happened.

I am sure I had been warned that Richmond streetcars were racially segregated. I had even been instructed, I believe, in the intricate system imposed by law: whites were seated from the front of a bus or streetcar, blacks from the rear, and when the races met in the middle, as she and I had done, black gave way to white, since we were not permitted to sit together. If I knew all that, I, a northerner, a Philadelphian from the Quaker City of Brotherly Love, had chosen not to pay attention to it.

I made what I meant to be a placating, apologetic gesture, but I could see from the woman's grim, set smile that I was only making matters worse. Fuming in helpless rage, I rode, head bent, to my destination. And so it was, in that demented minuet, that I was introduced to social custom in the South, in February 1946.

Unsettling incidents like the streetcar encounter made no difference. I was glad I had accepted Harry Bernstein's invitation to join him in his family's Virginia publishing venture. I was eager for new experiences and I could not want a better guide.

Harry was the first southerner I had ever known. Although we knew each other as fellow students of Japanese at Michigan, we did not become friends until our Washington tour of duty. Even so, I was aware of Harry back in our Ann Arbor days. I well remember my first impression of him. Harry was a lanky chap, just grazing six feet, of bony mien and freckled complexion, with auburn hair whose copper flame even a close-cropped GI haircut couldn't extinguish. His manner and appearance struck me as casual almost to a fault. I first noticed him, I believe, on a clear spring afternoon, on the sidewalk outside of Greene House, our dormitory; loose-limbed, joshing in elementary Japanese, he was playing catch—in ragged green fatigues and bare feet.

Arlington Hall, where we got to know each other better, was scarcely a "hardship post." Once an exclusive girls' school, its handsome buildings and wooded, well-groomed grounds were still recognizable under an army overlay of barracks, decoding centers, drill fields, messhalls, PXs, and the like. Although most of the Ann Arbor contingent was assigned to the night shift, that turned out to be no hardship, either.

We worked from 4 P.M. to midnight (or from 1600 to 2400 hours, as the Signal Corps preferred to say). However, soldiers on night shift did not have to fall out for reveille. They were also permitted to live off the base. Harry and I and three other Company D GIs decided to exercise that option.

We ran an ad in the *Washington Post* saying five army corporals, college students (a subtle touch, we felt, that suggested our respectability), were looking for a furnished apartment. To our surprise, we got a prompt reply. A recently discharged veteran, a Mr. Moses, was renovating a four-story red-brick row house, near Eighteenth and F Streets, Northwest, and invited us to come by and inspect the premises. From him we rented two shabby bedrooms and a sitting room, complete with a hallway hotplate and a small, second-hand refrigerator.

It was a scruffy lair, but it had its benefits. We could sleep as late as we liked. Mornings, with the shutters open, we could sit and read in a sun-filled bay. Just around the corner was the G Street YMCA, where, as soldiers, we were entitled to free use of the handball courts, swimming pool, and showers. And not far off, only a short walk across Lafayette Square, was the old Belasco Theatre, converted into a Stage Door Canteen, where friendly USO hostesses in red, white, and blue aprons plied us with coffee and doughnuts and where we could pick up free USO postcards and stationery.

In no time at all we were ensconced in our cozy nook, filling it with books and records and a carefree litter of olive-drab socks and underwear, empty Coke and beer bottles, old newspapers and candy wrappers. Since Harry and one other roommate smoked, butt-choked ashtrays were another decorative touch.

I hope I will not be accused of ethnic generalization if I say that while all of us chipped in to buy the drinks, it was Harry and I, the two Jews in the group, who kept the larder full with the delicacies our mothers pressed upon us whenever we got ready to head back to D.C. from a weekend spent at home.

It was in this shared experience, and our year together in Washington, that I came to appreciate the sharp, driving intelligence under Harry's rumpled, easy-going exterior. He had a brashness, a self-assurance that I admired and envied.

Both he and I wanted to be writers. Or if not writers, at least newspapermen. My three other roommates and I lolled about the apartment, reading; or else we spent the afternoons wandering through the halls of Congress on Capitol Hill, or visiting Washington's wonderful museums. Harry took part in these diversions, but he was not content with them. He dropped by the *Washington Daily News* and, in a beguiling southern accent distilled in his native Carolinas, talked them into taking him on as a cub reporter.

When the war ended abruptly, on August 14, 1945, in the black atomic rain over Hiroshima and Nagasaki, we, as Japanese code breakers, were suddenly out of work. Many of us slipped into an easy-going funk. We lay around the barracks on unmade beds (for by then my friends and I had had a falling out with Mr. Moses over the rent and bedbug-extermination and his intrusion into our privacy and had given up the F Street rooms). We read and napped and waited to be sent to an embarkation point, the Presidio of Monterey, California, where we expected to be absorbed into the Army of Occupation. Impatient, Harry made the rounds of the Pentagon and Armed Services and talked himself into a six-month assignment with the U.S. Strategic Bomb Survey, a special detail set up to determine which of our bombing tactics—pin-point bombing, scatter bombing, night bombing, and so forth—had had the most devastating impact on the Japanese people. The air force flew him over to Tokyo in a matter of days.

I and the other Company D alumni never got to Japan. The Signal Corps shipped us out to Monterey. But even while we were being outfitted and indoctrinated, word came from on high, at General Douglas MacArthur's level, that they didn't need any more Japanese translator-interpreters. I was sent back to Indian Town Gap, my induction center in Pennsylvania. Shortly after the first of the year, I was given an honorable discharge and sent home.

I missed the army. No, not the army, but the camaraderie of barracks and dormitory. Physically cramped as that life had been, I who had led a lonely, polar existence in Philadelphia, alternating between my father's kosher butcher store and Temple University night school, had discovered a liberating atmosphere in Ann Arbor and Arlington Hall. And that's what I longed for.

Physically and emotionally, I felt imprisoned. I found myself once again living behind and over the butcher store. I shared this three-story warren of boxy rooms with my parents, my younger sister, Bernice, my older sister, Blanche, and her husband, Harry Weinberg, a first cousin of ours. We all got along well enough, and Harry Weinberg was one of my closest friends. His intellectual attainments as a chemist and then as a pioneer in the linguistic discipline of general semantics were an inspiration to me as I struggled to find my own way. All I was certain of was that the army had carried me too far off from my old life to let me ever consider going back to it. And I had become too independent to want to submit again to my mother's watchful eye and hovering love.

So this is where Harry Bernstein found me when he stopped off in Philadelphia.

He was en route from New York to his home in Greensboro, North Carolina, to get his discharge. But his real destination, he told me, was Richmond. His father, I knew, published a monthly magazine for the Jewish communities in North and South Carolina. Now his dad was planning to publish a similar one for the state of Virginia. Harry was going to be the editor. And he was looking for someone to join him in the enterprise.

Join him! I loved the idea. To move to another town and start afresh must be one of youth's great dreams. And I was particularly interested when Harry outlined what he had in mind for us in the way of an editorial policy. From the pages of our magazine we were going to address Virginia's Jewish community and persuade its members to our point of view. We were going to win them to the support of the social and political reforms we had come to advocate with such zeal in Ann Arbor's Pretzel Bell and in long sessions of dormitory argument and deliberation.

I realized at the outset that I had no notable qualifications for an editorial position on a magazine of Jewish interest. My Jewish education had been a spotty one—Bible class, in English, every Sunday morning, and enough weekday-afternoon tutoring in Hebrew to enable me to read the Haftorah portion at my Bar Mitzvah. But I read Hebrew without comprehension, and I could not speak the language. Worse, after my confirmation at thirteen, I had quickly fallen away from Judaism. Except for our family seder, at Passover, I observed no holidays. I rarely entered a synagogue. Even though my mother kept a strictly kosher home, I had begun in my teens to ignore the dietary laws, and army chow lines and beer bashes completed my disregard of them. If I considered myself an agnostic, it was because I was too lazy and too indifferent to grapple with any serious religious question. If I was anything Jewish, I was "ah boyikh Yid"—"a Belly Jew"—whose attachment to the creed was entirely a matter of taking pleasure in Jewish dishes: kreplach, potato latkes, crusty rye bread, borsht (though come to think of it, I didn't care for borsht), and rich delicatessen fare.

Harry's editorial credentials were no better than mine. His Jewish education was just as poor. At least, though, he knew where he stood religiously: he was an uncompromising atheist. His newfound faith was social action. His undergraduate days at the University of North Carolina, Chapel Hill, had thrown him among radicals. Socialism attracted him. Even communism. In Ann Arbor and Washington, when we had talked of what we might do after the war ended, he spoke of enrolling in the London School of Economics and studying with England's preeminent Socialist, Harold Laski, paying particular attention to the anarchical theories of Prince Piotr Kropotkin.

But now he was ready, he told me, to respond to a new calling. As a southerner, he wanted to go back to the South and rouse the region from its economic stagnation; free it from the terrible scourge of racial segregation and discrimination. In Virginia, that meant taking up the fight against Senator Harry Flood Byrd Jr., a Democrat, but only nominally: as a fiscal conservative and white supremacist, Byrd opposed most of the domestic policies of the two Democratic presidents he served under, Franklin Roosevelt and Harry Truman. Senator Byrd headed one of the South's most powerful and reactionary political machines. It was Harry Bernstein's bold intention to bring the state's Jewish community into the struggle to unseat the senator and his henchmen in Congress.

Of course we did not realize, as we talked in my father's store that afternoon, how meager the forces were that we intended to mobilize. But how could we know? We did not learn until at least two years later that when it came to estimating Virginia's Jewish population, in the years of our activity, there were no accurate figures. An editorial in the November 1949 issue of our magazine offered brave guesses: 7,000 to 8,000 Jewish families in the entire state and perhaps 4,000 to 5,000 of them resident in Norfolk and Richmond, the two largest cities in the Old Dominion. In an effort to correct the situation, the editorial said, the Norfolk Jewish Community Council was about to undertake its own census. I never saw the final results, but I venture to guess they would not have increased the Jewish population figures for the state by more than a few thousand.

Yet even if we had known this at the very start of things for us, I cannot believe it would have dampened our enthusiasm. Certainly not mine. I was a new adherent to the cause, pure-hearted and certain of its rightness and too inexperienced to be daunted by the enormousness of the task Harry spoke of undertaking.

However, one thing gave me pause. The thought of leaving, and perhaps losing, a woman I had just met.

Naomi Weltman and I had become acquainted during the two weeks' furlough I had spent at home before going out to California. I had been given her name and phone number by the wife of an Ann Arbor classmate who knew I was from Philadelphia and was certain, she said, that I would enjoy meeting this old college chum of theirs who had just taken a job in my home town.

I jotted down the information to be polite, but was glad I had it after all. For what I found upon returning home after three years in the army was that either the two or three women I used to date before the war had lost interest in me or I in them.

I called Naomi up and we went out twice before I left for the West Coast.

We corresponded during the three months I was stationed at the Presidio. When I got back, we were pleased to find that an agreeable familiarity had developed between us through our exchange of letters.

Naomi was a psychologist by profession, employed by the Philadelphia office of B'nai B'rith to help that organization set up a counseling and employment program for Jewish teenagers. She was a short, plump, bouncy girl, with a New York openness and brassiness that I, who was shy and backward with women, found unexpectedly attractive. City College girls, of whom she was one, had a word of advice for their boyfriends, she told me: "A little more saxual and less intellactual." I was rather taken with that admonishment; I found it challenging. In the mid-town apartment she shared with another woman, I discovered the joys of heavy petting. We never went beyond that—we were both too innocent, inhibited, and inexperienced to venture into sex, and it was 1946, at least twenty years before the sexual revolution. But the promise of something deeper developing between us was always there, and I was loath to forgo that promise.

Yet even with Naomi in the balance, the improbable adventure Harry held out to me, the opportunity to do something socially useful, outweighed for me whatever Philadelphia had to offer. Naomi greatly endeared herself by saying that sorry as she would be to see me go, she thought that if I didn't take this chance, I'd always regret it.

So after mulling the matter over for a week, I called Harry in Greensboro and told him yes, I was ready to come south and throw my lot in with his. In our ignorance and arrogance, everything seemed possible to us.

To my surprise I liked Richmond. Or at least my first impressions of it.

Tired and apprehensive, I arrived late one January night in a cold daycoach, carried there in slow, meandering fashion by the RF&P, the Richmond, Fredericksburg, and Potomac.

But my first inspection of the city revived my spirits. There was a curious glamour about the place. I felt it as soon as I left the train and found myself in the dark, domed octagonal waiting room, its remote skylights framing fragments of starry sky. The cab that took me to the Hotel Jefferson, where Harry had reserved a room for us, went down Monument Avenue, and I strove to grasp the grand scale of that boulevard of old mansions from the few details that went flashing by—a lighted window high up in a looming facade, a lamp-lit portico and a broad sweep of white balustrade, the tree-lined park down the center of it, interrupted at intervals by bright-lit clearings, each commanded by the statue of a Confederate hero.

A little beyond the last bronze rider, where the avenue ended and traffic funneled into a much narrower street, we passed the columns and pediments of what could have been two Greek temples, almost side by side. Churches, I guessed. The first time I was right: it was St. James Episcopal. The second church was a synagogue. But since it was Temple Beth Ahabah, as I later determined, a Reform synagogue with a pipe organ and stained-glass windows (forbidden decor in the Orthodox synagogues of my youth), with a membership of mostly German Jews, who considered themselves part of Richmond's aristocracy, I may not have been far off the mark.

We came to a stop alongside a huge ghost-white brick pile. Its pillars and arches and soaring twin belltowers put me in mind of a Renaissance palace. We had arrived at the Hotel Jefferson. I entered through the upper lobby, from the Franklin Street side, and given the lateness of the hour and the dimness of the light I was sure my eyes were playing tricks on me when I passed what looked like a couple of baby alligators asleep in a white tile pool.

To reach the registration desk, I descended a red-carpeted staircase out of the Ziegfeld Follies or an old Busby Berkeley musical; and though the lobby seemed somewhat worn and seedy, the great columns of beige marble, the sky-light of multicolored glass, and the ornate iron railings of the balconies on two sides suggested a richness of decoration I associated with the Gilded Age.

The room the bellboy led me to struck me as another remnant of a bygone era. Harry was still in Greensboro, so I had the place to myself. High, white muslin–curtained windows looked out upon the street, white-painted plumb-ing pipes crossed close to the ceiling. Our bathroom, a fair distance down the hall, had a canvas-curtained shower in a claw-foot porcelain tub; and the bed I quickly fell asleep in was a double-sized brass fourposter.

My reconnoiters the next morning confirmed one thing. I really *had* seen baby alligators in the upper lobby. Outside the hotel, the weather being mild, I strolled along Franklin Street past a row of broad, four-story brick houses, many of them with pillared entrances. The trees along the curb and the gentle contours and twill patterns of the brick sidewalks underfoot reminded me of another old red-brick city, Philadelphia. At every cross street, I could look downhill at a thread of water glittering in the morning sun, a king's namesake, the two-century-old city's famed James River.

In the course of my time there, I found much else to like in Richmond. The smallness of it appealed to me. In 1946 it was a city of about 250,000, one-tenth of Philadelphia's population. The editorial office of Harry's and my magazine, a small, windowless cubicle in the basement of the Central National Bank Building, at twenty stories Richmond's sole skyscraper, was only a few blocks away from some of the other institutions that came to matter to us: the down-town YMCA, where we played handball and swam; the public library; Loew's, the city's midtown first-run movie house; and the two major department stores, Thalhimer's and Miller and Rhoads. Our printer, Keel-Williams, one of the city's few union printers, was only ten blocks away.

Even when we decided to give up our room in the Jefferson because it cost too much, our new lodging was still almost within walking distance of the of-fice. I left the Jefferson with a pang. I knew I would miss its elegance, however faded; the fresh towels and linens every night; and the quartet on the landing of the grand staircase, scraping out old Broadway show tunes at dinnertime as we walked through the lobby on our way out to an inexpensive cafeteria. But our new furnished room was larger than our room at the Jefferson. It offered us twin beds instead of a double, a large closet and a private bath, and best of all, it was on the second floor of a corner mansion on Monument Avenue.

The tales I had heard of the South's unhurried pace I found to be true. And whether it was feigned or not, southern salespeople and waitresses evinced a friendliness that I rarely found in my home town. I went back to Philadelphia a number of times in the course of the five years I lived and worked in Richmond, so I could make sidewalk comparisons. I remember walking along Market Street in Philadelphia one Saturday afternoon and noting the differences between the populations of the two cities. Richmond faces, both white and black, were more homogeneous. On Richmond streets I often felt I was looking at old farm faces, and old battle-scene faces, out of photographs I had seen over the course of years. But there was more to it than that. People in Philadelphia, besides being more racially and ethnically diverse, had other differences, I decided, not much to their credit. On the whole, they looked meaner and dirtier.

Affection for my adopted city let me accept some of its presumptions with forbearance: its tendency, for instance, to compare Monument Avenue to the Champs-Élysées and to compare itself, since it also rested on seven hills, to Rome.

What I could never tolerate, however, was the way law and custom forced us to live down there. For Richmond was a city riven by race. That was evident as soon as I set foot in it. A dusty corner of the Broad Street station was set aside for black passengers, and COLORED was stamped across the entrance.

A white cabbie was waiting on the taxi stand outside the station doors, ready to drive me to the Hotel Jefferson. A black passenger who arrived with me would have had to wander out into the darkness, whatever the weather, down a vast unlit stretch of lawn to Broad Street, where he could try to hail a passing black-driven cab. The equestrian statues I drove by that first night were statues of Generals Robert E. Lee, Stonewall Jackson, and Jeb Stuart, heroes of the white Confederate South.

There were no black faces in the armchairs of the Hotel Jefferson lobby the next morning and none among the diners in the restaurant where I had breakfast. Blacks were waiters, busboys, ash-try emptiers. Only whites were at the reading tables when I dropped in to take a look at the public library. And in Miller and Rhoads department store, where I went shopping for an appointment book, I encountered, to my disgust, my first segregated drinking fountains, two identical bubblers labeled "white" and "colored."

These were no more than the merest indications of the segregated society I was moving into. The streetcar incident was only one of many jarring moments that I experienced in the passing days. It was no surprise to learn, as I did soon enough, that not only was a black department store shopper assigned to a special drinking fountain and a special toilet, but the shopper could not try on clothing or eat in the tearoom. A black person, I was to learn for myself later, was not permitted to enter the Jefferson or any mid-town hotel by the front door. Out on Virginia's highways, the rare gas station that accommodated black travelers had three rest rooms: one for "White Men," one for White Women," and one for "Colored."

I recount these circumstances to suggest how segregation seeps into every aspect of a society committed to it. On a larger scale, segregation was often literally a matter of life and death: Richmond's schools and libraries and prisons and hospitals were segregated, of course, with the inferior ones assigned to "Colored." Race dictated where and how you earned your living, where you could live and eat and seek enjoyment in your free time. Even where you could pray. And poll tax and intimidation often kept you from voting. I had taken up residence in a society whose white members for the most part accepted these conditions as the natural order of things; and those decent whites who were appalled and sickened by the excesses of racial division—the Klan raids and the lynchings and the police brutality—seldom saw that the everyday slights and injustices to blacks arose from the same arrogance as the atrocities, and differed only in degree.

As a white person, I could never truly experience the terrible burden that segregation imposed on blacks. But what I could and did experience was what it was like to try to resist segregation as much as I could, and work to abolish it. It was exhausting. One needed to be aware of racial differences at every moment, as I had needed to be when I boarded the streetcar. I think of the countless hours we spent, in our organizational lives, finding rooms to meet in, eating places that would accommodate blacks and whites for working dinners or celebrations, campaigning for change, preparing testimony, and picketing.

It was possible, certainly, for a white person in Richmond to have a black friend. But it was a friendship without the most ordinary amenities of friendship. You could not meet your friend for lunch or coffee in a downtown hotel or restaurant. You could not go to a movie or play or concert together. You could not make a date to play handball at the Y. And if you walked down the street together, you could expect surprised or hostile stares from other white pedestrians.

And yet I consider myself fortunate to have been in Richmond at that time; fortunate that the reforms Harry Bernstein and I advocated when we began publishing the *Southern Jewish Outlook* were (at least to us) so self-evidently right. Race relations becomes a great deal more complicated once segregation and discrimination are prohibited rather than mandated by law. I was so certain *then.*

If I am certain of anything today, it is that I have few sure solutions to the problems of race. Each "solution"—affirmative action, for instance—often seems to generate new questions, new dilemmas. Racial integration—that shining goal—seems somehow to elude this nation's grasp. As growing numbers of African Americans make their way into the mainstream of our society, many of them find even these gains disillusioning or cause for cynicism. And if they glance back, they see millions of their black brethren hopelessly stuck in the quagmires of the inner cities.

But *then!* Caught up in the justice of our cause, I readily persuaded myself it did not matter that in Virginia I was twice an outsider, as a Jew and a northerner. Perhaps it was better that I didn't look into the matter too closely. Some propositions are best left unexamined. Sometimes, though, I caught a peek at how I must have looked to those I encountered in my daily work and daily living, uncomfortable glimpses that sometimes were provided by those I considered allies.

I remember gaining one such insight after I had been in Richmond, the capital of the Confederacy, several months; and after Harry and I had made many of the organizational connections with black and Jewish, labor and veterans groups that were to determine the direction in which our efforts on behalf of racial equality and social reform were to take us.

My role was defined for me one night by a young black man with whom I had struck up an acquaintance. He was a reporter for the *Richmond Afro-American,* perhaps its only reporter. We had encountered each other a number of times at meetings of the National Association for the Advancement of Colored People (NAACP) and at some of the meetings of other civil rights and liberal political groups that Harry and I had become involved in. After a while, even when a formal session was over, this reporter and I often found ourselves lingering on and talking to each other.

Spare, quiet, studious-looking, he was on general assignment; but what he most liked writing about, he said, was sports. All sports. Except boxing. "That's not a sport," he said. "That's murder." Although neither of us ever said a word about it, we both knew that employment was closed to him in the one place he could realize his ambition, the morning *Richmond Times-Dispatch* or the afternoon *Richmond News-Leader,* both operated by a single white corporation.

Harry and I intrigued him, I think. He couldn't quite figure us out, although he was ready to be friendly and advise us. He and I were having pie and coffee one night in the dining room of Slaughter's Hotel on Second Street. A black hotel, Slaughter's ignored the Jim Crow laws and served everyone without discrimination. It was after an NAACP membership meeting, and the talk turned to my preoccupation with race relations. I had to understand, he said, that no matter how well-intentioned I was, I had at least two strikes against me that would make most southern blacks look on me with suspicion. I was a northerner. And I was white. My being white was the main thing.

"They look at you and they think: 'Ofay.' "

"Ofay?"

"Yeah. It's a term Negroes use a lot among themselves. Especially when they're talking about whites. It's pig Latin."

"Pig Latin!"

Then I knew: Foe.

3

In the Company of Women

In the early months of 1946, as Harry and I buckled down to work, a succession of women entered our lives. Small in stature, large in self-assertion, their effect upon us was profound.

I wasn't in when the first of these women arrived, so Harry encountered her alone. She presented herself at our office one afternoon while I was out trying to sell ads. It was a task I detested. But I had to admit there was an unassailable logic to the argument Harry and his father, David Bernstein, advanced to me: without ads, we couldn't publish.

Harry's dad, a genial man of medium height, with a rosy-cheeked, spectacled, smiling countenance, was an old hand at selling "space." He had already sold enough to enable us to put out four introductory issues, starting with February 1946. But Dave couldn't continue to work for our publication. He had to go home and see to the financial underpinnings of the Anglo-Jewish magazine that he and Harry's uncle, Harry Sable, had been publishing for years in Greensboro, North Carolina. All Dave could do for us now was tutor me in the job by letting me accompany him on visits to likely prospects—dress shops, furniture and appliance stores, restaurants, florists, upholsterers, funeral parlors, auto repair shops—an assortment of merchandise and service establishments.

Why was *I* the one to undertake this assignment? Harry couldn't. He was the Editor. His name and title were on the masthead of the magazine, which we had decided to call the *Southern Jewish Outlook*. (We had meant to call it the *American Jewish Outlook*, but there was already such a magazine—in Pittsburgh, I believe—and its owners had let us know they would not look with favor on our use of the name.) My title was Advertising Manager, and though Harry assured me titles meant nothing and that I was to be, in every sense, his co-editor, as involved as he in the editing, writing, layout and production end of things, still . . .

I sighed. Put on a necktie and my freshly pressed good suit and followed Dave Bernstein into cluttered, tiny offices at the backs of stores and up the steps from the cement floors of small workshops and auto repair garages.

One aspect of this chore held a certain fascination: the opportunity to watch how a thorough professional operated.

By joke or artless comment on the weather, Harry's dad, that seemingly mild-mannered, affable man, would quickly ingratiate himself with anyone who granted us an interview. Store managers and firm presidents came under his spell as he spoke. Even I was taken in by the assurance with which he talked about the *Outlook* and his ability to suggest, without ever quite saying so, that Virginia's Jewish communities kept in touch through this one publication. It was trusted implicitly. Read closely. Surest way to reach Jewish customers (a lucrative market, by the way) and advise them of your wares.

Mesmerized, I sometimes had to remind myself with a start that we were not quite so well established as Dave Bernstein's words implied. Our "introductory issues" were sent out free to whatever local Jewish mailing list we could get our hands on, and although a year's subscription was only two dollars, we had, as yet, very few paid subscribers. But then I would quiet my qualms and give an artist my full attention. More often than not we left the premises with a signed contract, a contract that more often than not was for more ad insertions than our client had intended to approve.

After about two weeks, Dave Bernstein had to go back to North Carolina; my apprenticeship was over. I was left with whatever I had gained from my brief on-the-job training, which included a handful of notes I had scribbled after listening to Dave's sales pitch. I recalled that parody of old World War I movies, where someone says to the commander of a flying squadron, "Would you send a kid up in a crate like *that?*" I felt as nervous and unready as that kid as I went forth, solo, to sell space. I suppose I could have chucked it all and gone home to Philadelphia, but somehow I never entertained the thought. However onerous and discouraging the work might be, I was committed: to the *Outlook,* to its noble goals, to a section of the country that was somehow involving me in its problems. I had much to learn, even though there was much I didn't care to learn. Anyhow, I was beginning to learn something about myself. If a cause engages me, I tend to take root quickly.

So it was while I was out and afoot, going virtually from store to store along Broad Street and Grace Street, that Mrs. Anne Gellman knocked on the *Outlook* door and, when Harry opened it, marched right in. She was a petite, smartly dressed woman, dark-haired and dark-eyed, with a militant air that could sometimes be intimidating. Richmond-born but no southern belle, she was, as we found out later, a social worker by training who had committed herself to liberal causes.

She had read a couple of the introductory issues of the *Outlook,* and one or two of the liberal-leaning articles we had run and something in Harry's statement of purpose attracted her. She was there to see if her impression of where we stood politically was correct. As Harry recalls the meeting, she put him through a rigorous questioning. Satisfied that she and he agreed on many of the burning issues that confronted Virginia—civil rights, the rights of organized labor, social welfare, the oligarchic nature of the Byrd machine, to mention just a few of the broadest categories—her manner softened and she evinced a genuine friendliness.

Although by lineage and affluence she was entitled to a place in Richmond's highest social circles, that didn't interest Anne Gellman. It was evident, as we got to know her, that she had no use for what she called "the silk-stocking set."

She had spent the war years seeking to improve the conditions of working people and the black community. "We have tried to hold the fort while you boys were away," she told him. Now that Harry and other young southerners of his liberal bent were back from the front, she was ready to share her tasks with them.

She left, promising that we would hear from her. We did. Anne Gellman and her husband, Sam, a prosperous lawyer who shared her social views, were the first Jewish family in Richmond to befriend us. Shortly after her visit to the office, we were invited to dine with them and their two young sons. Evidently we passed Sam's scrutiny too, for we received other invitations from the Gellmans, to subsequent dinners and to meetings and gatherings they felt would interest us.

One evening the Gellmans invited us to hear and meet Dr. Channing Tobias, chairman of the national board of directors of the NAACP. That was not so surprising, though, Harry and I decided afterwards. Since the audience in Richmond, even for such eminent national figures, was a meager one and since we were two young liberals with credentials that satisfied her, Anne Gellman was ready to plug us in anywhere. She included us in more intimate soirées attended by Richmond's small but dedicated liberal circle. And it was through Anne Gellman that we made our first connections with other returning servicemen, with leaders of the Negro community, and with members of Richmond's nascent, struggling labor movement.

Our numbers were small. But in hindsight, I realize Harry and I and our liberal co-workers were among the forerunners of a newly emerging South.

The novelist Erskine Caldwell has left us a vivid description of the region he grew up in. The South, he said, speaking of conditions in the eleven states of the Confederacy from post–Civil War days to the mid-thirties, is "a retarded and thwarted civilization," a "worn-out agricultural empire," a reactionary land that has "purposely isolated itself from the world" and "taken refuge in its feelings of inferiority." Supposedly, it has been cured of slavery, hookworm, high tariffs, and boll weevils, but it is "still sick," still holding ten million people, white and black alike, in conditions "just above peonage."[1]

Even as he wrote, though, the region was transforming itself.

In 1938, President Franklin D. Roosevelt pronounced the South to be "the Nation's Number One economic problem." But many of his New Deal programs had begun to have a beneficial effect on the benighted area. And the process of social improvement quickened dramatically with the outbreak of World War II. Good weather and low production costs made the South an ideal location for training camps and burgeoning defense industries. The enormous demands of manpower for the armed forces and the new plants and shipyards drew hundreds of thousands of impoverished sharecroppers and tenant farmers away from the cotton and tobacco fields. Those who couldn't enlist thronged to the new industrial areas in search of better-paying jobs. Little rural towns expanded almost overnight into flourishing cities.

After the war, peace brought many questions. In his book *Speak Now Against the Day,* John Egerton delineates some of the imponderables that confronted the region:

"Nobody knew if the men and women in uniform or in war production would come back to the farms and small towns and take up where they had left off. Probably nobody imagined—not many, anyway—that King Cotton was permanently dethroned, that tenant farming and sharecropping would be replaced by corporate farming, or that the South in one short generation would

1. John Egerton, *Speak Now Against the Day: The Generation Before the Civil Rights Movement in the South* (Chapel Hill: University of North Carolina Press, 1995), 146.

be transformed from an overwhelmingly rural and agricultural society to a predominantly urban-industrial one. And only dreamers gave much thought at all to what white and black citizens of the region would do, if anything, to reduce discrimination and raise the living conditions and expectations of the vast multitudes of poor and needy people who lived among them."[2]

For Harry and me, what needed to be done was without question. We instinctively counted ourselves among the veterans who returned determined to remake the South. We would not realize until many years later that even as we arrived in Richmond, the oligarchic old despots of the region were beginning to feel themselves under attack. Each new progressive idea we championed—anti–poll tax legislation, union organizing, fair employment, an end to racial segregation and discrimination—threatened the waning powers of the southern reactionaries.[3]

Our great assets, as we took up the fight, were our youth and the certainty of our convictions—and our ignorance of the vast dimensions and implications of the tasks we faced.

It was our good fortune that experienced activists like Anne Gellman were on hand to welcome and direct us. Social brokering was one of her great talents. Harry and I got a demonstration of that when she invited us to meet other war veterans she knew.

One night in the spring of 1946, we found ourselves in the Gellmans' living room in a gathering of ex-servicemen. It was a diverse group of about four blacks and seven or eight whites. In conversation over cake and coffee we got some notion of our backgrounds. At least four of us were Jews: Harry and I; Anne Gellman's nephew, Phil Brenner, an optometrist; and Ed Fleischer, a desk man at the *Richmond Times-Dispatch*. Among the others were several lawyers, a German-American hairdresser, a Unitarian social worker, and the star of the evening, a young Episcopalian minister, newly assigned to Richmond, a decorated naval lieutenant—Anne insisted upon telling us despite his modest demurrer—who had served with distinction in the South Pacific.

We had one thing in common: we had all passed Anne Gellman's political test. Under Anne's skillful guidance, the talk turned toward forming ourselves into the Richmond chapter of a national veterans organization. For servicemen of our liberal stripe, there was only one group worthy of our affiliation: the American Veterans Committee, or AVC.

2. Ibid., 320.
3. Ibid., 278.

The AVC was a new assemblage of men and women of World War II who had little use for Fourth of July parades or annual convention horseplay or the fancy uniforms and lodge-hall trappings of such old-line veterans organizations as the American Legion and the Veterans of Foreign Wars. The AVC's more sober and thoughtful orientation was well expressed, we thought, in its slogan: "Citizens First. Veterans Second." The AVC was not interested in becoming a special-interest group. And that appealed to all of us there that night.

Harry and I had already read *The New Veteran,* by Charles G. Bolte, the AVC's most prominent founder and its national chairman. We found it to be an eloquent book. When Bolte wrote "the concept of a better world is not an idea or a dream; it is a matter of political necessity," we felt he was expressing one of our own fundamental beliefs.

Two of the men at the Gellmans', the *Richmond Times-Dispatch* desk man and one of the black veterans, were already members-at-large of the AVC. The black veteran made a strong impression on both Harry and me. Tall—well over six feet—powerfully built, with the shaven head and the bearing of a George Catlin Indian chief, Oliver W. Hill was a partner in the law firm of Hill, Martin and Robinson, the NAACP's Virginia lawyers.

All of us there that night were drawn to the idea of a veterans group that would bring a fresh viewpoint to the problems of defense and social welfare; that would, unlike its racially segregated old-time counterparts, welcome black servicemen into equal membership with whites; and that would invite servicewomen to join its chapters, too, instead of shunting them aside into a ladies' auxiliary.

It was never a question that night of whether or not to form an organization; all that was wanting was membership blanks and literature. One of our number readily took on the assignment of getting us such material.

When we left Anne Gellman's house we were well along toward the formation of Richmond Chapter No. 1 of the AVC. (In spite of our optimism, there was never to be a Chapter No. 2.) It was our triumphant belief that we were the first racially integrated veterans organization below the Mason-Dixon line.

Today I'm less certain we were first. I know now that upwards of two dozen AVC chapters were organized throughout the South, primarily in university communities like Chapel Hill but also in big cities like Atlanta and Nashville. But although in numbers we were far surpassed by the American Legion and the VFW, I am ready to say with confidence that those old-line groups were no match for us in energy as we pursued our reformist goals.[4]

4. Ibid., 468.

True to her self-imposed task of inducting Harry and me into the scanty ranks of Richmond liberals, Anne Gellman introduced us to Brownie Lee Jones. For both of us, it was an occasion of enormous significance.

Through Brownie Lee we connected with the Virginia labor movement. And very soon she became a close friend. In that capacity, she went on to enlarge our social circle by introducing Harry and me to two of the energetic women on the staff she was assembling, one of whom became more than a friend to Harry. She became his life's companion.

Brownie Lee Jones's connection with the labor movement was somewhat anomalous. She was the director of the Southern School for Workers. It was an organization largely funded by the Rosenwald Foundation of Chicago. Affiliated with neither the American Federation of Labor (AFL) nor the Congress of Industrial Organizations (CIO)—those two groups did not merge until 1955—the school was designed to provide services to both of them. Organized labor was just beginning to take root in the South, and Brownie's school sought to nurture its growth.

The school's general purpose was to offer training to union members—classes in parliamentary procedure, so that they could run their locals; in history, both American and labor; and in constitutional rights. Literacy classes and voter-registration drives were two of the other projects it engaged in. Once or twice a year the school would organize trips to Washington, D.C., so that union members could see, firsthand, how their government operated. And in times of stress, when a union went on strike, the Southern School was there to help instruct union members in the art of picketing and to set up soup kitchens.

Although the Southern School maintained careful impartiality, its policies and no doubt Brownie's personal predilections aligned it more closely with the CIO, the more progressive of the two federations. One indication of that was the school's attitude on matters of race. It was clearly and openly opposed to segregation. One of its stated purposes was to "sponsor projects bringing together members of Negro and white local unions on matters of common concern." Since the AFL trade unions and many of the CIO locals were racially segregated, this in itself made the school suspect. In that time, to be suspect meant only one thing to many white southern union leaders and their members: connection with the Communist Party or subject in some way to its influence.

Any of us who spoke or worked for racial equality could expect to be smeared with the red brush. An anti-Communist once put the situation we faced in blunt but accurate terms: "Integration," he said, "is the Southern version of Communism."[5]

No one—at least to us—seemed better able to surmount that kind of innuendo than Brownie Lee Jones. "Communist" attached more readily to Jews, people from working-class immigrant families, and easterners. But Brownie's origins were in the Midwest; generations of Oklahomans lay behind her. Thomas Hart Benton, that most American of artists, was a cousin. She had begun her career as a social worker and her first assignment was with the YWCA. But the Great Depression of the thirties moved her in a more radical direction. After trying to help young women who had lost their jobs because of business failures, she was drawn to the labor movement, like many young idealists of her time. Union organization, they came to believe, offered the likeliest way of bringing some security into the lives of working men and women.

Christened Fleeta McIlhenney Jones, Brownie early on adopted her nickname as her official signature. With her slight, boyish figure, her bobbed, greying hair, and her intense, bright gaze, and with a cigarette usually clamped between two fingers, she personified for me the flapper girl of the twenties.

She took Harry and me in tow and had us meet Richmond's labor leaders, who were in short supply. I cannot remember now who headed the AFL. But two of the CIO leaders seemed to welcome our interest: Ernie Pugh, the CIO's regional director for Virginia, a mellifluous-voiced southerner given to the recitation of such homiletic verse as the old Edgar Guest poem "Let me live in a house by the side of the road / And be a friend to man"; and the Reverend Charles C. Webber, Methodist "Chaplain to Labor," a trim, athletic man with twinkling eyes, who had once played semi-pro baseball and had just been elected president of the state CIO council. Webber was more our sort than Pugh. That became clear, I think, when we proffered both of them our services, free, for any writing or printing projects the CIO might have in mind, and Webber took us up on the offer.

Brownie, meanwhile, was ready to make use of us, too. She was organizing an "observers picket line" when she met us and immediately invited us to join it. What we were asked to observe was a strike at a large laundry and dry-cleaning establishment in an alley off Chamberlayne Avenue. Driven to desperation by low wages and poor working conditions, the black women who labored there had voted the union in and, when management refused to meet and bargain with them, taken their case to the sidewalk in front of the plant.

The strike had been going on for over a month. The Southern School had

5. Ibid., 301.

helped organize the picket line and had set up a soup kitchen. When militancy failed to bring the plant managers to the bargaining table, Brownie thought of trying a new tactic—shaming them. Her idea was to gather a number of white and black professionals, well-dressed men and women, and have us stand across the street from the plant. We were to watch the fired workers picketing and signify our solidarity with them.

So early one morning, around 7 A.M., about twenty of us set up the observation line. When Harry and I arrived to join the prominent gathering, I found, to my embarrassment, that I was facing a place Dave Bernstein and I had visited. It had been a successful visit, and there I was, in a demonstration against one of the *Southern Jewish Outlook*'s advertisers. Although it was unlikely that the plant manager would spot me in the group, I made a cowardly attempt to position myself in the rear. From that uneasy spot I witnessed my first strike.

It was a chilly morning, grey and overcast. On the sidewalk opposite us, a short width of cobblestone street away from where we stood shivering, the striking women began to march. They carried signs prepared for them by the Southern School, announcing their affiliation with the Laundry Workers Union and their refusal to work for starvation wages. Middle-aged, black, swathed against the cold in old coats and raveled sweaters and wool caps, they marched and sang. They trudged in an uneven, lurching circle, in broken shoes, on feet swollen and weary from their years of labor over laundry vats and presses. And yet they sang. A defiant song. An old song, although it was new to me: ". . . Just like a tree that's standing by the wa-a-ter, / We shall not be moved!" The words seemed to hover in the frosty air.

And as they marched, their replacements arrived. An old battered bus drove up. About a dozen slim young black girls, recruited from counties outside of Richmond, dismounted from the bus. They huddled together, shy, scared of the women they were scabbing on. When they caught sight of us, they whispered amongst themselves, mystified and afraid. Two broke and ran off. Two men came out of the plant and hurried the girls inside.

As I watched them going in, I realized with a sinking heart that the strike was lost. Management's strategy was plain: force the experienced workers out, since they were old and worn out and troublemakers; bring in a fresh new crew, at lower pay, and train them.

Brownie's observation line worked to some extent. The owners of the plant came out and stood on the back-entrance steps glaring at us. Then a truck from the parking lot alongside the plant came tearing down the street, so close to the curb that our observer line had to scramble backwards.

Our presence, I think, heartened the striking workers. They smiled at us and nodded when we shouted words of encouragement. Several of us held our fingers up in a victory sign. But after an hour or so, we left. It was no surprise to learn, as we did in due course, that management still refused to meet with the local's business agent, and that none of the strikers was rehired when the picketing finally petered out and stopped.

The office of the Southern School for Workers was situated on the third floor—two rooms at the top of a dark, narrow, rickety staircase—of an old brick building on North Ninth Street, directly opposite the black iron railing, old chestnut and magnolia trees, and close-mowed sloping lawns that surrounded the gleaming, snow-white Capitol Thomas Jefferson had designed for the commonwealth of Virginia.

Harry and I began dropping in at the school with some frequency—it was only six blocks from our office and on the way to our printer. The regularity of our visits increased as we got to know the members of Brownie's staff. Two in particular attracted us.

Helen Estes Baker was Brownie's one black staff member, a round-faced, pug-nosed, vivacious woman, golden-brown in color. Helen was a native Virginian, born and raised in the little town of Suffolk. Her father, James Estes, was a college graduate and held one of the highest-ranking jobs available to a colored man of his scholastic attainment. He was a letter carrier. He was the first member of his race in Suffolk to obtain such a position. Since he was colored, he could not aspire to a promotion. From time to time, during his working years, the local powers-that-be appointed a new postmaster. Whenever that happened, James Estes was taken off the street and brought into the office to instruct the new postmaster in his duties. Even after the post office was taken over by federal civil service, nothing changed for him.

One evening a day or two after Pearl Harbor, Helen's husband recalls, a group of family and friends had gathered together on James Estes's front porch, and in the course of conversation, somebody wondered aloud as to what would happen if the Japanese won the war.

"Oh," said James Estes, "it might not be so bad. Maybe I'd get to be postmaster."

Helen's college major was education. After her marriage, she worked for a while, in the late thirties and early forties, as a supervising teacher in an elementary school. The school was located in a poor working-class neighborhood in which most of the women were employed in the nearby tobacco factories. It was a source of some irritation to Helen that when these women came home from work, they would just *sit,* out on the porch steps, legs dangling, instead of going inside to fix dinner and tend to the needs of their families.

One summer, in the spirit, perhaps, of setting an example for these women, but also out of curiosity, Helen decided to take a job in a tobacco factory. After a day spent lifting and packing cartons of cigarettes into large corrugated cardboard boxes and getting the heavy boxes ready for shipment, she was exhausted. It took all her remaining strength to creep the few blocks home. She could not bear to bring the reek of tobacco into the house. She shed her clothes on the back porch, stumbled into the bathroom for a clumsy wash and went straight to bed. She did not return to the plant.

The summer experience convinced her that what those working women needed was a union. She bent her efforts to that end and somehow came to Brownie's attention. When Brownie invited her to join the staff of the Southern School, Helen readily accepted.

Helen was a person of great courage and common sense. Some people are fixed in our thoughts by an anecdote. One story Helen told us early in our friendship helped define her for me. She had been called to the witness stand in a trial and the attorney for the opposing side, a white man, asked her to state her name for the court record.

"Mrs. P. H. Baker," she replied, knowing that if she had said "Helen Baker," the attorney would have gone on to call her by her first name. That incident sums up for me her resistance to the humiliations inflicted on her race and the quick-witted way in which she fought them.

"P. H. Baker" was Dr. Percy H. Baker—"Bunny," to his friends—a geneticist on the faculty of Virginia State, the state-sponsored black college in Petersburg. By the time we got to know him, he had already won recognition in his field for the work he was doing with fruit flies.

Since Petersburg was about thirty miles south of Richmond, our circle of friends, once the Bakers were included, widened geographically as well as numerically.

The other member of Brownie's staff who became an immediate friend was a young woman from Nashville by the name of Joanne Farrell. She had a fresh-scrubbed, unpainted face, and kept her chestnut hair drawn tightly back over her ears, away from a broad white brow, and gathered behind in a snood. I mention these details for I feel they were, in a way, a political statement. A lack of makeup and a lack of interest in matters of hairstyle and dress, for a young person of our generation, were often indications of a commitment to a left-wing political orientation. For much the same reasons, young men like Harry and me never wore hats.

Joanne Farrell was another victim of the Great Depression of the thirties. Her father, an engineer, impoverished by the Crash, took to the road in search of employment, and Joanne pursued her grammar school education in five states before the family settled in Nashville. She was an apt student, however, and won a full scholarship to Vanderbilt University, where she majored in chemistry, was elected to Phi Beta Kappa, and graduated magna cum laude. For a while she worked as a chemist in a laboratory in New Jersey. But she came to realize it wasn't what she wanted.

The same impulse that brought Harry and me to Richmond—the postwar idealism in the air—brought Joanne there, too. Much the same impulse in the Kennedy years drew a later generation into the Peace Corps; and still later on in the sixties the same impulse brought other young people south, at Martin Luther King's summoning, to work in the civil rights movement.

Joanne Farrell's manner was so quiet that it took a while to get to know and appreciate the lively intelligence behind that brow. Harry and I were both drawn to her, to her swift, flashing smile and sturdiness of spirit. Among the pleasures of that friendship were the occasions when we lunched or dined together. Often, after an evening meeting or, on a rare free night, after a movie, as we drove Joanne back to her rooming house (on Monument Avenue, like ours) in an old car that Harry's dad had passed along to us, she taught us union songs.

"Which side are you on?" she sang in a clear, sweet soprano. "Which side are you on?"

Or another of our favorites: "There Once Was a Union Maid." Who never was afraid "of goons and ginks and company finks, / And the deputy sheriffs who made the raid." And finally:

> Oh you can't scare me,
> I'm stickin' to the union,
> I'm stickin' to the union,
> Till the day I die!

She sang songs she had picked up in the course of the Southern School's work with Negro churches:

> Farther along, we'll know more about it.
> Farther along, we'll understand why.
> Cheer up my brother! Live in the sunshine.
> We'll understand it all, by and by."

Her repertoire was limitless.

It is not wrong to say that both Harry and I were smitten. But by then my bond to Naomi was too tightly forged; I left the field to Harry.

Brownie had a gift for finding bright, attractive women to serve on her staff. Helen and Joanne were followed by two others.

Polly Hayden was the first true worker to join the Southern School's office force. She grew up in Roanoke, Virginia, child of a backwoods family of textile mill hands. Polly herself went to work in the mills at an early age. While still in her teens, she married a young sailor in her community. But perceptive people at the Roanoke YWCA recognized her capabilities. They felt her talents were being wasted in the mills and sought to guide her (there were, and probably still are, some in Virginia who would say the YWCA corrupted her). They got her a scholarship to Sweet Briar College, and when she came home she found she had outgrown her childhood surroundings and, sadder yet, her young husband.

Divorced and starting life in a new city, when Brownie hired her she was glad to become a member of our group. With her Virginia twang and her freckled, gamine face, she added an authentic working-class note to our social life.

Carla Meyerson, a grave, dark, young Jewish woman from New Jersey, filled the last slot on Brownie's staff and soon joined our social set. Carla brought her violin along with her, for music was one of her ardent interests. Literature was another. Needless to say, she was quick to introduce another opinionated voice into our political and intellectual discussions.

Brownie and her staff members shared one physical characteristic. They were all about five feet tall, an inch or so under or over. It was, I suspected, hardly a coincidence. After Brownie and I became good friends, I mentioned my suspicion. Brownie confirmed it.

"Oh, honestly, I don't know," she said, trying to explain her choices. "I guess tall people strike me as lethargic, somehow. Lacking in energy." She said that to me, and I am six-foot-two. I took her confidence as a compliment.

Our widening friendships were a source of support and consolation to Harry and me. If we felt embattled, confronted by an overwhelmingly segregated society and a Jewish community from which we too often felt alienated (even as we tried to cultivate it and influence it), at least we had the comfort of friends.

I expanded the number of little women in our group by one. After a year of many letters and many weekends of my commuting, first to Philadelphia and then to the Bronx, when she moved back to New York to become a psychology instructor at City College; and after weekends of her commuting, for she came down to Richmond several times, to test the social waters for herself and to see if she could find employment there ("Yes," they told her at the Virginia Commonwealth Department of Public Welfare, "trained psychologists are rare pearls in Richmond, Virginia"); and though we were never formally engaged, Naomi Weltman finally cried: "Enough!"

And so on January 23, 1947, we got married.

4

"You Boys'll Wear Yourselves Out"

Back in the post–World War II years I write about, the late 1940s and early 1950s, we liberals spoke a language that must sound like code today. Let an old cryptographer pause and sort through party names and party epithets and try to decipher the kinds of political affiliation available to Harry and me as we sought to advance our social goals.

Then as now, the two major parties were the Republicans and the Democrats. But the differences between the two seemed vaster then—as stark as rich and poor. Over the years these differences narrow from time to time, although after the Reagan decade and under the George Bush presidency, and even as I write today in the Clinton years, the gap between rich and poor has widened again.

Back in 1946, though, to liberals like Harry Bernstein and me, the Republican Party signified big business, outworn ideas, and reactionary politics. Almost two decades after the Great Depression, it was still, for us, the party of Herbert Hoover, he of the ruddy jowls and high wing collar, whose administration, we thought, had plunged our country into economic chaos. Since I believed his policies had brought my father close to bankruptcy and killed my hopes of going to college full-time, my grievances against him were highly personal. Thus I was startled to find, as we became involved in Richmond's political campaigns, that substantial numbers of the city's black voters were Republicans. It was instructive for me to become aware of the root of that allegiance and to realize that the party I despised was the party of Abraham Lincoln.

Although Harry and I professed to be independents, in the privacy of the the polling booth we usually voted Democrat. But what sort of Democrat? There were three options. One was unthinkable: Senator Harry Flood Byrd was a Democrat, but we abhorred his kind. He, however, soon distanced himself from the national party. At the Democratic National Convention in Philadelphia in 1948, Byrd and a number of other southern Democrats were so enraged at the strong civil rights plank their party adopted that they were ready to quit it, and they came to be known as Dixiecrats. But Dixiecrat was a nickname, not a ballot designation. Some Dixiecrats, most notably Senator Strom Thurmond of South Carolina, eventually switched parties and became Republicans.

If you stayed with the mainstream Democratic Party, and though infuriated, most southern Democrats did, you could be a Truman Democrat, more or less loyal to the president who succeeded FDR; or you could be a Wallace Democrat, a follower of former vice president Henry Agard Wallace, whom Roosevelt dropped for Truman, and who remained the nominal leader of the left wing of the party, an outspoken opponent of the nuclear arms race and our Cold War with the Soviet Union. Harry and I were Wallace Democrats.

Philosophically, I suppose, we were even farther left than that. The names of two other left-wing parties frequently appeared on ballots. Socialist and Communist. While Harry and I favored socialism as a system of government—the democratic socialism of the Scandinavian countries, for instance—the Socialist Party in America was so weak and so incapable of any kind of effective campaigning that participating in it would have been hardly more than a symbolic gesture. The Communist Party, on the other hand, had substantially more power and influence. Many liberals of an older generation had been attracted to its radical ideas during the Great Depression years, and many remained members even after the Soviet-Nazi pact. During the final days of World War II, when we and the Russians were comrades-in-arms, the Party acquired considerable legitimacy among liberals and attracted a large number of prominent intellectuals into its membership.

But America's disenchantment with Russia soon followed the peace. The distrust and animosities of the Cold War set in. And the American Communist Party came to be seen, even among liberals, as the Soviet Union's means for furthering its political goals in this country and as an instrument for subversion. Almost every progressive labor union and almost every liberal organization—the AVC, too, as we were to find out soon enough—struggled with the problem of how to avoid being taken over by aggressive and well-organized Communist cells.

There remained one other political designation to consider, sinister and most troublesome of all if you were not a Communist. And that was to be *called* a Communist. As a label slapped readily on any politically active person of progressive views (and in the South that would include almost anyone who fought for racial equality), it could have a sudden and chilling effect.

There were hardly any Communists in Richmond. Harry and I knew of only three: Alice Burke, state secretary of the Party, a brisk, outspoken, strong-minded woman; an ex-sailor, Louis Kalb, a noisome runt, who joined our AVC chapter and made a nuisance of himself, haranguing us on obscure political issues at meetings and, upon adjournment, proceeding to hand out flyers for some Communist Party event; and Kalb's patient wife, Mary. Three, then. Or four, if you counted the Kalbs' infant daughter, Buttercup, who accompanied her parents everywhere.

No doubt there were other Party members, too, secret and unknown to us. But Richmond's "radical network," in my experience, was a tiny one. If you included liberals like Harry and me in your "network" count, as people who disliked our politics were ready to do, the number grew. But it was never in my experience more than three or four dozen.

Once you were pegged as a "radical," you could anticipate being labeled Communist or, more likely, in the vituperative designations of those times, "pinko," "fellow traveler," "crypto-Communist," "Commiesymp." That was a risk you ran, particularly if, like me, you were repelled by the Communist Party's rigid dogmatism and stridency, yet still believed it was undemocratic and unproductive to revile the Party or outlaw it. The battle between Communists and anti-Communists was one of the most troubling and disruptive forces in the liberal political maneuvers of the era. Even in a backwater like Richmond, we felt the reverberations of those furious engagements in New York and other large urban and academic centers.

More than felt them. We saw with our own eyes, within our own liberal ranks, how destructive the Communist–anti-Communist struggle could be. The history of one regional organization, the Southern Conference for Human Welfare, exemplifies for me the lethal impact of our internecine strife.

The conference was organized in 1938 by a group of young white southern liberals, many of them officials in New Deal agencies. It was the first interracial civil rights body to emerge in the South since Reconstruction. High hopes attended its beginning. Such eminent, nationally known southerners as Justice

Hugo Black and fellow Alabamans like Aubrey Williams, a former director of the National Youth Agency, and attorney Clifford Durr and his wife Virginia, were involved in it from the start. Eleanor Roosevelt attended its first meeting in Birmingham. The CIO supported the conference financially as part of its new organizing drive, Operation Dixie.

Up in Richmond, Brownie Lee Jones took part in its activities, and Harry and I tried to attend whatever meetings and functions it scheduled in Virginia.

But in the end, its leading staff members were suspected, fairly or unfairly, of Communist leanings, and the organization's effectiveness dwindled. The conference's support of Henry Wallace's 1948 presidential campaign was a disastrous step. Within the year, the conference collapsed, done in, as many good causes of that time were, as much by suspicion as by fact.[1]

"The nice thing about having your own business," Harry said, "is that there's no limit to the hours you can work."

He said it often, and most times sourly, during the first half of 1946 as we got under way with the *Outlook*. Usually he said it around midnight when we were still reading galley proofs or working on the layout for an upcoming issue.

Days and nights ran together. The *Outlook* commanded most of our attention. Scarcely had one issue gone to press than we were slaving over editorials and feature articles for the next month's number. But we enjoyed writing those. What we chafed at doing and what took an inordinate amount of time was gathering Jewish community news, not only from Richmond (whose five or six thousand was still the largest Jewish population in the state) but from clusters of Jews all over Virginia. Social tidbits, Harry's father assured us, were what sold subscriptions; in his view, one wedding picture was worth a thousand words about some liberal Virginia Jew or a dozen paeans to kibbutz-living in Palestine.

We subscribed to two Jewish wire services, but used their canned stories sparingly. It was a matter of pride with us to print mostly original work. And not ours alone. Even though we offered modest payment, we found we could commission articles and book reviews from some well-established writers who were sympathetic to our point of view and interested in reaching a new audience. And writer friends from our Company D and Arlington Hall days were another source of material. Later on, within the year, we discovered a treasure:

1. This account of the SCHW draws from two sources: John A. Salmond, *My Mind Set on Freedom* (Chicago: Ivan R. Dee, Inc., Publisher, 1997), and Egerton, *Speak Now Against the Days,* cited earlier.

reprint rights. That enabled us to run some splendid things without cost, several of Martin Buber's Hasidic tales, for instance; a few Sholem Aleichem stories; new work by Yitzhak Shenberg, a rising young writer in Palestine; and a powerful John Berryman story about what it was like to be mistaken for a Jew.

More often than we liked, though, our news hunting and promotional efforts took us to organizational meetings where we sat through hours of dry business on the chance that a sympathetic chairman would recognize us and give us a few minutes to stand and plug the *Outlook*.

In more peaceful moments, at bedtime and in between times, we read. Aware of how little we knew, we read whenever and whatever we could. Books on Judaism and Palestine and the Holocaust, on any Jewish issue that seemed pressing, began to pile up on the office desks and overflow onto the couch and floor. We sought exchange subscriptions with various other Jewish publications. And with no army censor to stop us, we subscribed to such leftist periodicals as the *Nation,* the *New Republic,* the *New Masses,* Dwight Macdonald's *Politics*—and even George Seldes's *In Fact.*

In the interstices of these work-crammed days and nights we still, somehow, found time to pursue our interest in politics and social action.

The AVC began to flourish, and we were busy nurturing it. The naval lieutenant, the Reverend Ernest A. De Bordenave, to our great joy agreed to take the chapter chairmanship. Oliver Hill and I accepted subsidiary positions. Harry declined to take an office. The AVC helped me develop a few new skills. I, whose last public speech had been given at my Bar Mitzvah when I was thirteen, found myself addressing union locals, church gatherings, NAACP meetings—any group that would hear us—on the problems and aspirations of the returning veteran. I appeared before the Richmond city council as the one veterans-organization witness opposed to the erection of a World War II war memorial. The AVC wanted a living memorial, I said, a commemorative ward in the veterans hospital, scholarships for the children of Richmond men and women killed in battle. Two young men in the audience came up afterwards and gave me their dues checks on the spot.

In a small city like Richmond (population 250,000), it was fairly easy to become notorious. Harry and I found ourselves recognized on the street, sometimes by people who wanted to argue with us, sometimes by well-wishers. Chapters of Hadassah and Pioneer Women, two of the major national Jewish women's groups, ran subscription drives for us, and our mailing list of paid subscribers began to grow.

Ad solicitation, though, still made first demand upon my time. I spent most of every day, on foot and on the phone, doggedly pursuing potential advertisers. But I had little talent for such work, and though I did make sales, it was evident to Harry and me that if we relied on my efforts alone, we would be publishing some pretty slim issues of the *Outlook*; twenty-four pages at the most.

Then Providence smiled on us.

Harry and I were working at our desks one afternoon. I was on the phone, coaxing a reluctant businessman, no doubt, when we heard a knock on our open office door.

A woman stood in the doorway. Heavy-set, ample-bosomed, she gave us a dimpled smile as we both looked around. It was April; yet warm as the day was, she wore a long-sleeved, long black dress. A round, broad-brimmed black hat framed a kewpie-doll face. And her voice, when she addressed us and asked us if she might come in, was high-pitched and childlike.

She was Mrs. Fanny Kessler. She had received and read two or three introductory copies of the *Outlook,* and she was impressed. The magazine, she said, was just what the Jewish community of Virginia needed. It was a good-looking magazine. It addressed issues of importance, fearlessly. "As a Jewess," she said, "I would be proud to be associated with such an enterprise."

And what sort of association did she have in mind?

"Why," she said, "I am an experienced advertising saleswoman."

With admirable self-restraint, I did not rise at once and bestow the mantle of advertising manager upon Fanny Kessler. Instead, Harry and I asked her to please sit down and tell us more about herself.

Mrs. Kessler was a freelance saleswoman. She sold ads for high school and college yearbooks, for prom programs, for the souvenir booklets they gave out at organizational dinners and dances, things like that. She had lived in Richmond for more than thirty years. As a chapter member of Hadassah and a board member of the Temple Beth El Sisterhood, she knew the Jewish community intimately and felt certain she could be helpful to the *Outlook*.

We thought so, too. It took no more than a couple of hours to come to terms with her on a sales commission for a trial period of three months. She would draw up a contract, she said, and bring it by for our inspection the very next day.

Fanny had other talents besides one for selling; as we came to know her better, we discovered she was an amateur astrologer and a very good cook. Two healthy, hungry bachelors like Harry and me, tired of cheap restaurant food, were only too pleased to accept a couple of dinner invitations to the Kessler household.

Fanny was also devious. I chanced upon evidence of that shortly after she came to work for us. Happening into the office one day I found her alone at my desk. She was on the phone, talking, I gathered, to a prospective advertiser. And she was using an assumed name and holding a pencil in one corner of her mouth. When she hung up I asked her the reason for such subterfuge, and without a trace of embarrassment she explained that she had called someone to whom she had sold space only a few days ago in a program for the firemen's ball, so she felt it was necessary to disguise her identity and her voice. Sometimes, when we were on deadline and an extra ad or two would have carried us well into the black, Fanny was unavailable. Migraine. A sudden, vague indisposition. The thought did not escape Harry and me, though, that she was probably also on deadline for another of her clients.

Still later on, well along in our relationship, Harry and I caught her trying to play us off against each other. I can't remember the occasion; perhaps it had something to do with renegotiating her contract. But she took me aside, alone, and in her wheedling little-girl's voice said, "Marvin, I can't talk to Harry. He's all business. Abrupt. Curt. Impatient. Now you are a sensitive, caring person, Marvin, and I feel I can speak openly with you, heart to heart." I was flattered; but I felt I could not keep secrets from Harry and reported the conversation to him. He burst out laughing. "Harry," he said, in a fair imitation of Fanny Kessler's voice, "I can't talk to Marvin. His head's always in the clouds. He's a poet, a dreamer. Hopeless when it comes to numbers. Now you are practical. Down-to-earth. I can get to the core of the problem with you right away."

Although we couldn't quite trust her, we did like her. She had sales ability of a high order. And she made two important contributions to the success of the *Outlook*. First, she suggested that we run a "Cooking Page" and offered herself as its editor. An idea like that wouldn't have occurred to Harry or me in twenty years. It became one of the *Outlook*'s most popular features.

Then she informed us that she was trying to persuade her husband, Nathan, to sell ads for us. "I'm good," she said, matter-of-factly, without vanity, "but I'm simply not in Nathan's class. He's a super-salesman." Harry and I had met Nathan at one of our dinners at the Kesslers' and had been unimpressed. But Fanny knew better. She kept after him, and finally her persuasions worked.

Into the *Outlook* office came a whirlwind. Stout, on the short side, red-faced, his grey felt hat askew on a bald head, eyes magnified by lenses thick as the bottoms of shot glasses, Nathan Kessler was an arresting sight. He burst in upon us, jovial and booming. I cannot remember if Nathan ever wore a loud plaid jacket. But he was, without doubt, a loud-plaid-jacket personality.

"My Fanny thinks I gotta come down here 'n help you fellas out." How to describe his accent? His whole life was in it. Southern, middle-class American, a dollop of East Side Yiddish. It was June when he came by, and we had our eye on our first big holiday issue, the September 1946 number, the month in which Rosh Hashanah fell, the Jewish New Year. We hired Nathan on the spot and Fanny was right. Nathan was phenomenal.

With Nathan and Fanny at work selling ads, and with a part-time worker from a secretarial service to pick up and sort our mail, deposit checks, and tend to our elementary bookkeeping, Harry and I were free to undertake another major *Outlook* project. We decided not to publish in July and August. Instead, we stowed two small suitcases and a large batch of books and magazines in the trunk of Dave Bernstein's old Oldsmobile and set out to tour the state.

We did not confine ourselves to Virginia's major urban centers—Richmond, the Norfolk-Portsmouth area, Alexandria—where most of Virginia's 8,000 to 9,000 Jewish families lived. It was our intention to venture into all the byways, into small towns off the beaten track, looking for Jews wherever we could find them.

Sometimes, through our Richmond contacts, we came with an introduction to a local rabbi or to the president of the local Hadassah or B'nai B'rith chapter. If we came to a town where we knew no one, we would consult the phone book for a synagogue or a Jewish community center. If we found none, we would cruise Main Street until we happened on a store with a Jewish name—usually a dress shop or a furniture or dry goods store. Surprisingly, even when we walked in cold, right off the street, we seldom got a brush-off or a rude reception. Southern hospitality, perhaps. Half an hour with a talkative storekeeper and his wife usually provided us with a quick course in the town's history of the Jews. Any town with thirty or more Jewish families, we decided, was worth cultivating.

All that summer we criss-crossed Virginia, from Skyline Drive in the Blue Ridge Mountains down to the Tidewater and the Atlantic coast, impressed wherever we drove with the beauty of the state. A couple of times I'd break away for a quick trip north to visit Naomi and the family. And Harry would duck down to the Isle of Palms, off the coast of South Carolina, where his folks had a summer place. But for the most part we kept to the road.

In this way we ended up with a sizable number of loose two-dollar subscriptions and promises in six or seven towns to run subscription drives for us. We were able to develop, too, a network of social correspondents—housewives and storekeepers—who promised to send us monthly reports on weddings, Bar

Mitzvahs, births and deaths, and bridge and mah-jongg parties. All in all, the *Outlook* established connections with thirteen or fourteen Jewish communities.

Occasionally we would have a remarkable stroke of luck. In Alexandria, a city with a Jewish population of several hundred, we connected with the Bernfelds. Jules Bernfeld was a hairdresser by profession. But he was also an AVC member and active in local Democratic and Zionist politics. We were instantly compatible. His wife, Louise, who also took a liking to us, was president of her Hadassah chapter and an officer in the Seaboard Region. Every Hadassah member in Alexandria, she assured us in a manner that brooked no opposition, would become an *Outlook* subscriber. When we parted, Jules, who had a literary side, was ready to begin writing articles for us on weighty matters of politics and economics.

We returned to Richmond in a euphoric mood, which was enhanced by Nathan's sales report. It had been a profitable summer.

If there was any down side, it was having Nathan in the office with us, usually entrenched at the secretary's desk. Benign as Buddha he sat, contemplating a growing pile of sales contracts, ad layouts, and logo cuts. He was a Buddha who provided his own incense. A chubby smoldering cigar butt was always wedged between chubby fingers. Now and then his contemplative mood was broken by a phone call. In an office as small as the *Outlook*'s there were no secrets; certainly no secret phone conversations. You could tell at once from the disgruntled way he spoke that Fanny was on the other end of the line.

"Yeah, yeah. I know. Yeah." And then, though we could not hear her voice, we knew from his reply what she had said. "Nathan!" she must have said, urging him on to greater sales from whatever auguries she was consulting, "The stars are good!"

"Yeah, yeah," he said as he hung up, turned to Harry and me with a caustic smile and a shrug of humorous contempt. "Yeah. The stars are good."

For most of August and well into September, Harry and I toiled underground, in the salt mine of the *Outlook* office, putting together the holiday issue—at 60 or 64 pages our biggest issue yet.

When we finally emerged, the trees along Monument Avenue were bowed and heavy with the end of summer. And when we took up our organizational lives again, it was to find that Richmond Chapter No. 1 of the AVC was facing a crisis.

Our chapter had been growing at a moderate rate. We had nearly a hundred members, a good mix of blacks and whites and even one woman, a former WAC. But a week before our general membership meetings resumed in the fall, the Reverend Mr. De Bordenave invited the executive committee into his study and, with grace enough to look uncomfortable, informed us that the pressure of church work had grown so great he was compelled to resign as chairman.

When she heard the news Anne Gellman did not hesitate to put our dark suspicion into words. "His vestrymen must have gotten to him. I know that church. It's strictly a silk-stocking crowd. I'll bet they told him he had to stop hobnobbing with the radical element. People like the two of you."

Whatever the reason, we were without a chairman. But not for long. A delegation of three chapter members—the nominating committee—stopped by the *Outlook* office shortly after the meeting with De Bordenave and urged me to take the chairmanship. When I objected and suggested Oliver Hill, saying a native Richmonder would be more appropriate, the delegation, an interracial one, insisted that we were not ready for a black. I sighed, as is my wont when presented with a daunting task, and then went right out to the Baptist Book Store on Grace Street and bought a copy of *Robert's Rules of Order.* Harry, who had a strong distaste for holding office in any organization we got into, rose to the occasion and agreed to join the board.

When we dined at the Gellmans a few nights later and told her, Anne Gellman shook her head. "Chairman! Vice chairman! I declare. On top of everything else you're doing? Watch out, you two. You boys'll wear yourselves out."

But Harry and I were too caught up in what we were doing to worry about "burnout"—a word that I do not believe had entered the popular vocabulary yet. Besides, we felt the AVC was starting to catch on. An accountant and a couple of social workers in our chapter were staff members out at McGuire Veterans Hospital just over the city line in Henrico County. They were thoroughly familiar with all the opportunities available to veterans and had the happy thought of organizing a service that would offer guidance to ex-GIs seeking to claim their rights. It was a highly successful program. A grizzled veteran of World War II, Sam White, a Virginian with an unhappy penchant for saying "Nigras" instead of "Negroes," was so impressed with the help he got in filing for disability that he announced he was quitting the American Legion and joining us.

I had only been in office a month or two when I was presented with a stringent test of my abilities. Charles G. Bolte, a founder of the AVC and its national chairman, wrote to say that he was on a tour of chapters throughout the country and would like to visit Richmond, one of the foremost southern chapters. We were honored. Bolte was on the way to becoming a national celebrity.

But his announcement plunged us into a dither of activity. You would have thought a general was coming through on a white-glove inspection.

Two medical student members of the AVC were able to engage the Egyptian Building, a meeting-hall on the campus of the Medical College of Virginia; they assured us it would accept an interracial audience. The YWCA agreed to arrange a dinner for us. We plastered McGuire Hospital and black and white college campuses throughout the city with posters and handbills. And Ed Fleischer, our deskman member, managed to get a news item on the event into the *Times-Dispatch*.

Bolte and his wife Marian arrived at noon, on a Wednesday in November, the day before Thanksgiving. We had reserved a room for them at the John Marshall Hotel, a popular and fairly expensive lodging in the heart of downtown. Oliver Hill and I were designated to greet them and serve as their guides. It was a bold step. Since Negroes were not allowed to enter the John Marshall through the front entrance, we steeled ourselves for trouble. But Oliver was equal to the challenge. Six-foot-three, built like a football linebacker, he was a formidable presence. With him beside me, I feared no evil. And since I am over six feet and on the heavy side, I imagine I looked pretty tough, too, although I shrink from physical encounters.

Oliver and I entered and crossed the lobby, purposeful and stern-faced, paused at the desk while I asked a tight-lipped clerk for Mr. Bolte's room number and ignored whatever looks were aimed in our direction as we stood waiting for the elevator. The elevator operator, an elderly black man, stared at us but let us on, and we ascended to Bolte's room without incident and greeted our guests triumphantly.

That episode was the high point. The rest of the visit was an odd mixture of ups and downs.

The Boltes were charming, and Oliver and I would gladly have sat and chatted with them about Richmond, but we had a schedule to meet. On a wild chance, I had phoned the *Richmond Times-Dispatch* a week earlier and gotten through to the editor, Virginius Dabney, known pejoratively as a "Southern Liberal." I was agreeably surprised when he said yes, he had heard of Charles Bolte and his veterans group and yes, he would be pleased to meet him.

So Oliver and I escorted Bolte down to the lobby and across it and around the corner to the *Times-Dispatch*. It was a cordial interview, if guarded and non-committal, and we left encouraged by the thought that Virginius Dabney was now informed that the AVC had established an interracial beachhead in his city.

All the chapter members gathered at the YWCA to meet the Boltes and share a buffet dinner. Then we all went on to the mass meeting at the Egyptian Building. Alas, *we* were the mass. In spite of our valiant efforts to stir up publicity and despite promises from AVCers that they were bringing friends, Bolte and I, as we sat on stage, confronted an audience of about seventy-five people scattered about a large auditorium. Bolte was much more nonchalant than I about the whole thing. To my murmured apologies, he said, "I don't blame them. There's nothing duller than a public speaker. I know I hate to go hear one."

His speech, a good, forceful one laced with humor, improved the mood of the evening. But I, in my first public appearance in my new office, proved an inept chairman. When Bolte finished, I called for questions from the audience and, hearing none, and not being quick-witted enough to ask one of my own, adjourned the meeting.

I gave some of my impressions of Bolte and his wife in a letter home. Since my mother saved everything I ever wrote, I am able to quote from it:

Bolte is big. About an inch or so taller than I and huskier. His artificial leg (a war casualty) makes him walk like an old sailor but even so he never looks comical. He is only twenty-six years old. But his thick, black moustache helps age him and he has a wheezy, old man's laugh. He reminded several of the fellows in our chapter of Orson Welles. I am reaching the conclusion that most young public figures look like Orson Welles. E. J. Kahn does. Henry Morgenthau, Jr. Elliott Roosevelt. Not much of a theory, but I am stuck with it. No doubt I'll think of others from time to time who look like Orson Welles and I'll let you know.

Everyone liked Mrs. Bolte. She's tall, long-legged and looks a lot like Katharine Hepburn. When they produce the Charles Bolte Story, they won't have any trouble casting her role.

After the mass rally, Ed Fleischer invited us out to his place and since it is common knowledge in the chapter that he has one of the best liquor supplies in Richmond [which, at the time, had a law forbidding the public sale of liquor by the drink], about eight of us went out there.

Bolte was more fun to listen to off the platform than on it. Even drinking, though, you could never call him easy-going or relaxed. Alert, watchful—that's the way he seems. Ed Fleischer said something about men who were trying to make a living out of their war reputations, like Marion Hargrove, Bill Mauldin, or George Baker. "Or Charles Bolte," said Charles Bolte. Anyway, the important thing is everyone approved of him as our National Chairman.

The letter omits a final disappointment. One, on reflection, that has symbolic significance as I recall the evening. Ed Fleischer, another northerner, had thought to add a festive southern note to the occasion and decided to serve mint juleps. He did not discover, however, until we began drinking them, that somehow he had used powdered alum instead of powdered sugar. The whole evening had a sweet-and-sour taste.

Upon joining the NAACP Harry and I felt we had entered the frontline trenches in the fight for civil rights.

Founded in 1909 by blacks and whites, with Jews prominent among the first white members, the association was the oldest, largest, and most firmly based of all the national black service and civil rights organizations. In Richmond and throughout the South it was second only to the church in the devotion it inspired among its members. Indeed, the NAACP often met in churches, since there was a scarcity of black communal halls.

It wasn't hard to get ahead in the Richmond chapter. Tasks were so many and hands so few, any interested person could expect a warm welcome and opportunities for advancement. Once I had addressed the chapter on the AVC's program for returning veterans, and once I paid my dues and began attending meetings regularly, I was rushed right along. In six months I was co-chairman of the voter-registration drive. Within a year, I was a member of the board.

Even before we became active chapter members, Harry and I felt we had connected with the NAACP. Oliver Hill's firm was the association's chief advocate in Virginia, and Oliver had introduced us to his partners, to the jovial and exuberant Martin A. Martin and to Spottswood W. Robinson III, a wiry, pencil-thin, light-complexioned chap, whose off-hand and unassuming manner belied his crucial role in the firm. Spott Robinson had already acquired a national reputation for his work. He was one of the NAACP's major strategists in the school desegregation cases. The U.S. Supreme Court adopted a view Robinson had long expounded when it held, in its 1954 decision in *Brown* v. *Board of Education,* that racially segregated schools were inherently unequal and therefore unconstitutional.

In the Richmond chapter of the NAACP, three men were our mentors: Dr. J. M. Tinsley, chairman of the chapter and president of the state-wide conference; W. Lester Banks, director of the association's Virginia office; and John Drew.

Dr. Tinsley, a dentist, was a soft-spoken, courtly man, the first Virginia gentleman of our acquaintance. While he was always cordial, his natural reserve lent an air of formality to our relationship. Lester Banks, a ruminative fellow, a chain-smoker and a wit, was an easy person to get to know. But he was businesslike, too, frank to say he hoped Harry and I could become a source of funds and support in the white and Jewish communities.

With John Drew I went beyond a casual acquaintance into something deeper and, at first, more troubling. He and I co-chaired the voter-registration drive and in the course of working together became quite friendly. Drew was a compact, solidly built, bullet-headed black man, just above middle height. He had a moustache fine as a cat's whiskers and a smile as slow and bright as sunrise.

I'm not sure now what his office in the chapter was—treasurer or secretary, I think. But I noticed him at the first meeting I attended and was impressed from then on by his composure, by the clarity of his reports, and by the practical good sense of his comments on whatever business came before us. From the neatness of his dress, the sharp crease of his trousers, and the brilliant shine of his shoes, I would have guessed he was some sort of junior executive. I was so aware of Drew's abilities that even after months in Richmond I was still somewhat taken aback when I discovered how he earned his living.

As co-chairmen of the voter-registration drive, it was up to us to organize a committee of NAACP members who would go door-to-door in black neighborhoods shortly before elections, instructing prospective voters in how and where to pay their poll tax and register. Drew was remarkably adept at recruiting people and organizing the campaign. I devised report forms and instruction sheets for canvassers and voters. The Southern School for Workers readily put its mimeograph machine and office secretary at our disposal and cranked out several hundred copies of material for our committee's use.

Drew, I knew, worked for Pollard and Bagby, a large real estate and insurance broker on Main Street. His firm's office was less than a block away from the Southern School. So when I stopped by the school one afternoon to pick up our copies, I decided to walk Drew's report forms and leaflets over to him.

A receptionist sat at a desk just within the entrance. I approached her and asked, "Is Mr. Drew in?"

She looked at me blankly. "Mr. Drew?"

"Yes. I believe he works here. Mr. John Drew?"

She continued to stare at me. But then a smile of recollection burst upon her face. "Oh, *John* Drew. You must mean *John*. Yes, *John*'s here. I do believe he's comin' now."

And so he was, walking along the central aisle between the office desks, carrying a can of metal polish and rubbing cloths. He was dressed as I had never seen him before, in old army tans, clean, but rumpled from his chores.

Drew smiled when he saw me, raised his laden hands and motioned us toward the front door, wisely getting us out of earshot of the receptionist, who was watching us with rapt interest.

Out on the street we shook hands and I gave him his packets. It irked me to find a man of his capability engaged in such menial tasks. Yet it was evident from Drew's unassuming manner that he understood, as I would not, that in Richmond of that year a black wage-earner had few choices. I, at least, could chafe and fume inside for him when I saw how his natural organizational gifts were being wasted.

We made up as to when we would meet again and I left him there, setting his cans and rags down on the sidewalk, getting ready to polish the company's brass doorknobs and facings. Pollard and Bagby's "boy."

As our common enterprise progressed and I felt a growing intimacy between us, I began to call Drew by his first name. He, however, continued to call me "Mr. Caplan."

On reflection, I became aware of the nuances involved in the way we addressed each other in the NAACP. I never called Dr. Tinsley anything but Dr. Tinsley. His dignified presence, his high office, and his years required that. He called me "Mr. Caplan," although now and then, to my delight, for it suggested mutual affection, he slipped and called me "Marvin." Les Banks and I were on a first-name, bantering basis within a matter of minutes, for we considered ourselves contemporaries. But Drew couldn't have been more than ten years older than I. And I liked him too much to let his use of a formal—and subservient—form of address go unchallenged.

So I raised the matter with him during one of our lunches. It was in a coffee shop on Second Street. In my Richmond, Virginia, it could be nowhere else. Second Street was black Richmond's Main Street. Most of the necessary shops and offices were on that two- or three-block ghetto strip. Slaughter's Hotel was on Second Street; so were laundries and grocery stores, beauty parlors, dress shops, restaurants, even a mortician. And above the stores were many of the offices I began to frequent—the *Richmond Afro-American*; Hill, Martin and Robinson; and across a common landing from each other, Dr. J. M. Tinsley's dental clinic and the Virginia office of the NAACP.

John Drew and I had begun to meet in the NAACP office occasionally, during his lunch break, to go over the city map and association membership lists and determine in which of Richmond's fifty-five precincts to concentrate our efforts. Since his hours at Pollard and Bagby were long, he had some flexibility. So when we finished our work we would sometimes run downstairs and grab a bite. The restaurant was a black workingman's haven, a small, crowded greasy spoon, heavy with cooking odors and cigarette smoke. But it was one place that would serve both of us. And they made a pretty good Brunswick stew.

The first few times we went in there my alien presence attracted attention. But soon enough the regulars stopped looking at me. One noontime as we sat talking, John started to call me "Mr. Caplan." I stopped him.

"Hold on, John," I said. "Look. It seems to me you and I have had a good, close working relationship for some time now."

"Yes," he said, nodding. "I been wantin' to tell you how grateful I am to you for all you're doin' for our people."

"I don't do what I do for your people," I told him. "I do it for myself." And then, feeling I must have sounded abrupt, I quoted to him, from my current reading, the words of the ancient rabbinical sage, Hillel the Elder: "If I am not for myself, who will be for me? But if I am only for myself, what am I? And if not now, when?"

John liked that. He smiled and nodded approvingly.

"But that's not what I want to talk about, John. What I want to know is, if we're friends, and I call you 'John,' why do you keep calling me 'Mr. Caplan'?"

He shrugged and shook his head.

"Try calling me 'Marvin.'"

"Marvin."

But then he shook his head again, and smiled in what looked like an agony of pain. "I cain't," he murmured. "I cain't. It don't sound right."

"Well, then, if you call me 'Mr. Caplan,'" I said, "I shall have to call you 'Mr. Drew.'"

"Oh no!" he protested. "Don't do that! Everybody calls me 'John.'"

So I dropped the matter. Our working relationship and friendship continued throughout the five years Naomi and I lived in Richmond. When Naomi and I moved to Washington in 1951, Drew would come up to see us now and then and even stay overnight in our apartment. At some point in all that time, a moment unremarked by any of us, John Drew began to call Naomi and me by our first names.

5

Red Rumblings

Almost nothing is left of the *Southern Jewish Outlook* except memories. It isn't published anymore. Back copies of it are unavailable. I once owned two bound volumes of the first thirty or forty issues, but they have disappeared. Harry Bernstein, who after leaving Richmond went on to become labor editor of the *Los Angeles Times* and still lives in California, cannot imagine what happened to *his* volumes.

All that I have today are two loose copies of the *Outlook,* one from 1946, the other from 1950. They measure 10½ by 13½ inches, roughly the size of an old *Life* magazine. I also have a scrapbook of editorials, articles, essays, stories, and other samples of my work that I put together back in 1951 so that I would have something to leave with editors when I went job-hunting that year.

The editorials and articles are highly selective and scanty. But what my scrapbook does include is every "Office Diary" I ever wrote. The "Office Diary" was a monthly column, an informal essay in which I chronicled the goings-on in and out of the office of a group of characters identified, not by name, but by occupation. The Editor. The Advertising Manager. The Advertising Manager's Wife.

I cherish those columns. I think they are some of the best things I wrote for the *Outlook*. When I read them today it is like leafing through an album of old snapshots.

Our personal experiences, our interests, *ourselves* are reflected in them. Here's an excerpt. An anecdote told to me by a black member of Richmond Chapter No. 1 of the AVC:

Woman's Ingenuity

A friend of ours told us about his Army experiences, when he was the only Negro in a Headquarters company. He worked in an office with a WAC from Richmond, Virginia, who had all the genteel prejudices of the well-bred Southern belle. She never looked at or spoke to him directly. She avoided handing him things. And in the close quarters in which they and about a dozen others worked, she always kept the furthest distance possible. She even went so far, and this he felt was a bit unreasonable, as to Jim Crow the morning sign-in sheet. Whenever he signed in ahead of her, she would carefully locate his name and then write hers—a good ten spaces below.

And here, from another "Office Diary," is a look at The Editor (Harry Bernstein) in action:

"Ah, The Editor! Lying prone on the Office Couch, tossing sheets of newspapers and magazines up in regular spurts like a geyser, as he finishes reading them. Ah, The Editor! Imposing his complex, goading nature on the Office Help; turning the simplest discussions into tense, thought-provoking arguments." By contrast, in this same piece, I note that The Advertising Manager (me), unlike The Editor, "doesn't twist paper clips into odd shapes while he's reading. He doesn't stretch rubber bands between his teeth and forefinger and twang them till they break."

Since I wrote the columns, I had all the best of it. I was good-natured and reasonable; Harry, cynical and caustic. But I admit now it was a ventriloquist's trick; I was all the voices.

An undated "Office Diary," but one obviously written just before Naomi Weltman and I got married, suggests the hesitancy with which I approached the ceremony. It starts off with four lines of doggerel:

> Marriage is a chancey thing!
> It seldom turns out well.
> Sometimes you get more for a ring,
> On a carousel.

And once again, I, the noble spirit, must deplore the sordid details of daily life. The Advertising Manager, packed and ready to head north for the wedding, observes of his fiancée, "She used to write me such charming letters. Now all I get are lists of instructions."

I was a lucky man. Naomi took such joshing with amazing forbearance. After a mid-January honeymoon of one week in Warrenton, Virginia (a town I had come to know and like during my sojourn at Arlington Hall), and a few days in Washington, we returned to Richmond, and I discovered I had married a woman ready to accept me, crotchets and commitments and all.

A one-time "YIPSL" (a member of the Young People's Socialist League), Naomi shared my political and social convictions. She even took up a cause of her own. At the Virginia Commonwealth Department of Public Welfare, where she was soon employed as a psychologist, she became friends with the lone black social worker on the staff, a stately, self-possessed woman who had the same first name—Naomi Hardiman.

Mrs. Hardiman was accustomed to eating lunch alone in the department's small dining room. Without consulting anyone, and indifferent to stares or whispers, my Naomi began lunching with Naomi Hardiman, and so together they integrated the place. It was a small triumph and, as I see it today, a sad one. For it emphasized again how in a segregated society any friendship across the color line, however spontaneous and genuine to begin with, becomes, somehow, a social statement.

But then all our friendships as a married couple were a kind of social statement. Our friends were drawn almost exclusively from our offices and from the organizations we were active in, so that our work and play involved virtually the same people.

Harry and Joanne were foremost among the couples we saw socially. The Gellmans welcomed us. Another couple we grew close to was the Schiffs— Morris (or "Moe" or "Shifty," as he was known to his friends) and Betty.

Moe was one of the first southern whites to join our AVC chapter. However, despite a southern drawl, so broad it sometimes sounded like a comic put-on, Moe was not the genuine article. He was already three years old when his parents, Polish Jews, emigrated to America and settled in Richmond, where his father opened a grocery store in a colored neighborhood. Moe was a friendly, sociable fellow, always ready to do a favor for you or the AVC chapter; it was his and our misfortune that he wasn't always reliable. A characteristic gesture was to slap his forehead with his open palm and exclaim, "Ooooooh!" whenever he remembered something he had promised to do and hadn't.

Shifty was a self-confessed redneck. Or he had been one, he said, until he met Betty. She was the political director in that marriage. She and I shared an instant bond: both of us had been born and raised in Philadelphia. Up there, when she was twelve, she had gone to live with an older brother and his wife, and the wife, an avowed and active Communist, shaped Betty's political viewpoint. Moe's wife was a tall, striking brunette, in height almost equal to his six feet. In matters of social issue she seemed to operate by spontaneous combustion. Give her news of some event that struck her as an injustice, and her large grey-green eyes would flare up with ire; her broad mouth, so ready for laughter, would open in a burst of righteous anger.

Betty took a protective interest in Harry and me when, new to Richmond, we were still two lone bachelors. The Schiffs lived out in the West End in a new duplex, a wedding present from Moe's father, who was a real estate speculator as well as a grocer. Sunday breakfast at the Schiffs became a fairly regular event for us; and since Betty considered us unattached, she sought to introduce us to likely young women.

Before long it was our good luck to have Betty come and work for us. She was an excellent bookkeeper and soon took over most of the office business. When Fanny Kessler, that restless soul, decided she had had enough of "The Cooking Page" and resigned as its editor, Betty took over that assignment, too. "The Cooking Page" continued to be one of the *Outlook*'s most popular features. A misprint in one of the recipes brought us more mail and phone calls than anything else I can remember publishing.

The Schiffs were one of the first couples Naomi met when she moved to Richmond. She and Betty, an incongruous pair physically—Mutt and Jeff—hit it off from the start. Their warm, confiding, sisterly relationship and my own affection for Betty bound our two couples together.

We had other Jewish friends besides the Schiffs and the Gellmans. But there again, politics, not religious commonality, determined the selection: two AVC members, single men, northerners like me, Dr. Clayton Blum, a veterinarian, and Eli Horowitz, a patent examiner; a relocated Israeli couple, the Kochs—Fritz, a highly intellectual German refugee, store architect for Thalhimer's, and Anne, a native American, a saleswoman in Miller and Rhoads's book department. We found kindred spirits among other men and women active in liberal Zionist circles—Pioneer Women and the Farband (Workmen's Circle), organizations closely affiliated with the socialist Labor Zionist movement in Palestine. All of us were secular Jews, indifferent to shul or synagogue activity; we rarely attended services except on the High Holy Days. Looking back on that time I must admit, with a twinge of guilt today that I did not feel then, that Naomi, Harry, and I were more often in black churches than we were in synagogues.

I introduced Naomi to Spott Robinson, one of Oliver Hill's partners, and he insisted that we come out to the house that Sunday afternoon and have her meet his wife, Marian. The Robinsons became another regular stop on our social rounds. They had a brand-new TV set, still something of a novelty in 1947 Richmond. We took to dropping by occasionally on Sundays, after Spott and Marian got home from church, and we would sit around and snack and chat and view old movies with them.

Marian Robinson was a full-bodied, rose-freckled, handsome woman. The expression "Earth Mother" was in vogue then, and it seemed to me an apt description of her robust figure. She was often amusingly tart-tongued. "There goes old Spott, running his mouth again," she'd say when a phone call had interrupted us and her husband had become engaged in a protracted legalistic conversation with someone calling for advice. And though she was proud of him and his accomplishments and his impressive reputation as an interpreter of civil rights law, she once remarked in exasperation, after he had been honored for his work, "Yesss. Civil rights! You can't eat it! You can't wear it! You can't buy beans with it!"

Spott's easygoing, offhand, unassuming manner concealed his keen, exacting intellect. We had known him for quite a while before we learned from others that his scholastic average at Howard University Law School was the highest in its history, perhaps unequaled to this very day. But we did experience his perfectionism for ourselves.

Woodworking was one of Spott Robinson's ways of relaxing from the rigors of law practice. (Bricklaying was another.) When Naomi happened to mention one afternoon that she needed a duplicate set of wooden cubes for one of the tests she gave small children, Spott said, "Don't buy them. I'll be glad to make a set for you."

So the next time we came over, Naomi brought a box of the cubes, and Spott went to work copying them with his power tools. He had them for us the next time we stopped by. But he wasn't satisfied with them. Naomi thought they looked great. No, Spott said, he had just remeasured. The cubes were a few millimeters off. To our consternation, those cubes became a prolonged project, never quite right in Spott's opinion, never quite ready to be surrendered, until Naomi finally wrested them away from him one Sunday, refused to give them back, and assured him honestly, after she had used them for a while, that they suited her just fine.

Homemaking must be a feminine instinct. How else can one explain Naomi's dissatisfaction with our living arrangements? When we arrived in Richmond, fresh from our honeymoon, it seemed to me we had a perfectly adequate place to live: the large, second-floor bedroom at Mrs. Murray's that Harry and I had been sharing.

Harry obligingly turned the room over to us and moved into a smaller one on the third floor. But Naomi was unhappy. Although we spent little time in the place, she found the heavy walnut furniture oppressive and the romantic darkness of the richly curtained room depressing. She did not like sleeping in twin beds. (Now *there,* I had to concede, she had a point.) And though every morning we had coffee privileges in Mrs. Murray's kitchen, we ate most of our meals in restaurants. Naomi was simply aghast at what food was costing us.

To placate my bride I agreed to let her try to find us other housing. After countless ad perusals and phone calls, she did find us new lodgings. For half of what we paid Mrs. Murray, Nannie and Roger Hart, an elderly couple, rented us a bedroom and tiny kitchen on the second floor of their green-shingled bungalow on Hanes Avenue, over in Northside. The kitchen came complete with an ancient refrigerator, a two-burner gas stove, and a table and two chairs.

True, we and the Harts shared the same bathroom. But our room was good-sized and sunny. We also considered it a plus that it was underfurnished. It contained nothing more than a large double bed and an old bureau. Mrs. Hart assured us we could exercise our own taste in making it more livable, and we had her permission to decorate the place in any color scheme that suited us.

We could now have breakfast in our own abode and dinner at home on the nights we had no meetings and weren't working late. We could even have friends over for Sunday brunch (although it was evident to us, from things Mr. Hart said, that they had better be white friends). With the addition of two folding chairs and a little squeezing, four of us could crowd around the white-painted wooden table for lox and bagels. The kitchen had a door that opened onto a small back porch. On warm days one of our guests could sit in the open doorway, half-in, half-out of the kitchen and the place was positively roomy. Or so Naomi insisted.

Once the question of accommodations was settled, we could turn our attention to things that truly mattered: the *Outlook,* Naomi's work at the Department of Public Welfare, our busy organizational life, and the vainglorious notion of our little band of cohorts that it was up to us to remind Richmond how far it had strayed from the democratic ideals that had originated there.

I think I know some of the outstanding events a historian would enumerate if he were trying to convey the national and international mood in the year 1947.

Dominating everything was the onslaught of the Cold War. Only two years after the end of World War II, in which they had been allies, the Soviet Union and the United States were eyeing each other with bitter animosity. When Secretary of State George C. Marshall announced the Marshall Plan, a four-year, $17 billion program to help the recovery of a devastated Europe, the Russians denounced it as an attempt by capitalism to dominate the world. The Soviet Union organized a nine-nation Cominform to fight the plan.

New Deal liberalism felt the Cold War chill. Republicans controlled Congress for the first time in fourteen years. Over President Truman's veto they passed the Taft-Hartley Act, a measure that hobbled the labor movement with severe restrictions. The government instituted a loyalty check to purge its payroll of subversive personnel (i.e., Communists and their sympathizers). And the House Un-American Activities Committee instituted an investigation of communism in the film industry.

There were a few bright spots that year, however. For one thing, the U.N. General Assembly voted to partition Palestine into a Jewish and an Arab state. And since even we did not live for politics alone, I should note that for social activists the film of choice, and the 1947 Oscar-winner, was *Gentleman's Agreement* in which Gregory Peck portrays a gentile writer who assumes a Jewish identity so that he can experience anti-Semitism firsthand for an article he is writing. ("I looked at him [Peck]," my mother told me loyally, "and all I saw was you.")

Virginia surely had its own infection of anti-Semitism, yet so far as Harry and I could tell, the disease seldom manifested itself. As Jewish journalists, we preferred to concentrate on positive developments. We were greatly heartened by the U.N. decision on Palestine—one of the few times the United States and the USSR voted together. Harry and I could see in the forthcoming nation, Israel, the emergence on the face of the earth of another democratic socialist state.

But in 1947 Richmond, what soon eclipsed all other events for us was Oliver Hill's announcement that he was going to run for a seat in the Virginia House of Delegates.

Members of the Richmond Chapter of the AVC rallied as one to Hill's support. Harry and I were determined to do everything we could to help. Down in the bowels of the Central National Bank Building (and if you had ever heard the rumble of the heating and air-conditioning equipment, you'd know how apt my metaphor is) there was another tenant—a radio station. Because we all worked late, we became friendly with some of the radio staff members. An announcer, Bob Davis, shared our liberal views and helped us prepare a

record for the sound truck that we rented and drove through the streets of colored neighborhoods, urging people to "pay your poll tax, pay your poll tax, pay
your poll tax" and vote for Oliver W. Hill.

John Drew and I stepped up our voter-registration drive. I went out alone,
door-to-door, to form my own impressions of how our campaign was going. If
the blacks whose doors I knocked on were suspicious of a white NAACP can-
vasser, they certainly dissembled. I was met only with courtesy or, at the worst,
curiosity. Courtesy, curiosity—and probably evasion. For I could never know
how many of the promises to register I elicited ever translated into votes. One
thing I did know after my canvasses: Virginia's election laws were highly effective in the discouragement of all voters, white as well as black.

I already knew how small the electorate was. From a book I was reading
then, *Southern Politics,* by V. O. Key, Jr., I learned that from 1925 to 1945 an
average of only 11.5 percent of the people eligible to vote in Virginia ever went
to the polls.

If you wanted to vote in Virginia, you had to pay for the privilege. The poll
tax was $1.50 a year. If you had never paid it before, you had to pay the taxes
for two back years plus the current year. Plus interest. About five dollars. Not
an inconsiderable amount for a poor man.

It was easy to understand why so few black Virginians voted. In addition to
the poll tax, black voters also faced the prospect of having to take a literacy test.
And if you lived in a rural area, as many blacks did, you probably had to take
a day off from your job to vote, for polling booths were often situated in remote and inaccessible places and open at hours inconvenient for a working
person. Black voters frequently risked hostility and intimidation when they
went to register or to cast their ballots; most times none of the candidates running could ever be counted on to speak or act for them. Given such obstacles, it
was easy to understand why the Byrd machine was able to control the state so
effectively.

Despite all this, the August 5 primary turned out better than we had anticipated. Oliver was one of eighteen candidates vying for Richmond's seven seats.
He came in eighth. He got 6,310 votes, only 190 fewer than the candidate who
beat him out for the seventh place. Had he won, he would have been the first
Negro to occupy a seat in the General Assembly since Reconstruction days,
1889; and the first Negro Democrat ever to become a member of that body.

Heartbreaking? Yes. But we drew encouragement from the closeness of the
race. And we knew we would redouble our efforts whenever Oliver chose to
run for office again.

Almost every time Harry and I ventured out of Richmond for a meeting, we found ourselves caught in the Communist–anti-Communist crossfire.

Liberals had divided themselves into two camps. The Americans for Democratic Action (ADA) were vehemently anti-Communist. The Progressive Citizens of America (PCA) sought to maintain the old World War II common front between liberals and Communists, and it was no doubt true that the Communists controlled the organization.

Although Harry and I did not join either group, it is indicative of our sentiments that when the PCA called an all-day conference in Washington, we could not resist attending. Naomi and Joanne were interested, so the four of us drove up to the capital.

We found it an absorbing experience. The one-world views expressed at plenums and workshops were close to our own sentiments. And the highlight of the day was surely the unscheduled appearance at one session of Henry Wallace himself. It was the first time I had encountered him in person. That tall, shambling, soft-spoken man with a farmer's cowlick confirmed the favorable impression I had formed of him from newsreels and press stories. When he spoke of the need to reach some kind of peaceful accommodation with the Soviet Union, both Harry and I responded affirmatively. And when, emphasizing the need to explore our options, he quoted a German proverb, "Man muss immer umkehren" ("One must always make a fresh start"), I found myself nodding in agreement.

A wonderful concert ended the day. Woody Guthrie, that mythic American folksinger, sang some of his songs to his own guitar accompaniment. Then he introduced his protégé, a fresh-faced, sweet-voiced young tenor and fellow guitarist—Pete Seeger—and the two of them played and sang together.

We drove home exhilarated in spite of the lateness of the hour, with Joanne leading us in some of the songs we had just heard. When Wallace, at the urging of the PCA, announced at the end of the year that he would be a candidate for president in the 1948 elections, he had, in Harry and me, at least two firm votes in Richmond.

Communist domination was inevitably the central issue at the AVC's second national convention, held in Milwaukee, Wisconsin, near the end of June 1947. By then the organization's national membership had grown to comprise 102,000 World War II ex-servicemen and women. There were 1,000 chapters, spread throughout the 48 states, Washington, D.C., Alaska, and Hawaii. Fifteen hundred delegates and 600 alternates came together in Milwaukee, ostensibly in response to Charles Bolte's call to prepare "a positive program to halt the drift toward depression and war." But what really brought such an outpouring of members was the prospect of a showdown fight between Communists and anti-Communists over control of the AVC.

Four of us went as the delegates from Richmond: Harry, Moe Schiff and I, and Sam White, our chapter's crusty ex–American Legionnaire. It is more accurate to say three of us went with Sam, for he had the newest and roomiest car available. Sharing wheel-time, we drove day and night across one-third of the continent.

A pleasant surprise was the scattering of familiar faces we encountered at the Schroeder Hotel and in the various meeting centers: fellow alumni from Company D Ann Arbor and from Arlington Hall. Less agreeable, as we mingled with delegates from the power centers—New York, Chicago, Boston, Los Angeles, yes, even Philadelphia—was the realization, once again, of how politically provincial Richmond was. Our big concern down there was race, not reds. But in Milwaukee we quickly got caught up in the struggle for political control and set about choosing sides.

Like the rest of the nation's liberals, the AVC delegates were essentially split into two camps. The left wing, the Unity Caucus as it called itself, was reputedly dominated by Communists. The anti-Communist faction, or Independent Progressives, was a well-organized caucus whose leaders included Bolte, a majority of the AVC's governing body (the National Planning Committee), and some skillful operators from the ADA and the International Ladies Garment Workers Union. In contention was which group's candidate would be elected the AVC's new national chairman, since Bolte was retiring from office to take a Rhodes scholarship at Oxford University.

Harry, Moe, and I were put off by the vehemence of both caucuses. We were drawn to an alternative—Build AVC, a quickly organized coalition headed by Michael Straight that sought to stake out a middle ground between the two major factions. Straight was a dashing figure, a handsome, patrician, eloquent chap, publisher of one of the magazines we read most closely, the *New Republic*. The three of us decided to throw our support to him and his candidates, particularly his nominee for vice chairman, a black veteran, Franklin Williams, a counsel in the New York office of the NAACP. Sam White said he wanted to look around some more and hear all sides before he decided whom he'd vote for.

For me, one word described the mood of the convention: intense.

The *Milwaukee Journal* took note of that quality in a front-page box headed "Morpheus Absent." The heavily attended platform committee sessions, it observed, had continued throughout Friday night, ending at 8 A.M. on Saturday—"an eleven-hour grind."

The same passionate intensity was evident even at sessions set aside for relaxation. I have in mind the beer bash that the Milwaukee brewers threw in our honor. For the festivities they ushered us into a large hall, rich in beer-drinking decor. It featured a sawdust-sprinkled floor and round tables covered with red-and-white-checked cloths and laden with big bowls of pretzels and potato chips. Waiters in striped shirts and sleeve garters of Gay Nineties vintage moved about, plying us with thick meat sandwiches and pitchers of local brew. Up on the small, brightly lit stage was the entertainment—a couple of burlesque comics as MCs and a chorus line of pretty girls, whose ample natural endowments were enhanced by black net stockings, brief ruffled skirts, and low-cut, tight-laced bodices.

Most of these enticements were wasted on our delegates. A few partiers at the front tables hooted and whistled and carried on in credible veteran-convention style. But from there on back, as you walked away from the footlights, you saw the *echt* AVCers. These men and women were oblivious to the old vaudeville songs, the leg kicks, can-cans, and smutty stories; they sat deep in serious talk, grimly intent on the main business of our gathering.

The ideological split in the ranks of the AVC ran so deep it even divided families. When a rumor arose that Straight's Build AVC caucus (the "pink caucus," its disparagers called it) was planning to run Elliott Roosevelt for chairman, the Independent Progressives got the word out that if so, they would run Franklin D. Roosevelt, Jr., for top office. But the rumor was baseless, and that prospectively interesting confrontation between FDR's two sons never took place.

The candidates that Michael Straight's coalition finally did put forward, George Ebey for chairman and Franklin Williams for vice chairman, were defeated. The convention elected as its new national chairman Chat Paterson, the AVC's national legislative director, who, the *Milwaukee Sentinel* noted, "is often described as 'more realistic' than the retiring chairman, Charles G. Bolte." For vice-chairman, the convention chose the Independent Progressives' candidate, Richard Bolling, an ADA organizer and, in later years, a Missouri member of the House of Representatives and a liberal Democratic stalwart.

Sam White voted for Paterson and Bolling. One of Sam's motives was evident to us from some of the things he said. He couldn't bear to see Williams, a black man, as one of our national officers. The atmosphere in the car as we drove back to Richmond was strained. Yet today I have second thoughts about our readiness to condemn Sam White. Was his inclination to oppose a candidate simply because he was a "Nigra" any more an example of reflexive bias than Harry's, Moe's, and my predisposition to support a candidate, unknown to us, largely because we wanted to help advance a member of his race?

What prompts the question is my subsequent reading of a memoir by Michael Straight, in which he recalls the 1947 AVC convention and observes of Franklin Williams that he was "an ambitious black" who "proved in time to be a highly successful and most unappealing man."[1]

Not long after we returned from Milwaukee, Moe and Betty Schiff shocked their friends by announcing the breakup of their marriage of five years. Betty came into the office one morning, stood at her desk leafing through papers and without looking up said to Harry and me, "Moe and I are getting a divorce."

She was beyond any argument to the contrary or any consolation we could offer her. A few weeks later she left Richmond and moved back up to Philadelphia.

Before the year was out Brownie Lee Jones rallied all of us to a new project. In October 1947, President Truman's Committee on Civil Rights, after deliberating for almost a year, issued its final report. Entitled *To Secure These Rights,* it set forth in sober prose the facts of what racial segregation and discrimination were costing America in dollars and, worse, in lost and wasted lives.

To those of us accustomed to working for civil rights in a local atmosphere of indifference and hostility, it was good to see the issues addressed nationally. The prestige of the committee—fifteen national leaders, with Charles Wilson, president of General Electric, as their chairman—and the White House imprimatur commanded wide media attention. Anyone reading the news accounts or listening to the radio and TV broadcasts could no longer profess ignorance of the injustices that fifteen million black Americans endured.

Brownie proposed that we organize a forum to study and discuss the report. Encouraged by the enthusiastic response she got from those of us to whom she broached the idea, she and Joanne, indeed the entire Southern School staff, got to work arranging the endeavor. They engaged a conference room in the YWCA. They prepared a study guide. They sent out announcements and personal invitations. And Brownie persuaded Dr. Howard Davis, a professor of history at Richmond Professional Institute (RPI) to be our discussion leader. This last arrangement was no small coup, since Dr. Davis was highly regarded in his profession, and what's more, he was a native-born Virginian.

How those of us attending were chosen I can't remember now. But when

1. Michael Straight, *After Long Silence* (New York: W. W. Norton, 1983), 237.

Harry, Naomi, and I looked around that first night we recognized practically every one of the forty or fifty people sitting in the rows of folding chairs. Anne and Sam Gellman were there, Fritz and Anne Koch, John Drew and Les Banks and Dr. Tinsley; several of the AVC and the NAACP board members and rank-and-filers; a handful of CIO union officials, the Reverend Charles C. Webber prominent among them; several clergymen and churchwomen. Moe Schiff was there, accompanied by Phyllis Lindsay, a tall, good-looking young woman, as blond as Betty was brunette, who was soon to become his second wife. And no doubt some of those present were disgruntled to find a red contingent among us—Virginia's Communist Party secretary, Alice Burke, and the Kalbs, Lou, Mary, and little Buttercup.

For four consecutive nights under Dr. Davis's courtly, expert leadership, we made our way through the report and found that it confirmed our general impressions with harrowing details.

We had all been aware of the horror of lynchings. Lillian Smith had written a vivid book about them, and Billie Holiday sang a mournful and terrible song, "Strange Fruit."

> Southern trees bear a strange fruit.
> Blood on the leaves and blood at the root.
> Black bodies swinging in the Southern breeze;
> Strange fruit hanging from the poplar trees.

But the report brought home to us the extent and persistence of the phenomenon. It told us that from 1882 to 1925 lynchings were reported in 43 of the 48 states; the other five were New England states. In 1946, at least six persons, all Negro males, had been lynched by mobs. Three of the six had not been charged with any crime; of those who had been charged, one had been falsely accused of stealing a saddle, one had been accused of breaking into a house, and one had been charged with stabbing a man. That same year mobs were prevented from lynching 22 other people, 21 of them Negroes. The fear of lynching among Negroes, the report said, was "devastating."

In the account of police brutality and the administration of justice we were again presented with particulars: of confessions extorted by third degree, of false convictions by all-white juries, of Negroes whipped and shot by officers of the law. In Glynn County, Georgia, on July 11, 1947, eight Negro prisoners were shot and killed by white guards for an alleged attempt to escape.

We had known Negroes were underpaid and denied jobs because of race. The report told us, in the chapter "The Right to Equal Opportunity," that 80.8 percent of the complaints of job discrimination lodged with the Fair Employment Practices Committee (FEPC) in fiscal 1943 were based on race. An AFL survey showed the average weekly wage of Negro veterans in 26 communities (25 in the South) was 30 to 78 percent less than the wage white veterans received. We all had heard the catch phrase for blacks: "Last hired, first fired." From July 1945 to April 1946, the report said, while unemployment among whites increased one and a half times, it tripled among blacks. Close to the mid–twentieth century, minority workers were still held in peonage; prisoners in the South were routinely released into the custody of entrepreneurs who paid fines and posted bonds.

Things were no better for Negroes who joined the armed services. Black enlisted men were disproportionately denied commissions. In the U.S. Navy, Marine Corps, and Coast Guard, "almost 80 percent of Negro sailors are serving as cooks, stewards and steward's mates."

John Drew and I had known something about the problems Negroes ran into when they went to the polling booths. The report told us that because of such stratagems as white primaries, poll taxes, and literacy tests and because of intimidation, only 10 percent of all the eligible voters in seven poll-tax states voted in the 1944 presidential election, as against 40 percent in the states where the vote was free. In the 1946 congressional contests, 5 percent of the eligible voters cast ballots in poll-tax states, as against 33 percent where there was no tax.

In education, housing, and health care, the only thing blacks could be sure of was that any services available to them would be inferior. Nationwide, Negro life expectancy was ten years less than white.

Harry and I, as former residents of Washington, D.C., took special note of a cartoon summary of what awaited blacks in the nation's capital. Traveling from north to south, a Negro had to change to Jim Crow trains at Washington's Union Station. "He cannot eat in a downtown restaurant . . . attend a downtown movie or play . . . sleep in a downtown hotel." If a Negro chose to live in Washington, the report said, he was confined to segregated neighborhoods, where 40 percent of the housing was substandard (as against 12 percent in white neighborhoods); he had to send his children to inferior Jim Crow schools, where enrollment exceeded capacity by 5 percent (in the white schools, capacity exceeded enrollment by 27 percent); and his family's health was at risk in a city whose hospitals either did not admit Negroes or segregated them in overcrowded wards.

In the field of entertainment in D.C., the report noted what it called "ludicrous extremes": Constitution Hall, owned and operated by the Daughters of the American Revolution, admitted Negroes to the audience but not onto the concert stage (the DAR would not let Marian Anderson sing there in 1939); the capital's one legitimate house, the National Theater, allowed Negro actors onto its stage but refused to sell tickets to Negroes who wanted to attend performances.

Very few of our classmates dropped out during our exploration of the report. Our four nights together established a common bond. Sensing a sentiment that we not disband, Brownie proposed that we continue to meet and seek to implement the report's recommendations locally. Then and there we appointed a committee to draw up a statement of purpose and bylaws. A few weeks later, we reconvened at the YWCA and officially constituted ourselves as the Richmond Committee for Civil Rights, dedicated to "the abolition of segregation and discrimination in our state." Dr. Davis was elected president, Joanne Farrell, secretary.

But even as we launched the new organization and announced it to the press, the warning note of anti-Communism was sounded in our group. Two of the churchwomen telephoned Brownie a few days after our initial meeting and urged that the Richmond Committee amend its bylaws to deny membership to known Communists. After an agonizing consultation among Brownie, Joanne, Dr. Davis, and several of us board members, it was decided not to add a political stricture on membership. I could not then, and cannot now, see how we could espouse equal rights regardless of race and deny rights solely because of political affiliation. When we made our decision known to them, the two churchwomen dropped out.

I have no sense that our refusal to bar Alice Burke and her few followers affected the Richmond Committee adversely. But it may have played a part in a subsequent development. At some point in the next six months, Dr. Davis was advised that it was impolitic to be associated with the Richmond Committee, when RPI was so heavily dependent on state and local funds. So he resigned. And I was elected president of the Richmond Committee for Civil Rights.

Was I considered a Communist? In Richmond, where a prevailing civility often hid how people felt about each other and where nasty things were often said and done in secret, it was hard to tell. Virginia, like its sister states of the old Confederacy, certainly had its bigots. But in Virginia they tended to be gentlemen, not Klansmen.

Two incidents suggest how I was regarded.

One grew out of my new relationship with Alice Burke. She was one of the Richmond Committee for Civil Rights' most faithful members. She brought a wealth of information to our meetings. But being a forceful personality, she was not content with focusing on just Virginia. She was constantly trying to commit us, by resolution, to national and international issues that had nothing to do with our local purpose.

It became customary for Alice to call me in advance of our monthly meeting and suggest an item for the agenda. Most times I felt her proposal was irrelevant and told her so. But sometimes I thought she had a point and agreed we should bring the matter up. I mention this because it may help explain the story Brownie Lee Jones brought back to me.

Brownie had a remarkable talent for ingratiating herself and gaining the attention and confidence of a great variety of people. Somehow she had befriended someone she wouldn't name who was familiar with the FBI agent assigned to Richmond. This someone and the agent got into a conversation once about the number of Communists residing in the city. They quickly exhausted the list of known ones. The agent then went on to name a few he felt were crypto-Communists.

"What about Marvin Caplan?" asked Brownie's friend.

No, the agent said, he did not think Marvin Caplan was a Communist. "But," he said, "he's in a Communist communications net."

I could only guess that Alice Burke's calls to me were the source of that assessment; and that both our home phones and the *Outlook* phones were probably tapped.

The other incident that gave me an inkling of how people regarded me originated in a telephone conversation I had with a woman I scarcely knew. She and her husband, a young Jewish couple, were Moe Schiff's tenants. They rented the top floor of his duplex. It was my impression that they were an extremely conventional pair who disapproved of the bohemian and interracial happenings on the floor below. So I was astonished when she called me up one day and informed me that she had recently come into the possession of the complete writings of Nikolai Lenin.

"I was trying to think of somebody, Marvin, who would appreciate having them. And I thought of you."

I graciously acknowledged this dubious compliment.

Would I like to have them?

I thought I said I wouldn't. But several people, Naomi and Harry among them, have sometimes accused me of answering uncomfortable questions vaguely and not saying exactly how I feel.

At any rate, I came back from lunch one afternoon and found a pile of books outside the office door. About a dozen volumes bound in brilliant red. Everything Nikolai Lenin had ever written for *Iskra*.

Harry and I thought the whole thing was very funny. We often used a ledge across the back of the office couch as a bookshelf. We kept the new volumes there. I dipped into them now and then but soon gave up. They were heavy going. Still, they added a dash of color to the office furnishings and no doubt confirmed some casual browser in his suspicion of our politics.

Marvin Caplan with Sybil Baum at Ann Arbor, 1943.
Courtesy author

Harry Weinberg, Marvin's brother-in-law and first cousin, on leave from the merchant
marines, and Corporal Caplan, slated for embarkation to Japan, meeting for a night out in
Monterey, California, October 1945.
Courtesy author

Anne and Sam Gellman, two of the leaders and mentors of the postwar Richmond civil rights movement.
Courtesy Sue and Aaron Gellman

In 1948 Oliver W. Hill became the first African American since Reconstruction to be elected to the D.C. city council. Here he attends a fund raiser for the Richmond Committee for Civil Rights.
Courtesy author

"Our Gang" (*left to right*): Joanne and Harry Bernstein, Naomi and Marvin Caplan, Moe and Betty Schiff, Betty's sister Jan, and Dr. Clayton Blum, 1947.
Courtesy author

Brownie Lee Jones, founder and director of the Southern School for Workers (1945-51), a pioneer project in union workers' education in the South.
Photo by Wesley Swadley, courtesy Sue and Aaron Gellman

Joanne and Harry Bernstein, after they left
Richmond and settled in California, where
Harry became labor editor of the *Los
Angeles Times*.
Courtesy Joanne Bernstein

Spottswood W. Robinson III, one of the
NAACP's chief southern attorneys, who in
1946 was already laying the groundwork for
the argument adopted by the U.S. Supreme
Court in the 1954 Brown *vs*. Board of
Education decision, that racially segregated
schools were inherently unequal.
Courtesy Fran Wetzel

stay out of Hecht's

help end segregation at Hecht's lunch counter

..."I have visited the capitals
of many countries, but only
in the capital of my own country
have I been subjected to
this indignity."

Hecht's violates the law

D.C. Restaurants must serve all well-behaved persons
without discrimination - Law of 1873

Hecht's violates fair business practice

Millions of dollars are spent each year by Negroes at Hechts - yet
Negro Americans may not eat at the lunch counter

Hecht's violates democratic principles

Hecht's preaches brotherhood in full page ads, yet Hecht's
practices segregation at its lunch counter

shop at these
7th st. stores that
serve all

KANN'S

GOLDENBERG'S

KRESGE'S

WOOLWORTH'S

GRAND'S

MCCRORY'S

Coordinating Committee for the Enforcement of the D.C.
Anti-Discrimination Laws: 1103 Trenton Place S.E.

Mary Church Terrell is featured on this flyer distributed during the effort to desegregate
Hecht's lunch counter, 1951.
Courtesy author

Members of the Coordinating Committee for the Enforcement of the D.C. Anti-Discrimination Laws picket G. C. Murphy's on F Street near 13th Street, N.W., in May 1952.
Courtesy author

Mary Church Terrell and Annie Stein celebrate the U.S. Supreme Court decision of June 8, 1953, which upheld the validity of the "lost laws"—the public accommodation laws of 1872 and 1873. *Courtesy author*

6

La Guerra Alegre

If we had been superstitious or if aesthetics had mattered, Naomi and I might have shied away from buying the house, once we learned what its address was going to be: 13 Gross Avenue.

"Avenue" was something of an overstatement. When we first saw the thoroughfare, it was one of several muddy ruts across a corner of Henrico County, behind McGuire Veterans Hospital. "Gross" was Morris Gross, the developer, who gouged out the ruts and, on boggy fields on either side of them, was erecting about a hundred small brick bungalows, each one resting on a raft of concrete in a sea of mud.

Naomi, daughter of a Talmudic scholar who sold insurance for a living and granddaughter of the head of Telshe Yeshiva in Lithuania, a renowned rabbinical seminary, had her own name for what was to become "McGuire Village." "Tohu Wabohu," she said, quoting from Genesis 1:2: in the beginning the earth was "waste and void." But Eden sprang from that void, and we were hoping that Morris Gross could build somewhere, in all that muck, a little paradise for two.

For we had had it with the Harts. Living with them was becoming too cramped and too unpleasant. The common bathroom soon became an issue. Naomi was repelled by Mr. Hart's "dirty habits," as she called them, and shrank from using the facility. Then the Harts' daughter, a divorcée, dumped her two children on their grandparents and went off with her new boyfriend. They were nice kids, a girl and a boy. But the little girl was quickly drawn to Naomi and to our room, the brightest room in the house. To Mrs. Hart's consternation we had painted the ceiling and three walls marigold yellow and one wall a brilliant turquoise. Whenever we were home for the evening we had first, gently but firmly, to disengage the granddaughter from the premises and then lead her downstairs before we could be alone. Even so, we were scarcely alone. In that thin-walled cottage we had to talk in guarded tones. We had to keep the radio low and turn it off after 10 P.M.

What finally sent us packing was the realization, from Mr. Hart's offhand remarks, that we would be asking for trouble if we ever invited a black friend up for brunch or light refreshment.

No. We had to move. So early in 1948, with a down payment of five hundred dollars borrowed from my folks and a VA mortgage acquired with the assistance of a couple of the AVC's experts in such matters, we bought a place of our own. Moe Schiff and Harry helped us move. It took only two trips in the pickup truck Moe used in his linoleum-laying business to settle us in our brand-new house, a brick box with a slant asphalt-shingle roof. Architectural style? American Nondescript. But it had two bedrooms, fresh white plaster walls, polished hardwood floors (which we kept covered with heavy layers of newspapers until the lawn took hold and we could enter the house without tracking mud), and a gleaming, all-electric kitchen.

On our first night in our own home, in our new bed—a Hollywood box-spring and mattress that Thalhimer's had delivered that very afternoon—Naomi suddenly sat up, just as we retired, and yelled at the top of her lungs.

"What's wrong?" I asked.

She laughed. "Nothing's wrong. I just want to feel I can yell if I want to." So I yelled, too.

But there is discord even in Eden. Our house was second from the corner. The corner, or flagship, house, as Mr. Gross and his son preferred to call it because it had a double lot, was occupied by a retired couple, a sweet-looking, gentle little woman and a big blustery chap, a former army sergeant. Bill Mason.

"He has the warmest handshake of any man I've ever met," Mr. Gross's son told me when he took me over to meet Bill. I got to experience that handshake exactly once. For shortly after we moved in, we had a Sunday-afternoon housewarming to which we invited all our Richmond friends. And the next morning young Gross phoned me at the *Outlook* office in great distress. Bill

Mason had called him, he said, to complain about our party. "He says you had a house full of uh . . . uh . . . uh . . . colored people."

"Don't know where he got that idea," I said. "We just had some friends over for a housewarming."

Young Gross persisted. Bill had invested his life's savings in his house. A good neighborhood was important to him. When Gross went on to offer me well-meant advice about Richmond customs and the need to observe them, I cut him short. It was my house, I told him. I'd invite whomever I pleased. And I hung up on him.

There was no feud between Bill Mason and us. Simply cold silence. We couldn't count on the silence, though. On warm summer evenings when Bill got drunk we could hear him roaring, cursing, and singing as we sat in our living room with the windows open. However, the coldness thawed after a while. Naomi and I were surprised and touched to find a peace offering on our front steps one night when we got home from work: a little pile of fresh-picked tomatoes. And in the course of our three years at 13 Gross Avenue we and the Masons even got back on speaking terms again.

We were not the only ones to begin the new year with a cause for celebration. At almost the same time, Harry and Joanne got married. Joanne Farrell converted to Judaism, and we all drove down to Greensboro, North Carolina, for the ceremony and a gala wedding reception afterwards, in a swank roadhouse on the outskirts of the city.

Brownie Lee Jones returned from a visit to Manhattan and told us a story whose tagline became a watchword in our circle.

She had been staying with old friends, African Americans, the celebrated soprano Dorothy Maynor and her husband, the Presbyterian minister Shelby Rooks.

(Brownie's friendships, I must note parenthetically, never ceased to amaze us. She had come to know the writer Sherwood Anderson when he and his wife lived in Virginia for a while. And when the poet Langston Hughes came to Richmond to speak, a lucky few of us were invited up to Brownie's afterwards to join him for coffee.)

Anyway, while she was there a black colleague of the minister's dropped by the apartment. He had come from a board meeting where the obtuseness of the white board members on a racial issue had left him frustrated and furious. He was fed up with white stupidity. "Oh, I don't know, Shelby," he said. "Sometimes I think we ought to just cut ourselves off from them and let them drift."

Occasions were frequent in those Richmond years when a campaign against segregation came to naught. After hearing Brownie's story, we would often mitigate our depression by smiling ruefully at one another and saying, "Why don't we just cut ourselves off from them and let them drift?"

It is hard for me to recall any major victories in those years. Sometimes it seemed to me we were chipping away at a glacier with an ice pick. I remember, for instance, the attempt to end segregation on Virginia's buses and streetcars. Our leader was a freshman member of the House of Delegates, Armistead Boothe of Alexandria, who took his seat in January 1948. Boothe was an engaging fellow. A Rhodes scholar, a navy veteran, a native Virginian, he gave every evidence upon his arrival in Richmond of becoming a leader in the General Assembly.

He had the temerity, however, to challenge the status quo as it was enshrined and protected by Byrd Dixiecrats. One of his most provocative acts was to introduce a bill in the 1950 General Assembly that would have repealed the state segregation laws as they applied to public transportation. A subsidiary measure would have established a state civil rights commission to study problems of race relations.

Armistead Boothe was scarcely a flaming liberal. His principal argument when he introduced the bills aroused misgivings among many of us in the Richmond Committee for Civil Rights. Essentially he argued that if the state took no action, the federal government would. That could lead, he warned, to a federal statute or Supreme Court decision outlawing racial segregation in such places as public schools, where he felt it was necessary. "If segregation in primary and high schools is declared unconstitutional," he said ". . . it will usher into the South, including Virginia, an era of chicanery, hatred and violence." Virginia, cradle of presidents, should undertake the modest reform he was proposing of its own volition before it faced a court order. Since his reforms were the only ones available, we overlooked his reasoning and rushed to his support.

I well remember the public committee hearing at which his bills were considered. The room was so crammed with Boothe bill supporters it was impossible to segregate us. Boothe was the first to speak. He addressed the House Courts of Justice Committee with evident sincerity and feeling, urging the enactment of a law that would "lift a humiliation off twenty percent of our citizens." A dozen witnesses, white and black, joined him in this plea, and the white witnesses were not raggle-taggle liberals of the AVC and labor movement sort but persons of some eminence: an Episcopalian bishop, the vice president of a major bank, the president of the Newport News shipbuilding company, prominent women, church and civic leaders.

I stood at the back of the crowded hearing-room leaning against the wall, surrounded by a group of black students from Virginia Union College. One of our witnesses was Dr. W. L. Ransome, a venerable black Baptist minister, highly respected in the white community as a spokesman for his people. Although there was a kind of old-fashioned revivalist style to his elocution, I found his testimony eloquent and moving. So I was startled when I noticed that the black students around me were grinding their teeth and muttering against him. "Handkerchief head!" the student next to me said angrily under his breath. For an instant I thought I saw Dr. Ransome through his eyes. What sounded eloquent to me, I realized, sounded obsequious to him. If I were prescient, instead of annoyed, I would have known that I was standing among a new generation of southern blacks who in another ten years would be militantly demanding their rights in lunch-counter sit-ins and Freedom Rides.

The committee members sat and listened impassively to Dr. Ransome and to all of our witnesses. Not one question was asked of anyone who spoke for us. And no witness appeared in opposition.

The committee held a brief subsequent hearing at which an ex-governor of Virginia, Colgate Darden, testified in favor of the Boothe bills. It met one time more, and after hearing Boothe's final plea, went into executive session. Forty minutes later the chairman came out of the committee room smiling and announced to those of us waiting in the corridor that the committee had voted against reporting out the bills. He refused to say how the members had voted.

Several reporters protested. All votes had to be recorded, they reminded him. And it was against House rules to take a final vote in secret. One of the reporters said he had specifically asked the clerk to let us know when the committee went back into open session.

"Why, we *were* in open session," the chairman insisted smugly. Just before they voted he had asked the page to unlock the doors. It wasn't his fault if the reporters were so busy talking they hadn't heard the doors being unlocked.

And were the doors opened? Perhaps. "If the unlatching of the locks made any click," the *Times-Dispatch* man reported the next day, "it either was not heard or its significance was lost on those outside." He and others of the press were able to reconstruct the vote. The segregation repealer was killed by a vote of 9 to 7.

Several of us were standing with Armistead Boothe when the chairman emerged to tell us the bills were dead. Boothe was visibly shaken. "They do not understand what they are doing," he murmured, more to himself perhaps than to those of us he had come to recognize as allies.

"Oh, honestly," Brownie said as we brooded afterwards. "I think we ought to just cut ourselves off from them and let them drift."

Midway into 1948 Harry Bernstein resigned as editor of the *Southern Jewish Outlook*. He turned the post over to me and took himself and Joanne out to the Far West, to Tucson.

Their departure was a good deal less abrupt than I make it sound. From the beginning, Harry and I were aware of the incongruities and limitations inherent in the two of us publishing a liberal Anglo-Jewish publication in the Deep South. Domestic politics had a stronger claim on our temperaments than Jewish culture and religion. There was always an element of subterfuge in our use of an organ of the Jewish community to expound our political and social views. Both of us were uncomfortable with that. We also realized that with at most two thousand subscribers reading us, we were not about to exert much influence. Both of us thought we would be happier writing for a newspaper or magazine of general interest.

Besides all this, Harry had another reason for wanting to leave Richmond. He suffered from recurrent attacks of asthma, and several doctors advised him that his condition would improve in a dry, warm climate. His marriage to Joanne strengthened his resolve to leave the *Outlook*. Although she had converted, he still felt ill at ease as a spokesman for the Jewish community when it seemed to him he brought so little genuine conviction to the role. We had many long, soul-searching conversations before Harry concluded he would be happier elsewhere.

Harry and Joanne were two of our dearest friends. It was painful for Naomi and me to see them go. And Harry was my comrade in arduous times, in establishing the *Outlook* and becoming involved in Virginia. It was wrenching to part from him. But the immediate rush of events gave me little time to pine. Nineteen forty-eight was a crucial presidential election year. Israel, the country after America that most engaged me, had proclaimed its statehood on May 14 and was immediately attacked by the Arab nations surrounding it, plunging it into a war for its survival. And Oliver Hill announced himself an independent candidate for the Richmond city council. Those were sufficient claims to my attention.

Oliver's candidacy made the strongest demand on my energies. John Drew and I stepped up the voter-registration drive. We also got the word out on the strategy that all of us involved in Oliver's campaign had agreed to pursue. Twenty-nine candidates were running for nine seats. Although another of the independent candidates was black, he had little following. Oliver was the clear favorite among Negro voters. And so we advised everyone, black and white, who wanted to see him elected, to "single-shot": to vote for Oliver only, and not for any of the other candidates. The strategy worked. Oliver carried the black precincts overwhelmingly—the next candidate in those precincts got at most only thirty or forty votes. And Oliver picked up enough white votes to win the ninth and last seat on the council.

There was more to savor in Oliver's victory than the mere act of winning. This city council marked a break with the past. A public referendum the year before had sanctioned a streamlined, one-chamber, nine-member council to govern the city. The new council, the *Richmond Times-Dispatch* said editorially, would replace a "long out-moded form of government." The election, it declared, "is one of the most important in Richmond's more than two centuries of history."

The Richmond Citizens Association, a group of forward-looking Virginians, had led the successful referendum fight and then proposed a slate of nine candidates for the council. If it had chosen to include a Negro candidate in that slate, Oliver Hill would have been the obvious choice. The association, not quite *that* forward-looking, chose not to. A black candidate, it feared, would lose votes. Its one gesture toward the liberal electorate was to include a labor leader in the slate, T. D. du Cuennois, an area director for the CIO. And it was he whom Oliver nosed out for the ninth seat by 263 votes.

Oliver was the first Negro to hold public office since Reconstruction. The day after the election, the *Richmond Times-Dispatch,* in an editorial doubtlessly written by Virginius Dabney, hastened to assure white Richmonders that they need not view this "novel phenomenon with alarm." Oliver Hill was fully qualified, the paper said.

It questioned the propriety of "single-shotting" but admitted there must have been hundreds of white votes for Oliver Hill in the 28,143 ballots cast.

I know of at least one white voter whom I helped persuade. The polls were open from 6:30 A.M. to 7:30 P.M., and I spent most of that time in white precincts distributing Oliver Hill flyers. A little old white southern lady came creeping by as I was trying to drum up votes outside the Westhampton Engine House, and I handed her a flyer. She studied Oliver's picture for several minutes and then asked, "Is he cullud?"

"Yes ma'am. What's more," I said, "Mr. Hill comes from an old Virginia family. He was born and raised right here in Richmond. He's a fine lawyer and a veteran of World War II. He'll make a wonderful council member."

She thanked me and went on into the polls. In a little while she came creeping out. When she drew abreast of me she stopped, looked up at me with the gentlest and dearest of smiles and said, to my confusion, "Sonny. Ah jes want yew to know. Ah voted fo yewah nigger."

I couldn't bring myself to tell Oliver that story. I couldn't bring myself to tell it almost forty years later when an occasion presented itself. Duke, Oliver and Beresenia's son, who was a professor at Virginia State in Petersburg, came to Washington and gathered a group of old friends together to reminisce for a videotape he was making in honor of his parents' golden wedding anniversary. I recalled the time Oliver and I had defied official policy and had gone into the John Marshall Hotel through the front entrance in order to welcome Charles Bolte and his wife to Richmond.

I came out of the videotaping session with Spott Robinson, and as we walked back to our cars I said, "You know, Spott, there's another story I was dying to tell, only I was afraid it wasn't appropriate." And I told him of my encounter with the little old lady voter.

Spott chuckled. "You were right not to have told that story, Marvin. It wouldn't have been suitable. But, say, do you mind if *I* tell Oliver that story?"

When it came to the 1948 presidential election, Naomi and I ended up backing different candidates.

The Progressive Party had begun to organize for Henry Wallace in Virginia, and Naomi and I and several curious friends, John Drew among them, attended the state founding convention at the WRVA Theatre. Naomi also accompanied me to a couple of the meetings called to plan the Progressive Party campaign for Richmond, and we were surprised at how many new people we found there. Alice Burke and the Kalbs, John Drew and Moe Schiff and several union officials were about the only ones we recognized. Naomi felt uncomfortable at these sessions and said she was bowing out.

Prominent among the new faces were a young Jewish dentist relocated from New York City and a large, abrasive, trumpet-voiced black woman, Mrs. Senora Lawson. They were elected co-chairmen of the Richmond campaign.

I was not much taken with either of them. The dentist in particular irritated me. Each meeting included a reverent moment when he would arise and address us on the importance of our work. "The little people of America," he told us, with an ingratiating smile and a raised forefinger, "are looking to us for help." Or, "Watch. The little people in their might will rise up this November and smite their oppressors." I was not alone, though, in finding this sort of rhetoric annoying. I had occasion to call his home one night on some pressing party matter. His wife answered the phone. When I asked where he was and how I could reach him she said, "I haven't the vaguest idea." And then, in a weary voice that made me fear for his marriage, she added, "He must be off somewhere with his little people."

Naomi was certain the fellow was a Communist. That "little people" line, she felt, was a dead giveaway. I couldn't argue with her. As a student at the City College of New York she had received a thorough education in left-wing politics.

Naomi was supporting Harry Truman. The very thought of Thomas E. Dewey as president alarmed her; "that little man on the wedding cake," she said, repeating Alice Roosevelt Longworth's apt and witty characterization. Naomi had come to admire Truman for what she felt were his "spunky speeches." He at least, she said, was addressing the issues. "Listen to him," she said. "You ought to listen to him. I don't believe you hear a word he's saying."

I objected to that. I did hear him. Although I was impressed by some of things he had to say about civil rights, I also heard a strident anti-Soviet tirade that I feared would lead inevitably to war. Wallace's plea for negotiation and global cooperation was more to my liking. And on domestic policy, the Progressive Party's call for the nationalization of basic industries and for full racial equality was a summons to which I responded wholeheartedly. John Drew joined the Progressive Party, and his assertion that this was the first time in a political organization that he had ever felt welcome as an equal carried a lot of weight with me.

I was ready to concede that Naomi was right and that the Progressive Party was dominated by Communists. But I was not about to be scared off by red-baiting. I believed in Henry Wallace. I was staying in as a matter of principle. Taking a stand on principle was a big thing with me those days. I have seldom been more insufferable.

All through Richmond's tropical summer I worked for the party, writing press releases and leaflets. And on election day I was back at a post familiar to me, engaged in leafleting and last-minute curbstone proselytizing.

I was the only Wallace supporter on duty at my precinct, outside the Buick Motor Company on West Broad Street. A few men and women were distributing Truman literature. But the Dewey people were out in force: a sizable group of fair young men and women wearing special blue-and-white-banded straw boaters, carrying a blue-and-white Dewey-Warren banner, and offering not the kind of crude mimeograph appeal I was putting into voters' hands, but a nicely printed document.

I gazed upon them, and all my old fears of the Republican Party as the party of privilege were aroused. Only the day before, Governor Dewey had been named one of the ten best-dressed men in America, a choice that gave a slob like me one more reason to oppose him. But as I watched his confident supporters, I began to question my determination to vote for Wallace no matter what. My God! I thought. Suppose Tom Dewey wins! Not a pundit or pollster had given Truman a chance. The major national periodicals had already conceded the election. The only person who thought Harry S. Truman could win was Harry S. Truman. Suddenly principle seemed like an awfully wobbly thing to be standing on.

The polls closed at 6 P.M. I met Naomi after work, and we took a bus out to the Kochs' to listen to the election returns on the radio.

In Richmond, "Fritz Koch" was called "Fritz Kosh." When he first arrived in town he tried to insist upon the correct pronunciation of his name. "No, no," he'd say. "Excuse me. Not 'Kosh.' 'Koch.' As in 'Bach.' "

"And they would stare at me. And say, 'Bach'?" So he gave up.

We and about four or five other Richmond Committee stalwarts joined the Kochs for an evening whose outcome none of us looked forward to with pleasure. Still, if there is any consolation in creature comforts, the Kochs' apartment was a good place to be. Anne was a superb cook and Fritz a connoisseur of wines.

In the sybaritic atmosphere that Fritz, the master architect, had created out of books and records and paintings and the furniture and artifacts collected in his travels, we sat and sipped and snacked as we listened grimly to the radio. One early return broke the gloom.

The announcer was going down the list of states giving vote totals and when he came to Arizona and said, "Wallace: two," we collapsed in helpless laughter. We were sure we knew who had cast those two votes.

The contest was nip and tuck all evening, and the returns were still inconclusive when Fritz drove us back to 13 Gross Avenue.

Wednesday morning I opened the front door upon the *Richmond Times-Dispatch* and picked it up with dread. But to my astonishment the banner headline declared:

UNCERTAINTY MARKS ELECTION WITH HALF VOTE IN

Not till the following day did the paper proclaim the incredible outcome:

TRUMAN SCORES SURPRISING UPSET, WINS PRESIDENCY;
DEMOCRATIC MAJORITY RESTORED IN HOUSE, SENATE

Renegade Wallacite that I was, I whooped for joy.

When I got down to the office I called Brownie, who I knew had supported

Truman, and confessed to her my sense of relief. "Of course. Of course you're glad he won," she said, granting me dispensation. "It's not a matter of party, after all. You're a true democrat."

Wallace, whom the pollsters had predicted would win anywhere from 2 to 5 million votes, got little more than 1 million. In Richmond he garnered 307 votes, and if you had given me a pad and pencil and a little time, I think I could have accounted for most of them. The results of the election cured me. I have never again supported a third-party effort.

I lingered on in the Progressive Party with waning enthusiasm. The little people, in their unexpected wisdom, had ignored us and had sided with Harry Truman. John Drew's adherence to the party still kept me in. But even he was beginning to get disillusioned. He confessed to me that he couldn't stand Senora Lawson.

I stayed on the party list until the Korean War broke out in 1950. When the party denounced South Korea and declared that North Korea had been the victim of aggression, it was too much. I had followed Henry Wallace into the Progressive Party. I followed him out. Or rather, I was pleased when shortly after I resigned, he did too, for the same reason. We both felt North Korea had begun the war at the instigation of the Soviet Union and could not countenance the Progressive Party's (and the Communist Party's) stand. "When my country is at war," Henry Wallace declared, "and the United Nations sanctions that war, I am on the side of my country and the United Nations." It would not have occurred to me to put it that way, but I applauded the sentiment.

Israel's emergence as a nation was a thrilling moment to Jews everywhere, including Virginia's Jewish community—or at least to a sizable portion of it. For not every Jew rejoiced. Richmond, that bastion of conservatism, was also a stronghold of the American Council for Judaism. The council was formed in 1942 to oppose Zionism and the establishment of a Jewish state in Palestine. German Jews of the Reform movement were prominent among the council's leaders and members; I couldn't help noticing that the same German-Jewish Rosenwald family that bankrolled the council supplied most of the funding for Brownie Lee's Southern School for Workers.

Richmond's Jewish community was a very old one. The German Jews who immigrated to this country early in the nineteenth century may have been regarded as the Jewish elite in New York City. But not in Richmond. There, the Sephardic, or Spanish, Jews had preceded them long before. Sephardim had been soldiers and nurses in the Confederate Army, and one of their number,

Judah P. Benjamin, had been a member of Jefferson Davis's cabinet. The Sephardim looked upon Richmond's German Jews as parvenu and could barely countenance the other Ashkenazim, the Russian and East European Jews, who had not arrived in America in great numbers until the 1890s and early 1900s and only then began trickling South.

The Ashkenazim, though, were my *landslayt,* countrymen, for my father was one of them. They exhibited a strong Socialist strain, and in matters concerning Israel my allegiance was usually to them. As editor of the *Outlook,* I was invited to join the delegation that called upon Governor William Tuck to ask him to issue a formal proclamation heralding the new state. Tuck, a large, fat, jovial, pink-faced man, who had a special outsized record of old hillbilly tunes that he played as an accompaniment to his shaving every morning, welcomed us warmly. The inheritor of Washington's, Jefferson's, and Madison's commonwealth readily acceded to the request of his Jewish brethren. "But ah gotta tell you fellas," he said, laughing heartily, "for all ah know, Israel could be in Texas."

I was eager to do more for Israel than write favorable editorials. So when several young Jewish couples approached us and told us they were forming a Richmond chapter of the Labor Zionist Organization of America (LZOA), the American ally of David Ben-Gurion's and Golda Meir's Labor Party in Israel, Naomi and I joined them. Hy Newman, a veterinarian, and his wife Debbie, Zionists from childhood, graduates of and counselors at Habonim summer camps, headed the new organization. I became vice chairman for American affairs.

To indoctrinate and officially induct the new chapter, LZOA headquarters in New York sent Samuel Kurland to Richmond. Kurland was an agronomist and writer who, by happy coincidence, was also a Philadelphian. Naomi and I were fortunate to have him as our houseguest for a long weekend, from Friday afternoon to Monday morning. Kurland was a charming man, both entertaining, with his many stories of Israel, and useful. He insisted upon cooking Sunday breakfast and produced a marvelous cheese-and-onion omelet.

He and his family had "made *aliyah*"—that is, had migrated to Israel with the intention of living there. But his two small sons had trouble adjusting and his wife found the life onerous, so after a year they returned to the United States. Nevertheless, he thought Naomi and I should go. Israel, he said, could use independent couples like us. He certainly aroused our interest. At informal intervals in the weekend meetings—the workshops Kurland led and the lively swearing-in ceremony he conducted—we discussed our prospects with him. Naomi and I continued to deliberate for at least a month after Kurland left. In the end we decided, somewhat heavy-hearted, to stay put. But Kurland had planted a seed. From time to time over the years, going to Israel to live was an option that Naomi and I were never quite able to set aside.

As the new vice chairman for American affairs, I, with nothing but the best of intentions, touched off the most hectic meeting in the brief history of our LZOA chapter. It all began when the Newmans proposed that we have a social evening to which the thirty or forty of us already in the chapter would invite prospective members. I was designated to arrange a program.

As it happened, our social evening fell shortly after national attention was directed to an explosive episode in upstate New York. In August 1949, on the outskirts of the little town of Peekskill, the famous Negro singer, actor, and civil rights activist Paul Robeson was scheduled to give an open-air benefit concert for the Harlem chapter of the Civil Rights Congress, reputedly a Communist-led organization. The concert notices set anti-Soviet juices running in the Peekskill veterans' council. The council commander announced that its members would oppose the event with "a patriotic demonstration." In the ensuing free-for-all, one veteran was stabbed and another suffered a concussion. A number of concertgoers were injured and their cars were overturned. It took forty state troopers and the Peekskill police force to bring the riot under control.

Bob Davis, our neighborly radio station announcer, with whom I chanced to discuss and deplore the riot soon after it took place, told me he had an on-the-spot recording of the demonstration. He played it for me and I found it an upsetting experience. I already knew from news stories that the Peekskill chapter of the Jewish War Veterans (JWV) had marched with the other council members—the American Legion, the Veterans of Foreign Wars, and the Catholic War Veterans. I was particularly incensed, therefore, on listening to the record, to hear what the veterans were chanting: "Jew bastards!" "Commies!" "Kikes!"

I wrote a steaming *Outlook* editorial on the riot, roundly condemning the Jewish War Veterans for participating in a march that had unmistakable anti-Semitic undertones. I also resigned from the Richmond chapter of the JWV, which Harry and I had joined to further a subscription drive. And I borrowed Bob Davis's record and played it at LZOA's member-bring-a-member affair. My thesis that night was the inherent dangers, for Jews and other minorities, in the current wave of anti-Communist hysteria. Jews ran a risk, I argued, that right-wing allies would turn on them and link all Jews with reds.

After I concluded my remarks I invited questions. Only then did I realize how badly I had miscalculated my audience, at least the newcomers in it.

At the back of the Newmans' living room a huge, angry young man arose. "I have a question!" he shouted. "Can you deny," he asked, speaking through gritted teeth and shaking his finger at me, "that Paul Robeson's voice is a Communist *front?*"

Things got no better after that. I doubt if we picked up any new members that evening. Even so, my LZOA comrades forgave me. A month later they voted to send me as the chapter delegate to the national LZOA convention in Boston and paid my train fare. And when Hy and Debbie Newman decided to make *aliyah* and moved to Israel, I was chosen to be Hy's successor.

Finding myself the head of three organizations—the AVC, the Richmond Committee for Civil Rights, and the LZOA—left me bemused. Was I everyone's second choice for chairman? I wondered. But fleetingly. There was too much to be done to waste time pondering such questions.

Now it was my turn to think about quitting the *Outlook*.

By the summer of 1949 I felt I was at a dead end. I enjoyed many of my writing tasks—the editorials, the articles, the monthly "Office Diary." But I was tired of collecting social news, tired of rewriting and editing the tidbits our state-wide correspondents sent in, tired of reading galley proofs alone.

Even harder to bear than tedium was the realization of my shortcomings as an editor. In spite of my dogged reading of books and periodicals, I had to admit I had only a superficial knowledge of Jewish life and culture. I did not lead a very Jewish life: Naomi and I did not keep a kosher home, I was an infrequent synagogue-goer and an agnostic, and I seemed to have an instinctive aversion to going deeply into religious issues. Yet an intimate knowledge of and feel for Judaism was indispensable to much of what I sought to express in the *Outlook*.

On my own, I had begun to study Hebrew, but I was far from mastering the language; and my attempt was the first of many I have made over the course of years, all without marked success.

Then, too, I was running against time. I was almost thirty. Naomi was eager to start a family. I knew if I didn't move to free myself, I could get stuck in the *Outlook,* trapped by my own inertia.

Nathan Kessler unwittingly helped crystallize my determination to leave. He came back to the office one afternoon from an ad-selling expedition. And he was upset.

"For Crissakes! What's *this* doin' in here?" he demanded, slapping an open page of the latest issue of the *Outlook* with the back of his chubby hand.

"*This*" was an article I had written. Entitled "Sidney Hillman's Hatchet

Man,"[1] it was a warmly appreciative account of the work of our friend the Reverend Charlie Webber, Methodist chaplain to labor, whose leadership of the CIO's Political Action Committee had made that union an important force in Virginia politics. The title was the sobriquet bestowed upon Charlie by none other than Senator Harry Flood Byrd.

"Why, Nathan?" I asked. "What's wrong?"

"What's *wrong*?" he shouted, close to apoplexy. "A *minister* for Crissakes! What's a minister doin' in a Jewish magazine? An' a minister in a big fuss with Senator Byrd on top of it!"

So the unexpected had happened. Nathan Kessler had read an *Outlook* article. I had realized long ago that all he ever read were the ads to be sure the copy was correct and that I had given his best advertisers the positions he had promised them. But then he went to see one of his biggest customers, a local soft-drink wholesaler who handled the Coca-Cola franchise.

"As soon as I walk in he hits me with this! I was never so embarrassed in my whole life. 'Nathan,' he says to me, 'I thought you publish a Jewish magazine. And now I find this garbage,' he says. 'A real radical attack on my old friend Harry Byrd. I never thought I'd find anything like this in here.'"

"'You're damn right,' I tol' him after I read it over. 'This should never be in here.' An' I'm tellin' *you* that, mister. *You*, mister editor!"

My spirited defense of the article and my assertion of the freedom of the press cut no ice with Nathan.

"Yeah, yeah," he said. "You think you can print anything you want. Well, I'm tellin' you you *can't* print anything you want. The *Outlook*'s not that kind of magazine. The *Outlook* is a business. You're runnin' a business. And this thing has no business in here."

Nathan hit a nerve that time. I prided myself on my bold, outspoken opinions. Yet the very format of the magazine made them appear to have been inserted surreptitiously. How seriously could you take a journal of opinion when most of its readers skipped the editorials and went straight to the social news and "The Cooking Page"?

Ready as I was to go, my leave-taking was not so easily accomplished. First I had to find another editor—no simple matter given Richmond's limited resources. By chance I happened to mention my search to the Pologes, a couple

---

1. Sidney Hillman (1887–1946) was president of the Amalgamated Clothing Workers and a founder of the CIO. He was a supporter and confidant of President Franklin D. Roosevelt. Roosevelt's detractors claimed, no doubt wrongly, that Hillman dominated the relationship. As proof of that charge they would often quote a remark Roosevelt is supposed to have made to his subordinates: "Clear everything with Sidney!"

Naomi and I had come to know through the LZOA. Marge was a social worker. Conrad handled small advertising accounts. But somewhere in his résumé he noted he had worked as a reporter and held an editorial position on *Travel* magazine. He was as nominally Jewish as I was. That didn't stop him. It challenged him. He was eager, he said, to explore his heritage by editing a Jewish magazine. Considering the qualifications Harry and I brought to the position, that seemed sufficient background for an *Outlook* editor.

I yielded the reins to Conrad Pologe with relief and apprehension. I had been saying for quite a while that I wanted to devote myself full-time to writing. Now that the opportunity was thrust upon me, was I ready to grasp it?

Naomi earned enough to keep us housed and fed if we were frugal. So we made a pact. For one year she'd be breadwinner; I'd stay home and write and look to the cooking and housekeeping. And at the end of the year? Our pact had an unspoken codicil. We were not to raise that question until it became unavoidable.

Most weekday mornings after Naomi left the house to catch her bus to work, and after I washed the breakfast things, I went into the second bedroom, now my study, and took up my writing projects. Articles. A couple of brochures commissioned for the CIO by Charlie Webber. And short stories. Like many fledgling writers I was strongly drawn to fiction. It took most of the year to learn I had little talent for it. I did better with articles. My civil rights activities provided me with ready subjects for some of the publications I most admired. I became an unofficial Virginia stringer of sorts for the *New Republic,* the *Nation,* and the left-wing newspaper the *New York Compass.* It was exhilarating to find myself in their pages and disappointing to discover how poorly they paid. For bread and butter I depended on a local connection—the Sunday magazine of the *Richmond Times-Dispatch.* The editor was a fatherly chap who liked my writing style and my ideas for several local color features and who began to use me on a fairly steady basis.

My cooking became an accompaniment to these modest successes. I had two cookbooks. Mrs. Simon Kander's *Settlement House Cookbook,* indispensably basic for novice chefs like me who could use instruction even on how to boil water. And *Tante Marie's Cookbook,* a collection of elegant French recipes suitable for celebrations. By cheating, I got to use *Tante Marie* oftener than my infrequent publication warranted.

Although my days were taken up with writing, cooking, and cleaning, I was not about to drop any of the projects that mattered to me. The phone kept me connected. I could get almost anywhere by bus or bike. And Naomi and I kept our nights and weekends open to accommodate a heavy schedule of organizational meetings.

When I look back on those days, I count few victories. Our band of activists was so small that we were, perforce, guerrilla fighters. Our most ambitious campaigns were little more than sorties. We had as much effect as flea bites on the Virginia body politic. And yet these little episodes figure in my memory as triumphs. I get a lift remembering them. I find myself grouping them in my thoughts like chapters in an eighteenth-century picaresque novel:

In which we establish an interracial gathering place

It was Moe (Morris) Schiff's idea. He and a friend named Walter sold and installed linoleum under a corporate title drawn from their two first names. Walmarr Linoleum Company. Their retail showroom was in a large, ramshackle store on West Broad Street. Above the store was a loft, and it was Moe's happy thought, when the tenants living there moved out, that since Walmarr didn't need the space, we ought to transform it into a meeting hall for the American Veterans Committee.

Sheer inspiration. We AVCers, who looked with disdain upon the Elks and Legionnaires and their preoccupation with lodges and clubhouses, fell to work at once to make that loft our very own. We had scrubbing and painting parties. Moe and his new wife, Phyllis, who had come to share both his trade and politics, installed a glistening floor of tiles that followed, alas, the undulations of the old boards on which they were laid.

To pay for the paint and linoleum and clubroom furniture (folding chairs, mostly), we, who usually had nothing but contempt for raffles and bingo parties, announced a raffle of our own. We hit the streets selling tickets at 50 cents each for a drawing at which "For the Benefit of AVC Building Fund" we offered prizes: a Sonora radio-phonograph console, a table-model radio, and a twenty-five-dollar U.S. savings bond.

On the whole, our new hall was a useful place to have, even though heating it on cold nights was a problem and dancing on that old floor was difficult, and care and maintenance required a diversion of energy better used, I thought, in our social-action projects. Still, in Richmond, Virginia, at that time, where there were only two or three public spaces for interracial meetings, it was good to have one more place where people could gather without regard to color. And though our arms and backs and feet ached as much as any Elk's or Legionnaire's, the purpose of our hall was noble and justified our work.

Wherein my color confounds a segregationist

Martin A. Martin of Hill, Martin and Robinson told me about a case of his that sounded like material for a civil rights article, so I went along with him to the courtroom. Martin's client was a Negro college student. On a trip from Norfolk to Richmond this young man had been denied the last empty seat on the bus because it meant he would have had to sit next to a woman whom the driver took to be white. In the hearing before the State Corporation Commission, regulator of Virginia's transportation, Martin argued that by refusing to give full service to a legitimate passenger, the bus company was failing to perform its duty as a public carrier. The company argued that the driver was simply obeying the state's segregation law. To that, Martin replied with a question. How could the driver be sure the woman was white? Wasn't that a highly subjective judgment? Couldn't the driver have been making a mistake?

The hearing broke for noon recess. I met with Martin to discuss this last argument further. Martin, a chap with a lively sense of humor, said, "Wait. We're gonna have fun! I'm putting the bus driver on the stand when we come back. And I think I'll point out different people in the hearing room and ask him to tell us if they're white or colored. Heck, Marvin. I may even ask him to guess what you are."

It was summer. I had a deep tan from weekend yardwork around 13 Gross Avenue. And my hair was black. I grabbed a Baby Ruth bar, skipped lunch, went down to the basement barbershop and had them give me a GI haircut.

When the hearing reconvened Martin called the driver to the stand and elicited from him a firm assertion that he could always tell the race of his passengers just by looking at them.

"Look around this room, then," Martin said. "Can you tell us if that man over there is white or colored?" He pointed to me. I sat solemn and immobile, my glasses off. The driver squinted at me for a long time; pressed by Martin, he sighed and said at last, in a low, reluctant tone, "Colored." Martin called me to the stand, and after I was sworn in, asked me for my name and occupation. In my response I mentioned that I had, until recently, edited an Anglo-Jewish magazine. And was I colored? I don't recall if Martin won the case. Alas, he's dead. But I shall not forget the driver's sore, dour, disgruntled look when I answered the question.

In which we join Spott Robinson on a legal excursion

Spott Robinson needed a white "front" to help him arrange the purchase of a large tract of Tidewater farmland for a wealthy black businessman. He asked the Schiffs and the Caplans to help him. So one beautiful spring day, he and Marian and the four of us drove down to Portsmouth. The transaction, which required Moe Schiff to pose as the buyer and then resell the tract soon after to the actual purchaser, was a paper transaction of such intricacy I cannot begin to describe it. What I do remember, though, is the ferry ride.

The black businessman lived in Norfolk, across the Chesapeake Bay from Portsmouth. The most direct way to travel between the two cities in those days was to take the ferry. That day we made the round trip ferry ride—twice. After Moe made the purchase and we brought the papers to the real buyer, Spott, the perfectionist, reviewed the transaction one last time. He discovered a minuscule error that he insisted must be corrected. ("If we ever need a lawyer," I murmured to Naomi, "I know who *I'm* going to get.") So we had to go back to Portsmouth.

On the second ferry trip to Norfolk, in the late afternoon, we three men sat in the car, "running our mouths," as Marian Robinson would have it, while our wives went off to explore the boat. At one point they all trooped to the starboard rail to get a better view of a ship or shore sight. At once a guard appeared. "Hey!" he yelled. "You ladies can't go over there! That section's for colored!"

They turned upon him: Naomi, freckled and brown-haired; Phyllis, classically blond and blue-eyed; Marian a dusky rose.

"What makes you think we aren't colored?" Naomi asked.

"Yeah," said Phyllis, "how can you tell we aren't colored?"

"As it happens," Marian said, in grand, encompassing sisterhood, "we *are* colored."

The guard stared at them speechless, then slunk off in bewilderment.

Of a student experiment at Virginia State

In Petersburg one Sunday evening we heard a funny one. We were having dinner with Helen and Bunny Baker when two of Bunny's students at Virginia State dropped by to tell us of the latest campus escapade.

Some heavy construction work was being done on the highway near the college grounds, and the state allocated a large interracial crew of workers to the job. Two portable johns were dropped off to accommodate the men. A WHITE sign was hung on one, COLORED on the other. During the night the students crept out and switched the signs. Next day they watched. White and colored laborers, working side by side, dutifully segregated themselves whenever they heard the call of nature.

The next night the students switched the signs again. And again, white and colored workmen went unquestioningly to where the signs directed them. The students switched the signs on five successive nights. And on five successive days, when the men had to go, they switched johns according to the signs. Ivan Pavlov himself, Bunny the geneticist assured the students, could not have devised a better test of the conditioned reflex.

Wherein two courageous spirits are honored—and our suspicions are aroused

One of our civil rights heroes in those days was J. Waties Waring,[2] a federal district court judge in Charleston.

A southerner who could trace his family origins in his native state back to 1640, Judge Waring had the audacity to rule against his peers in a voting-rights suit brought by the NAACP.

The suit arose from South Carolina's attempt to evade a 1944 Supreme Court ruling that outlawed "the white primary."

The white primary was a stratagem—like literacy tests, poll taxes, and so forth—that the southern white oligarchy used to keep Negroes from voting. It was founded on a consequence of the Civil War, a kind of political self-segregation that arose in the South. White southerners came out of the war overwhelmingly Democratic; most southern Negroes, loyal to Lincoln, felt they owed their allegiance to the GOP. An additional incentive for this allegiance, among southern blacks, was the prospect of federal patronage when a Republican controlled the White House. A similar sense of self-interest drew many northern Negroes to the Democratic side. The election of Franklin Roosevelt with his more liberal views on race strengthened that commitment.

Over the course of years, the vanquished white South used the Democratic primary to reassert political control. Primary contests became the critical elections; victories in the primaries were usually final. To consolidate this power base, southern states adopted election rules and laws designed to keep Negro voters out of the primary.

In its consideration of an NAACP challenge to the Texas election laws, the Supreme Court held, in the 1944 suit *Smith* v. *Allwright* that it was indeed un-

2. Judge Waring is better known, perhaps, as a member of the three-judge panel that originally heard *Briggs* v. *Elliott,* the NAACP suit challenging the equality of the Negro schools in Clarendon County, South Carolina. Briggs was one of the five suits that the Supreme Court consolidated and heard as *Brown* v. *Board of Education of Topeka, Kansas.* Judge Waring filed a dissent in the *Briggs* case in which he sided with the NAACP and held that segregated schools were per se unequal. The historic 1954 Supreme Court ruling in *Brown* also took that view, thus vindicating Judge Waring.

constitutional for any state to use race as a criterion for participation in the primaries and that qualified Negro voters could not be excluded.

To get around that decision, South Carolina repealed its primary election laws. It put the Democratic Party in charge of the primaries, reasoning that a party was a kind of club, free to limit its membership, if it chose, to whites only.

Judge Waring, in 1947, held that privately conducted primaries that excluded Negroes were just as unconstitutional as the state-run contests they replaced. To argue that anything had been changed by repealing the primary laws, he said, was "pure sophistry." He dismissed the contention that the Democratic Party could be regarded as a private club. "Private clubs and business organizations do not vote and elect a President of the United States, and the Senators and members of the House of Representatives of our national Congress; and under the law of our land, all citizens are entitled to a voice in such selections." His decision was upheld by the higher courts to which it was appealed.

That decision brought Judge Waring to national attention. He and his second wife, Elizabeth, a northerner and therefore suspect in Charleston as a corrupting influence upon him, proceeded to compound his judicial misdeed by speaking out against segregation at meetings all over the country. In consequence, the judge was denounced as a traitor to his class and race; he and his wife were ostracized by Charleston society; their home was bombarded by brickbats, often enough to require the posting of a deputy marshall guard; and a movement was under way in Congress to have him impeached.

"Why don't we invite the Warings to be our guests of honor?" Brownie suggested when a few of us got together to plan a fund-raiser for the Richmond Committee for Civil Rights. No sooner said than done. The Warings accepted our invitation and one April weekend in 1950 arrived in the capital of the Confederacy. Following a public address, there was to be a member-bring-a-member tea and reception in their honor.

The Warings spoke to a large public gathering in one of the union halls and lived up to our expectations. Mrs. Waring, a vivid if somewhat emotional speaker, did most of the talking, describing for us the ordeal they were going through. Judge Waring, a man of sober and measured manner, was no less forthright in his speech. He repeated for Richmond his bold belief that "Negroes should be treated as American citizens" and welcomed the Richmond Committee as his ally in the effort to bring sunlight into the South's dim racial atmosphere.

The hostess for our tea and reception was Mildred Ansley, a relatively new member of the Richmond Committee. She was a graceful, willowy young woman, a descendant of a prominent Virginia family. She was either a lawyer or a legal secretary, and she lived in a beautiful, well-appointed apartment in a small building on Grace Street. I know very little about such things, but I was certain that the china and silverware that she and a colored maid used in serving tea were family heirlooms.

The thirty-five or forty people gathered in Miss Ansley's apartment that afternoon constituted about the whole of Richmond's active civil rights community. Miss Ansley's inclusion in that group was something I took particular pleasure in. She belonged to none of the recognizable groups from which the Richmond Committee drew its members—labor unions, church groups, civic groups like the NAACP and the YWCA and the League of Women Voters. She was sui generis, and winning her to our side was quite a coup, I thought. John Drew, Naomi and I learned later, thought differently.

On one of John's visits to us in Washington a year or so after the reception, we began asking about friends and co-workers back in Richmond, and when I asked about Mildred Ansley, John looked uncomfortable. He hesitated answering for a long while, and then he said, "I got to tell you about Mildred. I think she's workin' for the FBI." Naomi and I both expressed our astonishment.

"Yes," said John, "I hate to say it, but I think she's workin' for them." How could he know that? Well, it had taken him a while to become suspicious of her, he admitted. But there were some things she had said, things she had asked him for. "Like the membership list of the Richmond Committee. And the NAACP membership list." John said he hesitated, but finally told her he felt he could not give her the lists. After that, he said, Mildred Ansley stopped coming to meetings of the Richmond Committee. And so, and not for the first time either, Naomi and I were saddened to find ourselves suspicious of someone we thought we had won to our side.

In which we agitate the American Legion

Every summer the American Legion of Virginia sponsored the Old Dominion Boys' State, a summer camp that was also, the American Legion said, an institute for democratic living. The campers, young men of high school age, got to combine such summer fun as canoeing, swimming, and campfires with training in good citizenship. Within the simulated structure of a state and general assembly, they were instructed in the arts of political campaigning and election, parliamentary procedure and debate, and the legislative process through which a bill becomes a law.

Josephus Simpson, editor of the *Richmond Afro-American,* called me up one day to say that according to his reading of the Boys' State literature, the camp was open to young men of good character between the ages of thirteen and eighteen; neither race nor creed was mentioned as a qualification. Did I suppose, he asked, that Negro teenagers were eligible to become citizens of the state?

Josephus was a literate, humorous man, learned in Latin. He was the black counterpart of a white fellow Virginian, another editor with a Latin-sounding name, Virginius Dabney, editor of the *Richmond Times-Dispatch.*

I said I did not know the answer to his question but that I was sure the AVC would be interested in determining it.

With the *Afro-American* footing the bill for tuition, the Richmond Chapter of the AVC agreed to sponsor four Boys' State campers, two black and two white. We recruited our four candidates; however, when we met with them and their parents and explained what they might be in for, one of the white candidates promptly got cold feet and pulled out. So we sent in the money for two black high school seniors, Maurice Epps and Albert Scott, and one white, Ehud Koch, son of our friends Fritz and Anne.

The tuition fees were accepted. But when I brought the three candidates into American Legion headquarters for an interview, I could tell at a glance what the answer to Josephus Simpson's question was. The American Legion treasurer took me aside and asked me what kind of funny stuff was I trying to pull. I assured him our sponsorship was an expression of our interest in promoting a genuinely democratic Boys' State. He wasn't buying any of that crap, he said, and told me I could expect a tuition refund in the next day's mail.

To its credit, the *Times-Dispatch,* to which I took the story, assigned a reporter to look into it and ran a brief account of the affair. As for our three campers, *their* instruction in democracy began when I took them up to Washington for a three-day trip to reward them for participating in our test. We took the train up one Thursday morning and came back Saturday night. I wrote an article about our expedition for the *Afro-American.* In it I described a Washington that Harry Bernstein and I, to our discredit, were unaware of when we were stationed at Arlington Hall. It was Washington as it appeared to a Negro visitor in 1950, a heavily segregated Washington that the three young men and I found to be a social desert with only a few scattered oases.

Since the District streetcar lines were unsegregated, we could get around the capital easily enough. It was at our destinations that difficulties sometimes arose. For the most part we kept to a carefully charted course. We spent both nights in a commodious, Quaker-run residence on Wyoming Avenue, a lodging that a Quaker member of our AVC chapter was able to arrange for us. And we ate lunches and dinners at places we knew would serve us: Union Station; the AVC Clubhouse on New Hampshire Avenue, where the boys got a heroes' welcome from members who had heard about our Boys' State adventure; and the Supreme Court cafeteria.

Capitol Hill, the FBI, the National Gallery of Art, the Washington Monument, and—since Maurice and Albert were both interested in careers in science—the technical exhibits at the Smithsonian were all open to us for touring. But we were warned away from eating in any of the downtown public restaurants, since our Quaker hosts feared we would risk humiliation. And for our evening's entertainment in the downtown area near our lodgings, we were limited to a single choice: the one "white" movie house that would admit Negro patrons, an art-film house, the Dupont Theatre, near Dupont Circle. Its manager, I learned later, was an old-time leftist who was happy to strike this small blow against segregation. By a lucky accident of weekend scheduling, the bill changed overnight so that we could see two different films. Thursday evening we saw *The Chips Are Down,* a French film adapted from a Sartre script which my companions found tough going. On Friday we saw Sabu in *The End of the River,* an adventure movie much more to everyone's liking.

On Friday afternoon I suggested going out to Glen Echo, the D.C. area's one amusement park, a proposal that won enthusiastic approval from all three boys, even Ehud, who was the bookish sort. But the trip was shot down immediately, when a colored newspaper vendor who had taken a friendly interest in us overheard our plans and advised me that we could never get in. "Don't you know this is a real Jim Crow town? Glen Echo's just for white folk."

In spite of the restrictions and limited options that confronted us at every turn, we had a good time. Shared adversity brought us together. Toward the end of the trip we were joking and kidding around, and we came back to Richmond as friends.

When Naomi and I were living in Washington a few years later, a new friend, Angel Palerm, unknowingly gave me another way of looking at our Richmond experiences. Angel, an anthropologist, and his wife, Carmen, a psychologist, were refugees from Franco Spain who had settled in Mexico after the war and had gone on to pursue their careers in D.C. Carmen and Naomi met professionally, and soon after, the Palerms and Caplans began seeing each other socially.

The Spanish Civil War had captured the imagination and support of many young liberals of my generation, so Angel and I would talk about it from time to time. I was surprised to learn that Angel, a gentle, erudite fellow, had been a captain in the Loyalist army at nineteen. What's more, he recalled the experience with evident enjoyment.

"We called it '*la guerra alegre.*'"

The Joyful War! I couldn't believe it! My own impressions of that war, drawn from grainy newsreels of the destruction of Madrid, from Hemingway's *For Whom the Bell Tolls,* and, most memorably, from Picasso's harrowing *Guernica,* were anything but joyful. At best, the Loyalists' defeat was tremendously disheartening.

"Ah, yes," said Angel, "we lost. But before we lost, it was a good time. It was good to feel we were fighting fascism. Our spirits were high. We were young. And we had such wonderful songs."

La guerra alegre. It is surely straining to compare an actual war to our civil rights campaigns in Virginia. (It is less strained, I think, to compare to war the heroic demonstrations of the sixties, in Birmingham, Alabama, and Greenwood and Jackson, Mississippi, where brave souls were maimed and killed as they fought for freedom.) Even so, when I look back on those days in Richmond, the enemy was unmistakable and malignant; each small gain was an exultation; our spirits were high; we were young. And we, too, had wonderful songs.

I'm not the only one who looks back on those times with odd affection. In 1991, Oliver Hill and I happened to meet in the Israeli embassy in Washington and fell to reminiscing. The embassy observes Martin Luther King's birthday every year with a special celebration at which it give awards to prominent figures in the civil rights movement. That day one of the honorees, thanks to my suggestion, was Spottswood W. Robinson III, chief judge emeritus of the U.S. Court of Appeals. It was a joyful occasion for Spott and his family and friends and joyful for me personally to see Spott and Marian again, and Oliver and Bernie Hill.

Two young male students from the University of Virginia, one black, one white, approached Oliver and me as we talked, and we found ourselves recalling for them some of our early experiences.

"Those were wonderful days," Oliver said at one point.

"Wonderful days?" I exclaimed in disbelief. "Oliver!"

"Oh, yeah. I know what you mean. But we did have some wonderful times, then." And I knew what *he* meant.

Yet Angel Palerm was forced to leave Spain, and I had to leave Richmond.

At the end of my freelance year Naomi announced that she was pregnant and that the terms of our agreement had changed. After the baby came *she* would stay home and *I* would go out to work.

I heard this pronouncement with a mixture of sadness and relief. I regretted having to put aside a writing schedule to which I had grown accustomed. And yet I was meeting with such scant success that in fact I was about ready to give up. In the entire year I had earned all of five hundred dollars. My major project had been a long article on the Virginia NAACP's campaign to desegregate the public schools. It was an ambitious piece, based on many field trips I had taken to schools and courts with Hill, Martin and Robinson. The *Atlantic Monthly* had expressed an interest in it when I sent it a query. But the editors found the finished manuscript "too regional." Most of the article got printed, finally, in the NAACP's monthly magazine the *Crisis;* however, the *Crisis* was unable to pay me anything for it.

I began looking for work in Richmond but found no openings. I was already too notorious to be taken on as a reporter at either the *Times-Dispatch* or the *News-Leader,* and as for freelance work, I had managed to become persona non grata even at the *Times-Dispatch*'s Sunday magazine. That publication had printed four of my articles and had commissioned a fifth when Virginius Dabney ran an editorial on a civil rights issue that so angered me, I sent off a retort to the paper's letter section, "Voice of the People."

The Sunday magazine editor smiled uneasily when I brought my new piece in, an interview with a local artist who painted on china. He fiddled with the pages and then remarked, "That was quite a letter you sent in here the other day."

The *Times-Dispatch* printed my letter. It printed the article. But it didn't give me a byline. And its editors let me know in the osmotic way in which we communicated in Richmond that they'd never print another thing of mine again.

"Such is freedom of the press in America," said Fritz Koch sardonically when he heard the story.

"Oh, honestly, Marvin," said Brownie, "Just cut yourself off from them and let them drift."

But it was I who was drifting. I couldn't connect anywhere. My AVC buddy Ed Fleischer had left his desk job at the *Times-Dispatch*. He had played a prominent role in organizing a Guild chapter at the paper, and he was advised, circumspectly, that he could expect no further advancement. Now he was writing copy for the city's top advertising agency. The job paid well, he said, and he thought he might be able to get the company to take me on. But I knew for sure it wasn't what I wanted.

Josephus Simpson and Spott Robinson asked me up to the *Afro-American* office one afternoon and proposed that I write features for the paper and do legal research for Hill, Martin and Robinson. Between the two of them, they thought, they might be able to pay me a living wage. I was flattered but in the end decided it was too haphazard a deal for an incipient family man. I wanted a regular job with regular hours and regular pay.

And there was another consideration, although I didn't tell them about it: I was becoming discouraged with my work in Richmond. Every victory had to be won again. Oliver Hill had just run for a second term on the city council, and though his work had been greatly admired ("Any Richmonder who . . . studied Mr. Hill's Council Record," said the *Times-Dispatch* editorially, ". . . should have been convinced that he deserved re-election"), he lost the ninth seat by 44 votes. Many of us urged him to demand a recount. Oliver refused. In the announcement of his decision he said, "My objective is not to retain a position on the Council but to bring about better racial cooperation and understanding."

I began looking outside of Richmond, in New York, Philadelphia, and Washington, D.C. To pay my train fares I took a part-time job, driving a Red Top cab. There was a certain poetic symmetry to this, I think, in that my first and last impressions of Richmond came from a moving taxi.

Months passed and—nothing. "Oh, honey," Naomi said, feeling for me. "Every time you come home from a trip and look at me, I can see I must be getting bigger by the minute."

Then one thing led to another and I was put in the way of gainful employment. Down the hallway from the Southern School for Workers was the Richmond office of United Press International. It was a one-man operation, and Meyer Lurie, who ran it, had no opening and knew of none in Richmond. But a friend of his in Washington, he said, who worked for Fairchild Publications, a chain of business newspapers, had remarked in a phone conversation the other day that there was a vacancy in that bureau. I promptly called the friend, verified the information, and left for Washington at once. I stayed overnight with Eli Horowitz, a patent-examiner friend and fellow AVCer who had been reassigned from Richmond to Washington, and presented myself to the Fairchild bureau chief at 9 A.M. Chief Harry E. Ressiguie, a heavy-set, gruff old-time newspaperman who was better natured than he appeared to be, examined my résumé and scrapbook. Two days later he phoned me at Eli's apartment, where I was hanging around, and said he was ready to take a chance on me.

Ressiguie called me mid-morning on a Friday. I caught the late-afternoon train back to Richmond and, knowing that the Kochs had invited us for Shabbes (Sabbath) dinner, grabbed a cab and went straight out to their place from the station.

Naomi answered the doorbell when I rang. She took one look at my face and burst out laughing. Before I had a chance to speak, she turned to the Kochs and cried, "Yippie! Marvin's got a job!"

So we put 13 Gross Avenue up for sale and moved to Washington.

We left Richmond reluctantly. Certainly, from a racial and political perspective, it was a despicable place to live. But Naomi and I were both beguiled by its southern charm and unhurried pace. The civil rights activities we were involved in gave purpose to our lives there; and we were tied to the community by many bonds of friendship.

Even after we were settled in D.C., we kept revisiting Richmond: every few months at first, but then less frequently as friends moved away or died and as Washington made its own claims on our commitments and affections.

Yet Richmond always kept a strong hold on us. We looked back on our five years in the Old Dominion as memorable ones. What Naomi and I could never have imagined, even at our most hopeful, was how that bastion of white supremacy would someday be transformed.

But you didn't have to go back to see how things down there were changing. The changes were so dramatic that the whole country was aware of them. In 1990, Douglas L. Wilder became governor of Virginia, the first African American to assume that eminent office. And many hearts throughout the nation were touched when Richmond, in 1996, recast the nature of its most celebrated thoroughfare, Monument Avenue. To the ranks of statues of five heroes of the Confederacy, three on horseback and two on lofty pedestals, the city added still another commanding hero, the bronze-brown figure of the gentle, noble Arthur Ashe, armed only with his books and tennis racket.

Even though I didn't have to, I did go back. Not with Naomi, alas, for she died in 1981. But a dear companion and I went back, about a year ago, to revisit my old stamping grounds. And what I saw with my own eyes was more encouraging than anything that ever made the nation's front pages. We checked in at the Hotel Jefferson, where I had stayed on my first night in Richmond. That grand old pile has been completely refurbished, elegant beyond any dream or remembering. But even more astonishing were the human changes. Blacks are more than waiters or ash-tray emptiers today. The concierge was black. Young black men and women greeted us at the front desk. Black guests were scattered comfortably around the huge, plush lobby. Blacks were dining in the hotel's two fine restaurants.

Yet surprising as those sights were to a member of the Richmond Committee for Civil Rights, they didn't begin to prepare us for what we found when we left the Jefferson and took a walk down Franklin Street to another of my old haunts, the YMCA where Harry Bernstein and I worked off flab and tensions in the pool and on the handball courts.

Today, the YMCA has women members as well as men. And what is even more astounding, if old Richmond still clouds your mind's eye, is that it has black men and black women members, too.

We mounted the steps from the street to what had once been the Y's main lobby. But the lobby's gone. Instead, we found ourselves peering through a wall of glass into a gleaming fitness center. Row upon row of exercise machines stretched across a large, bright-lit chamber. Men and women, in scant gym clothes, were flexing their muscles on those shining steel contraptions. But even that is not what finally transfixed me. I looked again and saw a young white woman and a young black man seated side by side, indifferent to each other, pedaling furiously away on stationary bicycles.

Yes! In Richmond, Virginia! The millennium come to pass in only fifty years!

Jonathan Daniels, editor of the Raleigh *News and Observer* and one of the foremost southern liberals of Harry's time and mine, at a public forum once dubbed Richmond "both the cradle and the graveyard of democracy."[3] What I've seen happening there is almost enough to make me believe in resurrection.

Nowadays, when I hear a black person cry out in despair, "But nothing's changed!" I think of Richmond and am moved to say, "But you are wrong. Things have changed. They *have*."

3. Egerton, *Speak Now Against the Day,* 470.

Part II

Washington, D.C.: The Fight to
Desegregate the Restaurants
1951–1953

7

On the Hecht Company Picket Line

Once again it took a friend from my Ann Arbor, Michigan, days to involve me in a civil rights campaign. But where I had gladly followed Harry Bernstein down to Richmond and into the battle against racial segregation, in Washington our friend Ann Fagan Ginger had to shame me into taking part.

Ann was Ray Ginger's wife. Ray, Harry, and I had come to know each other as fellow members of Company D. Ray met Ann, who was a college junior at the time, soon after our unit arrived at the University of Michigan in 1944. Five weeks after their first date they got married.

Marriage entitled Ray to live outside the dorm where we were quartered. The little book-crammed apartment in which he and Ann set up housekeeping quickly became a favorite off-campus hangout for several of us Company D bachelors.

Later on, when our contingent was transferred from Ann Arbor to the Signal Corps unit out at Arlington Hall, the Gingers rented the first floor of a little house in Falls Church, a short distance from the post. And that was where we often gathered on a Saturday night, to gab and gorge and quaff large quantities of three-point-two beer.

After his discharge from the Army, Ray Ginger went on to establish himself as a promising young historian. His doctoral thesis became the basis for his first book, *The Bending Cross,* published in 1949, a widely acclaimed biography of the American socialist leader Eugene V. Debs. Western Reserve University, in Cleveland, Ohio, engaged him as a professor of American history. Before long, an appointment at Harvard appeared to be in the offing.

In the years after Ann Arbor and Arlington Hall, Harry and I still kept in touch with the Gingers. We commissioned a couple of *Outlook* articles from Ray. We had a happy reunion with him at the AVC convention in Milwaukee. When Ann graduated from the University of Michigan Law School, they advised us, and Harry and I sent her our congratulations and a present. When Naomi had to attend a psychological convention in Cleveland, I went along with her, and the trip became the occasion for a couple of evening get-togethers with the Gingers, who were living near the Western Reserve campus. In our first summer in Washington, Naomi and I were delighted, therefore, to learn that the Gingers and their five-month old son, Thomas Jefferson Ginger, were coming to D.C for an extended stay so that Ray could conduct research at the Library of Congress for a new book he was writing. What's more, they were renting an apartment not far from ours.

Glad as we were to see the Gingers again, I admit I was a trifle nervous at resuming the relationship. The Gingers were the most extreme left-wing of all our friends. While Naomi and I shared some of their political views, and though I had great respect for Ray, who played a role in my political education in the army, there were still strong differences between us. For one thing, I did not share his enthusiasm for the Soviet Union, or his notion that it was on the way to becoming a workers' paradise. By unspoken common consent we did not touch on our differences, and we shared several enjoyable evenings of supper and common baby care. Our daughter Freya was barely two months old by the time we met again. As the more experienced father, Ray had a word of comment on parenthood that he knew would be meaningful to a fellow army veteran. "Cap," he said, "it's like being on permanent KP."

Then, at one of our evenings together, Ann presented Naomi and me with a challenging invitation. There was a campaign under way, she told us, to compel the Hecht Company, one of D.C.'s major downtown department stores, to desegregate its basement lunch counter and begin serving Negro customers. She had begun going downtown every Saturday to walk the picket line in front of the store. Aware of our civil rights activities in Richmond, she said she was sure Naomi and I would like to join her.

"Ann," I said, "I can't."

My reasons seemed compelling to me. I was new to the city and felt no impulse as yet to involve myself in its civic life. I had a taxing new job and a new baby daughter. Both of them had first claims on my energies and attention. What's more, one of the eight newspapers Fairchild Publications published was *Retailing Daily,* a paper for the retail trade. Hecht's, like many major retailers, bought large numbers of that paper every day to distribute to officers and key sales personnel. I didn't think I would last long at the Washington Bureau, I said, if Fairchild discovered I was picketing a big subscriber.

Ann stared at me. Staring, I thought, was one of her most arresting characteristics. A slight woman of girlish aspect, Ann had long brown hair and large eyes that reminded me of Alice in the Tenniel illustrations. But when she looked at you at such a moment, a moment fraught with ideological implication, all her fervent feeling was concentrated in one candid, even pitiless gaze.

"Marvin," she said with a commissar's dispatch, "I'm sorry. Being afraid just isn't a good enough reason not to picket."

I thought about that after we parted. I mulled it over privately and aloud with Naomi. Independent of regret for any drop I had suffered in Ann's regard, I came to my own conclusion. Could I let fear compel me to be prudent? Could I ignore in Washington an evident injustice I would never ignore in Richmond? It was my own self-regard, not Ann's regard, I minded losing. I knew then where I would be the following Saturday.

The first thing that struck me as I approached the Hecht picket line was that I wasn't dressed for it. The month was August. The day was searing hot. I had come in an open-neck sportshirt, walking shorts, and loafers. But the two white and two black men carrying signs in front of the main Seventh Street entrance might have been dressed for church or some other formal occasion. They wore ties and jackets. A couple of them wore felt hats. The half-dozen women on the line, both black and white, were even more fashionably dressed. They may have been wearing walking shoes, and God knows I hope they were. But all of them wore pretty summer dresses and summer hats. Ann Ginger was already on the line, dressed as elegantly as the others, pushing Tom Jefferson in a baby carriage and handing out flyers to the passersby who paused to take a peek at him.

She broke away when she saw me and led me over to the command post, a pillar beside the entrance under the scanty shade of Hecht's iron and glass marquee. Picket signs were stacked upside down against a facing of reddish granite. Guarding them was a tall, rangy woman with a strong, bony face and a prominent nose. She wore a gay flowered dress and an immense broad-brimmed hat. If it weren't for the circumstances and her air of authority, she might have been the hostess at a tea party. She gave me a warm, radiant smile as Ann Ginger introduced us. The full significance of the moment escaped me. I didn't realize that in meeting Annie Stein I was meeting the campaign commander. She had a few cautionary instructions before I began. Pickets were to march about ten feet apart, as close to the curb as possible. And no smoking was permitted on the line. Formalities concluded, I reached into the pile of picket signs. My heart pounded as I grasped one, raised it, and fell in step as the circling picketers made way for me.

I held that shaft of smooth new wood as if it were a lance. I looked only upward as I marched. All I saw as I walked was a strip of white wood and the grey back of the cardboard sign. I was too nervous to try and read the message. I felt as if the sign, like a sail, were carrying me along. It took several turns around for me before I dared to lower my gaze. To my surprise no one was staring at me. If anything, most passersby ignored us. Most people tended to quicken their steps and keep their eyes fixed straight ahead as they went by. Now and then I caught a smile of sympathy or a hostile stare, but nothing more. Not a Fairchild face anywhere. In less than an hour, light as the burden was, and though I switched the sign from hand to hand, my arms and shoulders ached. My steps grew mechanical. I was bathed in sweat. And lulled by my own cadence into boredom.

When my two-hour stint was up, I returned my sign to the stack against the wall. Only then did I read what my sign said. FAIR-MINDED AMERICANS, I had advised Saturday shoppers, HELP END SEGREGATION AT HECHT'S LUNCH COUNTER. Annie Stein thanked me with another radiant smile. The Coordinating Committee was meeting Wednesday night, she said. Would I like to come? I jotted down the time and place. In spite of my misgivings, it felt good to be back on the front line again.

The full name of the organization I was about to join was the Coordinating Committee for the Enforcement of the D.C. Anti-Discrimination Laws. Its whole history and purpose were in that cumbersome title.

The anti-discrimination laws were two statutes enacted in 1872 and 1873, in the wave of Reconstruction reform that followed the Civil War and brought black Americans new legal rights. Such reforms came to the District of Columbia earlier and in greater measure than elsewhere, when the first postwar Congress, controlled by the Radical Republicans, used the nation's capital as a proving ground for new social legislation. The 1872 and 1873 laws were enacted by a bicameral territorial legislature—partially elected, partially appointed by President Grant's administration—that Congress set up to govern the District from 1871 to 1874.

The laws required restaurants, hotels, "ice-cream saloons," barbershops, and certain other places of public accommodation to serve "any respectable, well-behaved person without regard to race, color or previous condition of servitude" or face a $100 fine and a loss of license for a year.

Toward the end of the century, however, new Jim Crow laws in the South and indifference or hostility to the plight of Negroes elsewhere were eroding the civil rights advances of Reconstruction throughout the nation.

A prominent leader in the Washington Negro community, Mary Church Terrell, who at the age of eighty-six assumed the chairmanship of the Coordinating Committee, could still remember a time "in the 1890s [when] a colored person could dine anywhere in Washington." Succeeding Democratic administrations, she recalled in a newspaper interview, brought to power "cruel Southerners" who ignored the District's laws and imposed racial segregation on the capital by political pressure and administrative action.

One of those "cruel Southerners" was Woodrow Wilson, born in Staunton, Virginia. Upon assuming the presidency in 1913, Wilson adopted a code of rigid segregation in federal government, barring blacks from holding high office, even those positions that had been reserved for them since the start of the Reconstruction era.

Wilson's actions, however, were only a continuation of a process of racial segregation in the District that had already begun years before. The anti-discrimination laws of 1872 and 1873 were soon ignored with impunity by public establishments. In 1901 the laws were simply omitted from a recodification of the District of Columbia Code.

Common sense suggested, however, that a city could not repeal laws just by dropping them. From time to time in the ensuing years those "lost laws" were remembered by local blacks in sporadic agitations against segregation and discrimination. However, a broad-based community campaign to reestablish the laws did not get under way until after World War II.

The "rediscovery" of the laws was a consequence of a new national report. The 1947 report of President Truman's committee, *To Secure These Rights,* which inspired us to form the Richmond Committee for Civil Rights, had already documented the terrible toll of racial injustice nation-wide. The new study, which came out a year later, concentrated on the District only. It drew an equally disturbing picture of the impact of racism on the black community in the nation's capital. Entitled *Segregation in Washington,* the report was the work of a committee of ninety nationally known citizens, Eleanor Roosevelt, Hubert Humphrey, Walter Reuther, Helen Hayes (a native Washingtonian, incidentally), and Melvyn Douglas among them.

The report described, in excruciating detail, the injustices and indignities that a black resident of the capital had to endure. In a paragraph whose consequence he could not have anticipated, the author, Kenesaw Mountain Landis II, observed:

> Some people say that the time is not ripe for colored people to have equal rights as citizens in the Nation's Capital and that white people are "not ready" to give them such rights. But in 1872 . . . the popularly elected Assembly of the District passed a law giving Negroes equal rights in restaurants, hotels, barbershops and other places of public accommodation. Stiff penalties were provided for violation. As late as 1904 this civil rights law was familiar to the correspondent of the New York Times. But around the turn of the century it mysteriously disappeared from the compiled statutes of the District and it cannot be found in the present codes. Since there is no record of its repeal, some lawyers speculate that it may well be technically in full force and effect.

One of the readers of the report whose imagination was stirred by this passage was Annie Stein. She was, at the time, chairman of the Anti-Discrimination Committee of the local chapter of the Progressive Party. It was only one of the many positions she had held in a lifetime devoted to left-wing causes.

Annie Stein grew up in New York City in a poor Jewish family. Her parents were radicals who had long since substituted social protest for religious affiliation. A graduate of City College of New York, trained as a statistician, Annie Stein was always deeply committed to political action. In New York during the 1930s, she worked for the National Women's Trade Union League, organizing the lowest-paid workers in the city—laundry and domestic help and restaurant and hotel employees. In Washington during World War II, she represented the CIO on an Office of Price Administration panel and worked to see that grocers and restaurant owners observed ceiling prices. After the war she worked for the Washington Committee for Consumer Protection. To protest the rising costs of milk and meat, she organized a city-wide consumer strike that succeeded in keeping the price of meat down for many weeks. She was a government employee for a time, until she lost her job in a dispute over her refusal to swear to an anti-Communist loyalty oath.

Free from the restrictions of a daily job (her husband, Arthur, who also left government service over a loyalty oath dispute, supported the family as an independent building contractor), Annie Stein was able to devote her considerable energies to exploring the implications of the Landis report's observation on "the lost laws."

She began by phoning her lawyer friend Joseph Forer, chairman of the District Affairs Committee of the D.C. chapter of the National Lawyers Guild, the left-wing equivalent of the American Bar Association. Forer readily agreed to undertake the legal research necessary to establish the continuing validity of the old statutes. His strongly affirmative conclusion spurred Annie Stein on to the next step. Recognizing the need to build broad public support for enforcement of the "lost laws," she became the catalyst for the formation, in 1949, of the Coordinating Committee, a coalition that eventually included some sixty-one civil rights, labor, religious, and social groups.

No one now knows how she did it, but in what turned out to be a master stroke, Mrs. Stein persuaded Mary Church Terrell to accept the chairmanship of the committee. Annie Stein was content to be the secretary.

Mrs. Terrell brought enormous prestige to the office. At the age of eighty-six, she was nearing the end of a life rich in public service and honors. After her graduation from Oberlin College, where she majored in the classics, she came to Washington to teach Latin and German in the M Street High School, a black secondary school of exceptionally high academic standards. She went on to serve as a member of the D.C. school board for eleven years. She was the founder and first president of the National Association of Colored Women's Clubs and was in great demand as a speaker at international women's conferences. She was president of the Women's Republican League of Washington. She and her husband, Robert H. Terrell, were prominent figures in Washington black society. Robert Terrell was, for a time, principal of the M Street High School. He later became a judge of the Municipal Court and, after his death in 1925, was memorialized when Terrell Junior High was named after him.

Mrs. Terrell was a tall, white-haired woman of regal bearing and surpassing eloquence. Her complexion, in her late years a pale ivory, was not one to alert strangers that she was colored. A friend of hers, the writer H. G. Wells, in his introduction to her autobiography, *A Colored Woman in a White World,* observed that Mrs. Terrell might have been more explicit about a matter that he says a perceptive reader could figure out anyway. Mollie Church's African American ancestors had intermarried with whites, and she grew up in Memphis, fully aware of the problems attendant on being the product of two races.

What gives Mrs. Terrell's autobiography its strength and poignancy is the author's unflinching recognition of what it means to be black. It never occurred to her to "pass" for white; she would have rejected such a choice as cowardice. She asserted her racial identification proudly and never shrank from the obligations she felt it imposed on her.

A passage in the autobiography, which was first published in 1940, almost seems to foreshadow Mary Church Terrell's involvement in the campaign for "the lost laws." Mrs. Terrell observes that as a colored person she could walk from the Capitol to the White House (a distance of some sixteen blocks) and not find a restaurant that would serve her. She recalls being hungry and weary and reading the posted menu outside a restaurant longingly but being unable to summon the "grit" she needed to enter and risk refusal. "But," she says, "I have never stopped trying to get what I knew was just and right for me to have."

One senses here the impulse that brought together two women as unlike as Mary Terrell and Annie Stein—the southern aristocrat and the New York leftist. It was in Mrs. Terrell's lifelong battle against the injustice of racial discrimination that she and Mrs. Stein found common ground.

Mrs. Terrell's frequent characterization of Annie Stein as "the greatest secretary in the world" was an appropriate expression of her affection for the other woman and her recognition of talents of a very high order. If Annie Stein had been a West Point cadet, a member of the Coordinating Committee once observed, she would have ended up a general. She was a superb strategist. She proceeded to demonstrate her gift by mapping out a course of action to make the public aware of "the lost laws" and to set in motion the court test necessary to determine whether the laws were still in effect.

Joe Forer's research was done, he recalled, in a single afternoon. It took four years after that to get a court decision upholding his conclusions.

Six other lawyers joined him in signing his opinion. Among them were two highly regarded African Americans: Charles H. Houston, the dean of Howard University Law School (and one of Spott Robinson's teachers and inspirations); and Margaret A. Haywood, who went on to become one of the first women judges of the D.C. Superior Court.

That the laws had never been repealed seemed fairly evident to everyone; a crucial issue in the ensuing court debates, though, was whether Congress had the power to delegate its authority over the District to the legislative assembly that had enacted the laws.

Forer asserted that Congress had such authority. His opinion recalled that, in 1908, a conviction against a man charged with mistreating a horse was upheld by the U.S. Court of Appeals even though the law under which he was convicted, was, like "the lost laws," enacted by the legislative assembly in the early 1870s and omitted from the 1901 code. The appellate court held that the law against mistreatment of animals was a "police regulation" enacted in the interests of law and order and that the 1901 code explicitly exempted such regulations from repeal. That conclusion, too, Joe Forer anticipated, would work in favor of upholding "the lost laws."

In May 1949, the National Lawyers Guild opinion was submitted to the D.C. corporation counsel, Vernon West, who announced that he would take the matter under study. And there the matter rested. After repeated failures to get any action from the counsel, Mrs. Stein and Mrs. Terrell went into consultation with the Coordinating Committee's chief attorneys, Joe Forer and his partner David Rein. Their conclusion, quickly verified by the entire Coordinating Committee, was that the time had come to prod the corporation counsel by presenting him with a specific violation of the old laws.

On the afternoon of Friday, January 27, 1950, Mrs. Terrell, accompanied by three friends, entered Thompson's Cafeteria on lower Fourteenth Street in downtown Washington, picked up trays, and proceeded along the counter.

Thompson's did not often have such distinguished patrons. The cafeteria was one of a chain of four and was known among Washingtonians as a place where you could dine cheaply—during the 1930s, for instance, it sold ham-and-egg sandwiches for five cents apiece. Thompson's usual clientele consisted of footsore shoppers, secretaries with twenty minutes for lunch, tourists looking for an inexpensive meal, and men down on their luck, who came in on a cold day to sit for an hour or so and warm their hands on a mug of coffee.

Accompanying Mrs. Terrell, who brought her usual elegant presence to the place, were two men, the Reverend W. H. Jernagin, pastor of the Mount Carmel Baptist Church and president of a national Baptist training program, and David Scull, a government worker active in the civil rights programs of the Society of Friends; and another woman, Geneva Brown, secretary-treasurer of the Cafeteria Workers Union. It was an interracial group, for Scull was white.

While the four of them were engaged in loading their trays, the manager confronted them. He took one look at the two unmistakably dark faces, the minister's and the union official's, and told the group grimly that it was against Thompson policy to serve colored people.

Armed with his refusal the testing party took the next step. One of the principal reasons for choosing Thompson's was that it was next door to the building in which Forer and Rein had their offices. The lawyers were waiting for Mrs. Terrell and her friends. They got their sworn, signed affidavits and took them right down to the corporation counsel, arguing that Thompson's had violated the Equal Service Acts of 1872 and 1873.

Technicalities raised in the preliminary stages of the complaint and in its first consideration by a court required Mrs. Terrell to lead two more testing parties into Thompson's. Each time the manager obliged by restating his rea-son for refusing service. Eventually, the *Thompson Restaurant* case was launched and on its way through the courts.

The Washington Restaurant Association girded itself to do battle on the side of Thompson's. It sent a letter to its members urging them to continue to refuse service to colored persons and asking them to contribute at least $25 to a de-fense fund. The *Washington Afro-American* estimated that the fund eventually amounted to about $100,000. The Washington Board of Trade joined the asso-ciation in the suit as a "friend of the court."

Arrayed against these powerful forces was the Coordinating Committee's hand-to-mouth operation, which sought to marshal public support for the D.C. government's suit against Thompson's. Its meeting hall was the storefront headquarters of the Laundry Workers Local 471, on M Street, N.W. The com-mittee's office was located in Annie Stein's two-bedroom apartment in the Trenton Terrace complex in Southeast Washington, which she shared with her husband and their young son and daughter. She kept the committee's records in a filing cabinet in her bedroom; that was also where she kept the commit-tee's mimeograph machine. Her dining room table was often pressed into ser-vice for stuffing and mailing parties and for evenings devoted to the lettering of picket signs.

Neither Mrs. Terrell nor Mrs. Stein was content to sit by and wait for a court ruling. Despite her age and eminence, Mrs. Terrell was no figurehead, al-though it is true that her prestige alone was an enormous asset. It enabled the Coordinating Committee to operate fairly free from red-baiting during the hysterical heights of the McCarthy era. Mrs. Terrell's chairmanship and the committee's concentration on a single issue—the desegregation of the capi-tal's eating places—quieted the fears of some of the more conservative organi-zations that joined the committee. Apprehensions could easily have been stirred in those uneasy days by the fact that Forer and Rein were, in addition to being local officials of the National Lawyers Guild, also attorneys for many left-wing notables in trouble with the House Un-American Activities Commit-tee. And Annie Stein's prominent role in the Progressive Party was another cause for anxiety among some of the Coordinating Committee's supporters.

Besides her indifference to any whispers of Communist influence, Mrs. Ter-rell had another important quality. She was Annie Stein's match in militancy. Her and Mrs. Stein's co-equal relationship—reflected in their mutual trust and their affection and high regard for one another—was one of the Coordinating Committee's great operational strengths.

As they saw it, their task was to foster community awareness—in the black community especially—of the existence of the anti-discrimination laws and their probable validity. Member organizations were the network for advancing this point of view by scheduling committee speakers and distributing committee literature.

Through a systematic program of testing and negotiation, the Coordinating Committee sought to expand the list of eating places open to everyone.

One afternoon a month the committee would send out small interracial testing parties, groups of two or three, and was agreeably surprised to find that, in spite of white hostility and restaurant association opposition, there were more restaurants in Washington than generally supposed that were willing to serve anyone who came in.

To the known and scant supply of places that served without discrimination—Union Station, the zoo, federal government cafeterias, organizational eating places such as the dining rooms of the YWCA and the American Veterans Committee clubhouse—the Coordinating Committee was able to add a growing number of regular commercial establishments.

In June 1950, the Coordinating Committee issued its first list of white-owned District restaurants that served without discrimination—about twenty of them. The list was an immediate best-seller. Among its adherents were foreign embassies and the State Department of the United States, which found the prevailing discriminatory policy of most capital restaurants a continual source of international embarrassment. The list was rechecked, revised, and expanded periodically. By the time the Thompson case reached the Supreme Court in 1953, the Coordinating Committee was giving its stamp of approval to more than sixty restaurants. It was not uncommon for Annie Stein to get a call at home from a State Department official who wondered if Mrs. Stein's new list was available and if he could send a messenger over for it as soon as it came off the mimeograph.

In the opening campaign to reestablish the old laws, it was Annie Stein's brilliant tactical suggestion to concentrate on lower Seventh Street. The numerous department and variety stores in a six-block stretch of that street were heavily dependent on black trade. It became the Coordinating Committee's task to point out to the stores the injustice of refusing lunch-counter service to many of their best customers. And on the street and in committee member organizations, "Don't Shop Where You Can't Eat" became the dominant slogan.

Several of the department and variety stores desegregated their lunch counters after meeting with Coordinating Committee representatives. But even negotiation had its limits. The first confrontation on Seventh Street arose when

Kresge, of the national variety store chain, refused to meet with a Coordinating Committee delegation, and a subsequent leaflet distribution outside the store, urging a boycott, produced negligible results. Some of the Coordinating Committee's more aggressive members then proposed that the organization picket the store.

At first the proposal met resistance. Some of the committee's organizations felt picketing was undignified and that it would take them in a more militant direction than they wanted to go. Even some of the committee's union members were reluctant to picket, since they knew firsthand that walking the line was no pleasure and that lines were difficult to maintain.

Mrs. Terrell met this organizational crisis grandly. Ignoring the warnings of the uselessness and vulgarity of picketing and the fears expressed that it would provoke riots and racial violence, she put on her ankle-length fur coat, wrapped a scarf around her head, and with her cane in one hand and a sign in the other, led the first picket line in a snowstorm. Occasional threats and insults were the worst things the pickets experienced. In eight weeks Kresge's trade was so seriously hurt the store capitulated. The pickets were invited in to have a cup of coffee and to sit at the lunch counter that had denied black customers service for so many years.

Victory convinced the Coordinating Committee that picketing, used as a last resort, could be a powerful weapon in the fight for desegregation.

The Hecht Company became the next target of a picketing campaign. Hecht's unwittingly invited the Coordinating Committee's attention. During World Brotherhood Week in February 1951, the store ran a full-page ad in the local newspapers featuring a message from Eric Johnston, Economic Stabilization Administrator and general chairman of the event. Under a large photograph of a white hand and a black hand clasping, Mr. Johnston called on everyone to work to build "bridges of brotherhood." He declared: "We can't blind ourselves to the disturbing and undermining racial and religious antagonisms in America. They will defeat our good intentions for world brotherhood until we cast them out and live as brothers in our states, communities and neighborhoods—not for a single week in any year, but day by day and year by year."

The ad prompted Mrs. Terrell and Mrs. Stein to visit Hecht's and meet with a high official. Heretofore Hecht's had refused to serve black customers at the basement lunch counter. Did the ad mean the company was now ready to drop the color bar and build "a bridge of brotherhood"? Apparently it did not.

The ad, the official explained, was "a purely commercial gesture." The lunch counter would continue to be reserved for white customers only.

Discussions with Hecht's continued for many weeks; then the store broke off all negotiations. The Coordinating Committee responded by mobilizing a boycott against Hecht's. When it became evident that the boycott was having little effect, out came the picket signs.

The line got under way at an unpropitious time—on a tropical Saturday in July 1951. In spite of that, the Coordinating Committee undertook to keep the line going in front of the store's main entrance near Seventh and F Streets every Thursday night, every noon hour on Friday, and all day Saturday.

Ann Ginger was right. Picket-line volunteers were badly needed. So the Caplans signed up. I reluctantly, Naomi exuberantly. For my wife felt as committed to this cause as I did. Neither of us wanted to wheel Freya on the line. So we took turns, marching on alternate Saturdays for two hours each.

Picketing, for me, was a painful obligation. It was not only the exposure to public scrutiny that I dreaded and my fear of encountering a Fairchild colleague. I also hated having to get dressed up to march. For what I soon discovered was that it was no coincidence that the other men on the first line I joined were wearing ties and jackets. Annie Stein, strategist, had decreed a dress code of exquisite cruelty. Since "the lost laws" required service for "any respectable, well-behaved person," she reasoned, the pickets ought to underscore that fact by looking particularly natty.

So, sighing and kvetching, I would go off to discharge my duty. Naomi, on the other hand, looked forward to picketing as a social occasion. Although not usually preoccupied with dressing up, she always prepared herself for the line with great care. You would have thought she was going off to some high-style formal affair in which it was somehow important that she look as fashionable as any other woman in attendance. Silk stockings on a summer day was not what she usually wore. But she drew them on uncomplainingly when she was getting ready to circle in front of Hecht's. She was in high spirits even as she marched. She enjoyed the fellowship of the line. She didn't mind occasional stares and insults from passersby. More aggressive than I by nature, she gave as good as she got. Not the least of the pleasures of the line for her was that it got her out after a week of being cooped up in the apartment with the baby.

For me, however, picketing was only one aspect of my work with the Coordinating Committee. I began attending business meetings, and when Annie Stein learned I was a newspaperman she charmed me—I cannot think of a more accurate description—into becoming chairman of the Publicity Commit-

120 / Farther Along

tee. Attendant to that office was a position as a Coordinating Committee executive.

The Publicity Committee chairmanship was a frustrating job. I sent out releases on what I considered newsworthy events, but except for those picked up by the *Afro-American,* they were rarely used.

The Hecht line was enlivened from time to time by guest appearances, all of which I attempted to publicize. Once a prominent black boxer took a turn on the line. On another occasion our featured guest was Josephine Baker, the celebrated black American singer and dancer, toast of Paris, and friend of Mrs. Terrell's (who seemed to know everyone). Mme. Baker took time during a visit to the capital to come down to Hecht's and try to get served at the lunch counter. Failing that, she joined our march for a while. The city's black ministers came out several times. Black-run labor unions, notably Local 471 of the Laundry Workers, sent trained pickets out to demonstrate their solidarity with the campaign. I could not get a word of this into any of the city's three daily newspapers. Hecht's, after all, was a major advertiser.

The picketing dragged on for six months, from the first tropical Saturday in July through a slushy Christmas season. The climax of the campaign came on the Thursday night before Christmas. A picket line of about a hundred people marched in a snowstorm outside the main entrance. Led by a committee member dressed as Santa Claus and carrying picket signs that had begun to swell and run, the cold and dripping pickets circled the sidewalk in a jaunty lockstep, singing words that several of us had set to the tunes of well-known folk songs and Christmas carols.

To the tune of "Down in the Valley," I remember singing:

> Down in Hecht's basement,
> The basement so lo-ow,
> The lunch counter won't serve you,
> If you're not white as snow.

A hostile woman shopper tried to grab Santa's sign and he retaliated by taking a swipe at her with it. Although a couple of policemen were standing by, no arrests were made. As one of the pickets observed afterwards, how could you arrest Santa Claus so close to Christmas?

Shortly after Christmas the Hecht Company capitulated. Annie Stein predicted it. Addressing a meeting of the Coordinating Committee in the Laundry Workers hall, just before the big Christmas demonstration, she said it was her opinion that Hecht's had had enough. They were losing tremendous amounts of business, she said. That was evident from "the fabulous sales" they were running in an attempt to lure boycotting customers back to the store.

"They'll put up with us during December when business is good and during the Christmas rush and maybe a few weeks after that," I remember her saying. "But you'll see. When the January white sales start and we're still out there . . ."

January came and still the store management refused to meet with a delegation from the Coordinating Committee. The pickets knew the basement counter was still refusing service because it was our practice to check the counter every week on the chance that the store might have quietly dropped the color bar.

Then one Saturday, in about the middle of the month, a black porter came out to sweep the pavement while the line was in progress and softly and casually mentioned to a couple of the pickets that they didn't need to picket anymore. The store, he said, had changed its policy.

The following Tuesday a black picket-line leader presented herself at the lunch counter. Instead of being ignored or rebuffed, as she had been during all the months she had been checking, she was able to buy a sandwich and a cup of coffee from a white waitress, who seemed to pay no attention to the color of her skin. A day or so later, Mrs. Terrell, Mrs. Stein, and three black women reporters from the *Afro-American,* the *Pittsburgh Courier,* and the Associated Negro Press enjoyed a lunch at the basement counter.

The store refused to admit it had changed its policy. Reporters from the black press inquired and I personally inquired, identifying myself as a reporter for *Retailing Daily.* Officials told each of us that there was nothing to the story. The store, they said, had never discriminated against its black customers.

A short while later, Hecht's removed the counter stools. Apparently the management had decided that if customers had to eat, it would get fewer complaints if whites and blacks stood rather than sat next to each other. Thus Hecht's chose to act in earnest on what Harry Golden had meant in jest when he proposed his system of vertical integration![1]

1. The wry suggestion of humorist Harry Golden, that the way to accomplish the mixing of the races without rancor was to see that whites and blacks never had to sit down together, was widely quoted during the 1950s and '60s. In one of his books, *The Best of Harry Golden,* he observed, "The white and Negro stand at the same bank teller's window, pay phone and light bills to the same clerk, walk through the same dime and department stores and stand at the same drugstore counters. It is only when the Negro 'sets' that the fur begins to fly."

8

Life in a ''Leftist Nest''

The Coordinating Committee had no official headquarters. But its center of operation was unquestionably Trenton Terrace, the Southeast apartment complex in which Annie Stein, Joe Forer, and David Rein lived as neighbors. Other Coordinating Committee officers and many volunteers active in the campaign to desegregate the D.C. restaurants lived in the project, too. And before long, in 1953, Marvin and Naomi Caplan and their infant daughter, Freya, moved in.

In his memoir, *Loyalties,* his story of growing up in a Communist household, the journalist Carl Bernstein of Watergate fame mentions Trenton Terrace—disparagingly. Writing in 1989, Bernstein recalls a time shortly after World War II when, he says, many of his parents' friends "clustered in Trenton Terrace, a wretched new development of small Colonial-style brick apartments built across the Anacostia [River] in Southeast Washington. The House Un-American Activities Committee (HUAC), in a 1954 report, described the enclave as 'a leftist nest.' "

Many of us who have lived in Trenton Terrace have one reaction to that.

"Leftist nest"? Okay. But *"wretched"*?!

"How can he call it wretched?" one former tenant demanded, after reading Bernstein. She spoke for all of us who have agreeable memories of the place.

She remembered, with pleasure, enjoying a morning cigarette and a cup of coffee as she looked out of her sunny second-story kitchen window at the green tops of trees and the glitter of a brook below. "Wretched? No! Carl Bernstein has it all wrong."

But then, how could Bernstein, a child back then, have any idea of what Trenton Terrace, or TT, came to mean to young couples like Naomi and me?

I am writing, remember, of the late 1940s, early 1950s, when Washington, like most large American cities, was suffering a severe housing shortage aggravated by almost two decades of depression and war. The nation's capital was undergoing explosive growth. Thousands of young middle-class couples had been drawn to work there by the great expansion of government under the New Deal and by the demands of World War II.

Decent places to rent were scarce. And even for whites, prejudice compounded the difficulty of finding suitable housing. Some landlords would not rent to couples with infants or young children; some would not rent to Jews. Those homeseekers who found their way into TT often came from cramped or squalid quarters. ("We had one hotplate and had to wash our dishes in the bathtub," a fellow TT tenant told us once, recalling the first Washington apartment he and his wife were able to rent. "We moved. One night in our next place, I caught four rats in mousetraps. While they were clattering around on the kitchen floor, I killed them with a broom.")

To those renters, to us and others like us, TT seemed an incredible bargain. Built on a hillside in 1945, its twenty 3-story red-brick buildings encircled a green embankment thick with shrubs. The complex had an agreeable pastoral setting. If you walked down Mississippi Avenue in one direction, you came to a full-scale working farm with a horse and cows to thrill the kids. If you walked the other way, you came upon the broad parade grounds of an army installation, Camp Simms. And across the avenue, directly opposite TT, was our own personal park, a wooded area called Oxon Run after the little creek coursing through it.

Greenery, newness, good maintenance were available for relatively modest prices—we paid seventy-five dollars a month for a two-bedroom flat. But more precious than price to all of us was another thing—the project's communal spirit. And while that was not a consequence of a conspiracy to bring left-wing radicals together, as the HUAC or the FBI might have supposed, it was not entirely accidental, either.

Given the lasting impression many former tenants have of TT as one big happy family, it's appropriate to observe that the project was very much a family enterprise.

Karl Gerber, who took the lead in building TT, was one of a close-knit family of five brothers and five sisters. They were Russian-Jewish immigrants who came here from the Ukraine early in the century and settled in Baltimore. A few family members moved on to the Washington area and operated businesses there, some with considerable success. Karl Gerber was co-owner of Tower Pharmacy, a thriving establishment in downtown Washington.

Several things prompted this successful pharmacist to become a builder. The Federal Housing Administration, in an effort to stimulate housing construction in the postwar period, was offering an attractive, virtually no-risk program of loans and insurance. And a lawyer friend of the family, who may have ended up with a 10 percent interest in the deal, is said to have had an "in" with government housing officials.

Other co-owners of TT were two of Karl's older sisters and their husbands. To manage TT he chose the youngest member of the Gerber clan, his sister Lillian, and her husband, Herbert Benjamin. With that he put an indelible stamp on the character of the undertaking.

For the Benjamins were Communists.

Herbert Benjamin, who claimed he was a socialist by the age of twelve, went on to join the Communist Party of the United States and become one of its national officers. He was best known as "the supreme commander" of the 1931 National Hunger March, when he led three thousand jobless men and women in protest to Washington. Lil Benjamin didn't have her husband's prominence, but she was active in numerous Party programs during the thirties and forties.

When TT opened for rentals, a lot of the Benjamins' friends were among the first applicants. The project drew from other sources, too. Bolling Air Force Base and several other government installations in Southeast Washington supplied most of the tenants. But securely lodged in about 60 of the project's 214 units were friends with whom the Benjamins shared close political ties—and friends of friends. One told another or interceded with the Benjamins on an acquaintance's behalf. Which is exactly how Naomi and I ended up there.

Our first residence in the District of Columbia was a furnished bedroom in a Petworth-area boardinghouse. It was up to Naomi to find us a better place to live. I couldn't help. I was too busy trying to hold on to my job at Fairchild Publications. My first assignment was to cover federal regulatory agencies and the courts. To the vast complexities of that beat, I brought something close to total ignorance.

Fairchild Publications, a family empire, had a motto propounded by its founder, Louis Fairchild: "Our salvation depends upon printing the news."

My salvation, I was certain, depended upon my *comprehending* the news. Consider some of the issues I had to deal with: the Federal Communications Commission was in the midst of hearings to determine which color television system to authorize; the Federal Trade Commission was conducting a truth-in-labeling proceeding on furs (many pelts with exotic-sounding names—lapin and Persian lamb, to name just two—were, I discovered, simply rabbits' fur) as well as a conference on new anti-trust regulations; the Tariff Commission was in the midst of renegotiations of GATT (the General Agreement on Tariffs and Trade); the Securities and Exchange Commission and the Interstate Commerce Commission confronted me with an esoteric mix of issues involving stocks and bonds, rates and carrier regulations; and the dockets of the courts I covered were full of complicated cases in which bankruptcies, taxes, customs, and patents were in hot contention.

Eight hours a day I worked out of the Fairchild Bureau, a single large room cluttered with the paper and document-laden desks of eight reporters, a desk-man, and our bureau chief. Most evenings after a hurried bite I would rush off to the Library of Congress, where I would send for technical books and magazines from which I sought enlightenment.

Though she was almost six months pregnant when we arrived in Washington, my plucky wife set out each morning to roam the city by bus and streetcar, wherever the apartment ads in the *Washington Post* took her.

Exhausted and desperate, we finally moved into a Cafritz project in Southeast Washington, though we didn't much care for what we settled for. It was a two-bedroom apartment on the top floor of a three-story walk-up. Naomi had to drag infant and stroller up and down three flights of stairs whenever she wanted to take Freya outdoors. Since the unit lay under the Bolling Air Force Base traffic pattern, it was not uncommon to be blasted out of a night's sleep by the roar of a transport overhead. The living room faced an inner court so dim that if you wanted to read you had to switch a lamp on, even in broad daylight. And the apartment walls were a battleship grey (though the management promised to repaint in a year). At ninety dollars a month, it seemed overpriced to us.

We brought our furniture up from storage in Richmond, and three months after we moved in, we brought our new daughter home from Doctors Hospital. But we never felt comfortable there. And when, after a year, the management reneged on its promise to repaint, we decided it was time to move.

By then I had become involved in the Coordinating Committee. When I confided our dissatisfaction with the apartment to Annie Stein as she drove me home from a meeting one night, she had a ready solution.

"Why don't you move into Trenton Terrace?" she asked and proceeded to expound on TT's sociable delights.

"I'll speak to Lil Benjamin," she said. Sure enough, she did. And in less than a month an apartment became available. Everything Annie Stein had told us about the convivial atmosphere of TT appeared to be true. The day we moved into the first-floor apartment on Mississippi Avenue that was to be our home for the next four years, Rita Fleisher came down from the second floor, introduced herself, and invited us up for tea and cake.

All at once we found ourselves among "kindred spirits," as one woman dubbed the fellow tenants in our group.

Within the little circle, the political spectrum, while generally leftist, was still broader than you would suppose from the assertions of the HUAC and the FBI. It ranged from actual CP members to Truman Democrats (e.g., Naomi and me, reconstructed) and to other moderates who professed nothing more political than a vaguely liberal inclination. The anti-Communist left was not in evidence—members of Americans for Democratic Action, for instance, or members of some of the strongly anti-Communist unions. And there were no black families. You might suppose, given our liberal bent, that the absence of African Americans would have become an issue. But we were so accustomed to a Washington composed of rigidly segregated racial groups that none of us thought to raise the matter.

The sixty or so members of our circle shared another common identity. Something like 80 percent of us were Jews. And most of us were New York and East Coast Jews, usually of working-class origin. Our families were part of the last great wave of Jewish immigration—the nearly 2 million who arrived in this country between 1881 and 1914, "the overwhelming bulk of them either directly or indirectly from Eastern Europe."[1]

Members of the earlier Jewish migrations to America in the eighteenth and early nineteenth centuries were, as I well knew from my Richmond experience, largely of German or Sephardic origin. A good proportion of these Jews—think Rosenwald, Lazarus, Baruch, Cardozo, Frankfurter, Warburg—established themselves in merchandising, finance, and the professions.

Trenton Terrace's Jews, on the other hand, were no strangers to poverty. Those with college educations were often, like Naomi, graduates of New York's great institution, City College, which was free in their time. Their Jew-

---

1. Irving Howe, *World of Our Fathers* (San Diego: Harcourt, Brace, Jovanovich, 1976), 58.

ish orientation, for the most part, was not religious but secular; if there was one faith whose tenets many of them held to religiously, it was socialism.

The well-known American writer and critic Alfred Kazin, whose family came to New York from Minsk in White Russia, tells what it was like to grow up in such a milieu:

> In America an innocent democratic socialism was to have prodigious effect on the immigrant Jewish working class. When I was growing up on the Socialist religion, among the most excited messianic believers since primitive Christianity, it never occurred to me that there might be Jews who did not believe in socialism. Or that a time would come when Communists would so harden this religion that it would produce suicidal fanatics like the Rosenbergs and then equally vehement ex-radicals who, in their hatred of their past, became far-right extremists all too useful to the Reagan era but understandably distrusted by their conservative Christian allies.[2]

On the whole, there appeared to be little friction between our insular left-wing minority and the rest of the TT residents, who outnumbered us. Our nods and greetings when we encountered each other in hallways, on house-steps, or at bus stops, were perfunctory but cordial enough. However, our little enclave was scarcely immune to the prevailing anti-red hysteria of the fifties.

Apprehensive disapproval lurked under seeming neighborliness. A kindred spirit recounted a telling incident. Her fourteen-year-old daughter greeted a couple of neighbors who were sitting outside on a summer evening as she left the building. And when she was out of earshot, one woman, not of the inner group, remarked to the other, who was a member and who got word back to the girl's mother, "She's a wonderful child. But, unfortunately, her parents are Communists."

Carl Bernstein and HUAC were not the only ones who attempted to characterize Trenton Terrace. It was even something of a pastime among those of us who were living, or had lived, there. In a conversation I once had with Abe Tersoff, Karl Gerber's son-in-law, who was a resident for three years, he remembered TT as "a nice, intellectual community."

One of the central members of the inner circle observed that it was "as close to a commune as you could be and still live in separate apartments."

The Benjamins' son, Ernst, who went on to become general secretary of the

---

2. Alfred Kazin, "From Father Abraham to Columbus," *The Forward,* December 25, 1992.

American Association of University Professors, recalled another suggested use for TT in a 1991 speech he gave at Wayne State University, "On Being a Red Diaper Baby." Sometime in the fifties, he says, there was talk of establishing an internment camp for Communists in southern Pennsylvania, and a book he read proposed that when they got to TT, "they wouldn't have to round us up. They could just put a fence around the project."

I myself once remarked to Naomi that it might be appropriate to rename TT "Little Birobijan," after the Soviet Union's Jewish autonomous region.

Whatever we chose to call it, those of us who liked living there agreed that the sense of community was one of TT's most agreeable features. "A home away from home," said one of our neighbors, an anomaly in the group, a non-Jew, a Catholic woman from New York's Little Italy. That was more than platitude. Most of us who took part in the project's active social life were young couples in their thirties and new parents, and we often did feel as though we were members of an extended family.

The buildings themselves could not contain all our activities. In good weather, the garden court out back was our town square and a children's paradise. It had swings and seesaws, a jungle gym and a sandbox; the steep hillside was fine for sledding—on real sleds in winter and on sheets of old cardboard in summer. A broad public alleyway ran through the center of the project; it was along there that we gathered for talkfests or barbecues or, on the Fourth of July, for the enjoyment of the fireworks and watermelon we all chipped in to buy.

If you wanted to go farther afield, Oxon Run, across the street, was a great place for hikes and picnics. Some of the more energetic souls began farming again in the "victory gardens" left over from World War II.

Baby-sitting was never a problem. Someone was always staying home. If you wanted company, you could always drop in for a shmooz somewhere. And scarcely a week went by without a holiday or birthday celebration. Sometimes the parties got boisterous. At a New Year's Eve party in our apartment, the men stripped to the waist, and the wives, blindfolded, had to identify their husbands by touch.

There were several excellent musicians in the group. One of them played bass in the National Symphony Orchestra, so we occasionally enjoyed a living-room concert. Chess and checker partners were easy to come by. And a bi-monthly poker game begun back then has continued to this day, attended by TT friends who have kept in touch through the years.

Lillian Benjamin presided over the establishment to mixed reviews. Almost every one of us had a Lil Benjamin story to illustrate what "a character" she was. Like the time a worried mother, afraid of accidents, complained of the lack of railings on the steps going down to her basement apartment, and Lil replied, "Well, I'm insured." Or the time she ordered a group of girls to stop chalking up the sidewalk for a game of hopscotch, yelling, "Where do you think you are? The Lower East Side?"

But another mother remembers the time her daughter came home from school with the Benjamins' daughter, Jessica, and showed Lil a note from the school doctor saying she had a heart murmur, and Lil, without consulting the parents, immediately arranged to move the family from the third floor to the ground floor so that the girl would have fewer steps to climb.

And a young man who grew up in TT remembers that one of the big gripes he and the other boys had was that she "was always planting bushes where we wanted to play baseball."

We parents owed her a debt of gratitude when she let us convert an apartment into a cooperative nursery school, a remarkable innovation for those times.

I realize as I write that I make TT out to be more idyllic than it was. Yes, social bonds united us. But so did fear.

This was the Cold War era. The *New York Times* (August 13, 1992) spoke for many of us in an editorial comment on those days. It observed that "many Americans grimly recall the fearful 1950s, when the mere allegation of Communist sympathies could destroy careers and reputations. Nobody was immune from suspicion and it made no difference that accusers were frequently anonymous—and mistaken."

Many in our TT group can react to that observation in a personal way, particularly the large number of government workers. In the hysteria of the time, somehow they all got lumped together—actual members of the CP or of organizations suspected of being Communist-dominated, along with non-political types, who, however innocent, were still suspected of being subversive.

That the Soviet Union in those days posed a grave threat to the security of the United States is, I believe, beyond question. Shortly after the end of the Second World War, in which we and Russia had ended up allies, Joseph Stalin, in a speech on February 9, 1946, declared that communism and capitalism were incompatible and another war was inevitable.[3] Winston Churchill, in an address he gave a month later in Fulton, Missouri (a speech for which the left accused him of being a warmonger), warned the West that an "iron curtain"

---

3. David McCullough, *Truman* (New York: Simon and Schuster, 1992), 486.

had descended in Eastern Europe and that a new menace was rising behind it. Vivid images of subsequent events remain with me: images of Nikita Khrushchev pounding a desk at the U.N. with his shoe and shouting to the West, "We will bury you!"; of American schoolchildren cowering under their desks during simulated nuclear attacks.

But if the dangers the United States faced were real enough, I feel it is evident today that we overreacted in dealing with them. There is no better example of that than the U.S. loyalty program.

Beset by Republican charges that he was soft on communism, and ill-advised by J. Edgar Hoover (a man he detested) on the extent of the domestic Communist threat, President Truman with much misgiving instituted a loyalty program for federal workers in March 1947. His misgivings were justified by the results. By 1951, three million federal employees were investigated and cleared by the Civil Service Commission. Several thousand resigned, and only 212 were dismissed for questionable loyalty; not one of them was indicted, and no evidence of espionage was found. Truman admitted afterwards that his own program "had proven the loyalty of 99.7 per cent of all federal workers," and that "the program had been a terrible mistake."[4]

Such concessions after the fact are cold comfort today to surviving TT tenants who lost their jobs in loyalty purges, found themselves and their families exposed to public disgrace when their names turned up on blacklists, and were summoned before HUAC and the Subversive Activities Control Board and other investigative committees.

You get an idea of the capricious, vengeful nature of these witchhunts when you look at what happened to some of the TT tenants who got caught in them:

• An electronics engineer at the Bureau of Standards was dismissed for no other reason, apparently, than that he had been active in the United Public Workers, a union suspected of being Communist-dominated.

• Another Bureau of Standards employee, a physicist with no interest in politics, was accused of subversive activity and summoned to a loyalty hearing because, he believes, he occasionally rode to work in a TT carpool with a known Communist. Intervention by Eleanor Roosevelt, to whom his wife appealed, finally got the charges dropped.

• A public school teacher lost his job after an investigation uncovered evidence of leftist political connections. To support his family, he became a piano tuner. When an FBI informer at a HUAC hearing named him as a member of a CP cell, his tuner's license was revoked.

4. Ibid, 551–52.

• An accountant at the Department of Agriculture was investigated and marked for dismissal when it was discovered that as a young man he had once run for Congress on the CP ticket. He fought the charges, arguing that at the time the CP was a legitimately recognized party. After an inquiry that lasted several years, he was allowed to keep his job. But his daughter believes the stress he underwent "killed something vital in him."

• A teacher of French and Spanish in the New York City school system, winner of several citations for excellence, was forced to resign when during a loyalty investigation he refused to answer questions about his political beliefs. He ended up in D.C., where he earned a precarious living teaching English to diplomats at the Romanian legation.

It was an ironic convenience for such TT tenants to have Joe Forer and David Rein as neighbors. Representing government employees caught in loyalty probes became their firm's all-consuming specialty. When a staff attorney at a HUAC hearing asked Joe Forer how many times he had appeared before the committee, Forer couldn't remember. Too many times, he said, to be able to give an exact figure. The staff attorney then went on to compliment Forer for his "decent" and "courteous" behavior in the course of his numerous appearances.

Trenton Terrace was something of a haven for all of the tenants under suspicion. Although we were sure TT was under FBI surveillance, today few of us can remember being accosted on the project grounds. It is my own hunch that the FBI purposely sought us out elsewhere in order to embarrass us. I have a vivid recollection of the time two agents appeared in the Fairchild newsroom one afternoon and tried to question me about a neighbor I barely knew. Three of my fellow reporters sat within earshot while I, obstinate and red-faced, refused to answer the agents.

We were all convinced that our phones were tapped. And many of my neighbors assumed, as a matter of course, that whenever they drove to a meeting, the FBI would be lurking in the street to jot down license numbers.

Yet those who were fired somehow made other lives for themselves. Some became salespersons. Some became cabdrivers. Several of them borrowed from family and friends and pooled their money and opened laundromats. A resourceful former employee of the Navy Yard opened an auto repair shop that had a largely TT clientele. Some scored spectacular successes. A woman whose husband was dismissed from a government job opened a china and pottery store that became widely recognized as a trendsetter for those interested in contemporary wares. She proudly numbered among her regular customers such notables as Lady Bird Johnson, whose husband, Lyndon, was Senate majority leader at the time, and Joan Mondale, Senator Walter Mondale's wife.

Seasoned activists in the group refused to be intimidated. Political and social causes still claimed much of their energies. In 1948, they were prominent in the Progressive Party's campaign to elect Henry Wallace president. In 1950, they were involved in the protests against the Korean War. In 1953, they sought to stay the execution of convicted atomic spies Julius and Ethel Rosenberg.

The campaign to desegregate public eating places was foremost among the local causes for which they worked. Trenton Terrace provided a faithful cadre to staff two aspects of the Coordinating Committee's ongoing project—pickets to march in front of department and variety stores that would not let black customers eat at their lunch counters, and recruits for the committee's testing parties, the little interracial groups that visited downtown restaurants to determine which ones were quietly ready to serve any black patrons who dropped in.

All through the fifties, TT was home to many of us active in D.C.'s civil rights movement. But then the close-knit social group began to disintegrate. Trenton Terrace was never intended to be more than a temporary residence, one that most of us outgrew as our families and incomes increased. Naomi and I were typical. We moved into TT in 1953 with just Freya. While we lived there our second daughter, Anne, and our son, Bennett, were born, and soon we felt cramped in just two bedrooms.

Fortunately we could afford to start looking for larger quarters. Though my position at Fairchild was never my dream job, it kept us solvent. In the course of working for the publications, I won several commendations and a few raises. The staff position I coveted—to be one of the bureau's two Capitol Hill reporters—was still some years away. I didn't get that plum until 1960. But meanwhile, I found some satisfaction in mastering the technical challenges of my beat. And in the course of my rounds I occasionally picked up material Fairchild couldn't use but that I could turn into freelance magazine articles, and so supplement our income.

There were even occasions when the courts and regulatory agencies I covered put me in the way of some marvelous experiences. Most memorable of all was the time, in December 1953, when as Fairchild's Supreme Court reporter I was able to witness the rearguments in *Brown* v. *Board of Education,* the school-desegregation case, one of the legal landmarks of this century.

During the three days that the justices heard argument on the issue, in a consolidation of five school-desegregation suits, Fairchild got very little work out of me. I would tear through the lower courts and commissions of my responsibility, dictate urgent stories over the phone, keeping them terse as possible, skip lunch if I had to, and head for the press box to try to be there when the high tribunal convened, around 1 P.M.

Seating in the chamber was tight. The three hundred public seats were filled in minutes. Out in the main corridor, hundreds waited, ready to fill any vacancies that turned up.

The press box was jammed, too. And not just with reporters. Members of the public, with friends in high places, were sometimes squeezed in among members of the press. The afternoon that the high court heard argument in the Virginia school case, I found myself sitting next to a broad-bottomed dowager, beautifully garbed and coiffed. Her estate was surely far above the fourth estate. I got a quick impression of pearls and furs and rare perfume, of ringed hands free of pad and pencil, before I turned my full attention to the drama unfolding before me.

My old Richmond friend Spott Robinson was already at the lectern when I sat down, engaged in sharp parry with one of the justices.

Unfortunately, the lady beside me was in a chatty mood.

"Do you know who that is?" she asked.

"Spottswood Robinson."

"And do you know who he represents?"

"Virginia. NAACP," I mumbled distractedly.

She was quiet for a brief while and then she asked, "Is he a *Nee*-gro?"

Now, Spott was light-complexioned. Even so I considered the question impertinent. But go make a federal case when I wanted to hear one.

"Yes."

She nattered on beside me, while I tried to listen and keep a grip on my temper.

Then she said proudly, "Do you know? John W. Davis is a personal friend of mine."

Oho! So that's how she got in! John W. Davis! One of the nation's foremost appellate lawyers! The Democratic Party's nominee for president in 1924. And on this day, South Carolina's advocate on behalf of its segregated schools.

"Is that so?" I said. "Well," I said, "Spottswood W. Robinson the third," I said, "is a personal friend of *mine*."

I heard the rest of the argument in peace.

Yet another reason compelled Naomi and me to think of leaving Trenton Terrace. When we first moved in, the apartments were rent-controlled. Sometime during the mid-fifties the controls were lifted. TT regulars were not ones to take that lying down. We immediately formed a tenants' council to fight rent increases. That only exacerbated the ill feelings that had been growing between Lil Benjamin and tenants she had once considered friends.

Another factor in the dissolution of our sociable enclave was an easing in the housing shortage. New housing projects, reasonably priced, began opening in the suburbs. They were limited to white home-buyers only. Even so, quite a few of the TT kindred spirits were not going to let principle deter them when it came to finding a good place to live.

Naomi and I and our three children left TT in 1957. Like many of our old neighbors we carried fond memories with us. Trenton Terrace's special appeal is captured, I think, in the experience of one of its youngest tenants. That "wonderful child" whose parents "unfortunately" were "Communists" grew up in TT and knew no other residence before she left its sheltering atmosphere and went off to college, to the University of Chicago.

"Mom!" she exclaimed, on one of her first phone calls home. "The world is nothing like Trenton Terrace!"

9

Eat Anywhere!

Not long after our successful Hecht campaign we took on another retailer, an even more formidable opponent, a giant store in the G. C. Murphy's variety store chain.

A pencil vendor, a white man, who sold his wares in front of our target, the Murphy store on F Street near Thirteenth, explained to a few Coordinating Committee pickets one afternoon why we could never hope to win. This vendor was a small, legless fellow who took up his post outside of Murphy's every business day, propelling himself and his little pet monkey on a wooden platform mounted on casters. He was a debonair dresser who, even in the hottest weather, wore a spotless long-sleeved white shirt, a black bow tie, and a jaunty boater. His russet hair and moustache were always neatly trimmed.

As a Murphy's institution, he seemed to feel he could speak for the company. Murphy's, he told us, was "hard."

"And they're too big for you," he continued. "They're bigger than Hecht's. You're dealing with a big national chain. They're not going to mind the few dollars you may make them lose."

In spite of this well-meant advice, the picketing was initiated in May 1952 and continued throughout the summer. The Coordinating Committee came to Murphy's buoyed by both its victory at Hecht's and a subsequent victory at another Seventh Street department store, Lansburgh's, which had agreed to open its lunch counters to everyone after two visits from a delegation headed by Mrs. Terrell and Annie Stein.

At the time the picketing began, the F Street Murphy's was the only chain variety store in the District that still refused to serve black customers at its lunch counter. Two other Murphy stores in Washington had already dropped their exclusionary policy. But the manager of the F Street store seemed determined not to budge. He refused to discuss the issue. When the Coordinating Committee appealed to Murphy's home office, it got back a letter saying such policy matters were left to the discretion of the manager of each individual store.

On a sunny Saturday, with Mrs. Terrell looking on from a little canvas stool set out for her near the pencil vendor, members of the Coordinating Committee took up their signs again and began marching in front of Murphy's. The huge store ran straight through the middle of the block, from F Street to G Street, with entrances on both thoroughfares. Even so, with rare exception, the committee was able to keep pickets in front of both sides of the store every Thursday night and all day Saturday.

Occasionally we staged sit-ins at the lunch counter. An interracial group of us would take seats as they became available and tie up the counter for several hours by having the white members of our party refuse to accept service unless our black companions were served, too. Mrs. Terrell sometimes took part in these demonstrations. But though the counter supervisors were clearly vexed with us, they never summoned the police. On the whole, though, we found we could make our point better by picketing. And here our ranks were often strengthened by guest appearances.

Once a group of local ministers came to march. Another time, on my invitation, Lester Banks and John Drew brought up an interracial busload of marchers from the Richmond, Virginia, chapter of the NAACP. For the most part, however, the line was maintained by the faithful: the veterans of the six months at Hecht's and the eight weeks at Kresge. Despite the muttered threats and shouted epithets of some of the white passersby, the pickets were often encouraged by expressions of sympathy from other pedestrians, white as well as black. Occasional gifts of money were pressed into our hands.

No one foresaw the end of the Murphy picket line. It came suddenly, early in September. I had my first intimation of an approaching victory when Annie Stein called me at work. That morning she had received a phone call from the Murphy store manager, C. P. Kerley. He had just come back from his vacation, he said, and had a different slant on things. Could he see her alone?

Annie said she would be glad to see him. But, she added, she couldn't see him alone. Mrs. Terrell, as chairman of the Coordinating Committee, would have to be invited, too. Kerley hemmed and hawed a bit but finally agreed to see them both. "I think he thought we white folks could work out some sort of deal," Annie said. Anyhow, she was polling me and other members of the Executive Board to determine what stand she and Mrs. Terrell should take. I told her not to budge an inch from demanding the immediate end of Jim Crow at the counter. Annie laughed. "Everyone I've called so far," she said, "has been giving me the same advice."

That night, when Naomi and I dropped by the Steins' apartment to learn the outcome of the meeting, Annie told us the whole story.

"Kerley received us very nervously. To make things worse, Mrs. Terrell had forgotten her hearing aid. So she made speeches. On democracy. On ethics. On this and that. A bit off the point, but still good."

In the face of such "elemental force," Annie said, Kerley could do nothing else except give in. He did, finally, but by slow degrees.

He began by saying there had never been any need for matters to come to this, the picketing and sit-down demonstrations at the lunch counter. "Maybe if I had given a little and you had given a little at the beginning, this need never have happened."

"It could be," Annie said, choosing not to mention that in her telephone conversations with Kerley before the picketing began he had never given her an opportunity to give a little. All she'd asked for was a chance to meet with him, and he had flatly refused every time.

At first Kerley suggested a trial settlement: pull off the pickets for a week or so and he would discuss desegregating the counter with the supervisors. When this didn't work, he said, "Well, just don't picket this Thursday or Saturday." (It was Wednesday, then.) "Monday morning we'll start serving everybody."

Annie was sorely tempted to agree. But then she said, "Mr. Kerley, we just can't call off the picket line without telling our pickets something. They're pledged to picket until Murphy's changes its policy. We've got tens and tens of children and their parents ready to march on a picket line this Saturday. We're making up leaflets and signs. Thirty-six ministers are planning to preach sermons this Sunday urging their congregations to boycott Murphy's. We can't call the whole thing off just like that."

Kerley was glum. He said he had taken a look at other lunch counters that had desegregated—Woolworth's, Neisner's, Hecht's. "Neisner's counter, the others. They're all colored, now. And do you know? Since you started picketing us, business at our lunch counter has doubled."

"I don't doubt that it has doubled," Annie said. "But who're you getting at the counter? You're getting the single, spiteful southern ladies who buy lunch there just out of meanness. You aren't getting the families. Those single little old southern ladies aren't buying your dungarees. It's families that buy your dungarees."

Kerley didn't deny this. Annie gathered he had been checking his sales against sales in the two other Murphy stores, and that even though they had desegregated, business had fallen off throughout the chain's Washington outlets. Finally he said, "I'll tell you what. We'll start serving everyone tomorrow. And now I'll have to speak to Bausch and Daniel [the counter supervisors] and make them think the whole thing's their idea."

He left. Fifteen minutes later Bausch and Daniel came following him in looking, Annie said, like whipped dogs. Mrs. Terrell had been speechifying all this time, exclaiming over the humiliation of being denied lunch-counter service in the capital of democracy and saying such things as, "If it weren't so tragic it would make a cat laugh."

Now, Annie said, Mrs. Terrell made her finest speech of the afternoon. "Can't you businessmen ever look past your counters? Can't you realize that you're sowing hatred in the hearts of thousands of young colored people? I worry for America. . . . I am the widow of Judge Robert H. Terrell, a judge of the Municipal Court of Appeals for twenty years. I am eighty-nine years old. And I have to stand and eat in a shabby little five-and-ten."

The men listened to her in silence. Afterwards Kerley escorted Mrs. Terrell and Annie to the lunch counter. He inaugurated the new policy by treating them to coffee and to strawberry shortcake, a favorite of Mrs. Terrell's.

The two women passed the pencil vendor as they left the store and, jubilant, stopped to buy a pencil from him. Annie laughed as she recalled the moment. "You should have seen his jaw drop when we told him we had won!"

Only four months later the Coordinating Committee suffered a staggering blow. On January 22, 1953, after a year's deliberation, the U.S. Court of Appeals for the District of Columbia ruled 5 to 4 that the old anti-discrimination laws were no longer valid. Mrs. Terrell told the press that the majority ruling was "a tragedy for the United States. The four-fifths of the world's population who are colored people will be shocked by this ruling and by the moral justification given to the evil of segregation."

The appellate decision was one more sharp turn in the case's zigzag course through the courts. On July 10, 1950, after the first argument in the case, Judge Frank Myers of the Municipal Court for the District of Columbia had ruled that the laws were no longer in effect, since their omission from the D.C. code was evidence that they had been repealed "by implication." He was reversed by the D.C. Municipal Court of Appeals on May 25, 1951, in a 2-to-1 decision. The January 1953 reversal of that court's opinion by the federal appellate court was, fortunately, still subject to further review by the U.S. Supreme Court.

By then there was tremendous pressure on the District government to appeal. The pressure came not only from the Coordinating Committee and the liberal groups it represented. It came also from influential groups in the city that were working for home rule. The U.S. Court of Appeals had based its ruling in part on the argument that Congress did not have the right to delegate any of its governmental authority to a lesser body, in this instance the territorial legislature that had enacted the "lost laws." In doing so, the Court of Appeals raised serious doubt that Congress could ever permit the citizens of Washington to govern themselves.

Then, too, what had begun as a local dispute between a group of District residents and a restaurant had become a national symbol in the fight against racial discrimination. Both the Democratic administration of Harry Truman and the Republican administration of Dwight D. Eisenhower found it politically expedient to add their weight to that of the many groups, both local and national, urging that the "lost laws" be reinstated. The Department of Justice during the Truman administration filed a "friend of the court" brief with the U.S. Court of Appeals in defense of the validity of the old laws. The Justice Department under Eisenhower filed a similar brief when the case reached the Supreme Court, and the U.S. Attorney General Herbert Brownell took part in the argument there.

The District appealed the case a few weeks after the adverse ruling by the federal appellate court. The Supreme Court heard argument in April, and on June 8, 1953, it reversed the U.S. Court of Appeals in a unanimous eight-member ruling.

The power of Congress to grant self-government to the District, the court said in the decision by Justice William O. Douglas, "would seem to be as great as its authority to do so in the case of territories." Furthermore, it concluded, "the acts of 1872 and 1873 survived, we think, all subsequent changes in the government of the District of Columbia and remain today a part of the governing body of laws applicable to the District."

EAT ANYWHERE! the *Washington Afro-American* commanded its readers in a banner headline. The two major dailies were more restrained in their reactions. The *Evening Star* deplored the "fuzziness" of the procedure by which a civil right was won through an appeal to a "lost" law. That, it said, was "something less than ideal." However, it observed, "restaurants will be open to all and this—procedure aside—is as it should be."

A *Washington Post* editorial saw the Supreme Court ruling primarily as "a sweeping victory for home rule." It went on to say that the decision would accelerate the trend in the capital to obliterate "all enforced segregation and discrimination." And finally, in a lofty admonishment to the principal parties in the fight, it declared: "We hope the restaurant owners will cooperate and put the law speedily into full effect and that those who have led the civil rights fight will give them a fair chance to make the required changes smoothly and harmoniously." In its news stories on the decision, the *Post* made no mention of the Coordinating Committee; it identified Mrs. Terrell as merely "one of three Negro plaintiffs in the case." It reported that the reactions of restaurateurs "ranged from relief to blunt acceptance. Only a few reported that any white waiters or waitresses planned to quit."

The *Star* quoted Mrs. Terrell as saying that the Coordinating Committee would continue its efforts as long as necessary to see that no restaurant would be permitted to violate or evade the laws.

Now that the validity of the "lost laws" was established, the case went back to the Municipal Court for a trial on the merits. If Thompson Restaurant was found guilty of a violation, as it surely would be, it faced the possibility of losing its license for a year. But the Coordinating Committee saw no need to be vindictive. Four days after the Supreme Court ruled, Mrs. Terrell and the three other original complainants went back to the Fourteenth Street restaurant on a prearranged visit. Joe Forer followed them in. As he recalled the moment, the manager himself came over and personally, even obsequiously, Forer felt, carried Mrs. Terrell's tray to the table.

Satisfied, Forer went back to his office and wrote a letter to the corporation counsel on behalf of his clients saying that since Thompson's was now complying with the law and since its behavior in denying service had been no different from that of most of its competitors, there was no reason to single it out. He was therefore withdrawing the complaints.

Anyone who lunched with Mary Church Terrell when she was eighty-nine, in one of the newly desegregated restaurants shortly after the Supreme Court ruling, and watched her sprinkle a teaspoon of sugar over her strawberry shortcake, would have supposed that she would live forever. Alas, that extraordinary woman died on Saturday, July 24, 1954, at her summer home in Highland Beach, Maryland, little more than a year after the *Thompson Restaurant* case was decided and only two months after the *Brown* v. *Board of Education* school decision.

The Coordinating Committee barely survived her. It was a victim of its own success. It could not bring the coalition it represented to bear on other matters of discrimination, such as job discrimination, and went out of existence about two years after the decision.

Annie Stein went on to champion other causes. A few months before the Supreme Court decision came down, she and her family moved to Brooklyn, where she soon became active in the fight for school desegregation. She died there in 1981 at the age of sixty-eight.

In a way, the Steins' departure was a portent. Two or three years after they left, force of circumstance prompted many of us in the old Trenton Terrace gang also to think of leaving. The end of rent control made the apartments less of a bargain. Many of us began to outgrow them, anyway, as our families increased in size. Our two daughters, Freya and Anne, already shared a room. When our son Bennett was born, we had to squeeze his crib in right next to our bed. Two bedrooms for a family of five was too tight a fit for us.

So Naomi and I, like many of our neighbors, began house hunting. I complicated the search by insisting that we live inside the District. I disliked the idea of commuting from the suburbs. I also wanted our children to attend Washington's newly integrated schools.

After many months of looking, we found a house: a three-bedroom, green-painted, cedar-shingle bungalow in a modest residential neighborhood in Northwest Washington. Not long after we moved in, even before we were settled, we discovered that the next civil rights issue to engage Naomi and me came with the property.

Part III

Washington, D.C.: Neighbors, Incorporated
1957

10

The Last White Family
on the Block

The *Atlantic Monthly,* which ten years earlier had rejected my article on the fight to desegregate Virginia's public schools because the editors felt it was "too regional," now looked with favor on a piece I wrote about my own small neighborhood. It accepted and published, in July 1960, my account of what our lives were like when Naomi and I and Freya, Anne, and Bennett moved into Manor Park, in Northwest Washington.

I can think of no quicker way to convey the problems we faced in those early years than to quote that article here:

THE LAST WHITE FAMILY ON THE BLOCK

On how many white and how many Negro skins does integration depend?

J. Lindsay Almond, governor of Virginia, believes the presence of a single Negro child in a student body of a thousand is unconscionable mixing. Until the courts stopped him, he shut down any school threatened with racial blemish.

Morris Milgram, the Philadelphia builder who specializes in integrated suburban housing developments, set a quota in his first project of

55 per cent white and 45 per cent Negro. In subsequent ones the proportion has varied, but he has kept them about two thirds white.

"Percentages, percentages," says my wife. "It's all a matter of percentages." She thinks Governor Almond is absurd. But she looks with favor
upon Mr. Milgram.

The neighborhood we live in was an all-white one for about thirty
years. Five years ago Negro families began moving in and soon occupied
about half the houses. Perhaps by now the percentage has shifted in their
favor. That's too many, says my wife. She says it with a heavy sense of
confusion. For she wants integration. She welcomed the U.S. Supreme
Court school decisions. With a feeling of pride and rightness we saw our
eldest child go off to a recently integrated public elementary school. But
the first year that she went the school was 56 per cent white. Last year it
was 70 per cent Negro. This year it is about 85 per cent.

When the first Negro families appeared many white families fled
from the neighborhood into the suburbs surrounding Washington.
Counter to that trend, and after the first panic had subsided, we moved
here three years ago, attracted by the roominess of an old house. White
families are still moving out, but at a slower rate, circumspectly, as if
their moving now is a betrayal of those old neighbors who still remain.
The PTA loses three white board members during the school term. The
publicity chairman resigns (shamefaced) from the Citizens Association.
Membership drops in the white churches. Percentages shift.

"If only a white family would move in," an old resident cries, as a
marooned person cries for the sight of a sail. (We have been there so long
we don't count.) "I have nothing against the Negro. Some of the families
moving in are lovely. But if only a white family would move in!"

Like most good middle-class city neighborhoods ours has a serene,
substantial look. The houses, one-family, detached, most of them with
porches, stand back from the street upon well-tended lawns. Old trees
shade the yards and sidewalks.

The advent of Negro families has made little change in the physical
appearance of our streets. Houses still get painted regularly. Grass is cut.
The pavements are swept, the gardens cherished. The streets are empty
in the summer. An occasional child, no matter what its color, will look
well-cared for. And if it is a Negro child, he or she is almost certain to be
particularly well-dressed and neat.

Even our next-door neighbor, a staunchly Southern widow of seventy-five who has lived most of her adult life here and can recall when

the high school across the street was vernal wilderness where you picked huckleberries in the summertime and went ice skating on the creek in the winter; even she concedes that the four Negro families on our block are not objectionable. She hated to see them move in. "But," she says, with a strange pride, "*our* Negroes are different."

Then what is it we fear? Why does the heart of almost every white person drop when a new For Sale sign goes up? Speak to an old-timer on our block or down the street, where the change has been more rapid, and almost invariably, except for an occasional complaint about the increase in children's noises, since most of the newcomers are young families, you will hear stories of how industrious our new neighbors are, what good care they take of their homes.

Yet each small disturbance is magnified in the wide eyes of fear. A new neighbor has a noisy party, cars drive up late at night, people appear on the street talking loudly or laughing, or two boys, or two gangs, one white and one Negro, get into a fight and rumor runs through the neighborhood like fire. That's what we fear! Negro turbulence. Where is it? Next door? It is seldom next door. But it's down the street, next to old Mrs. Grandy, who lives there all alone, poor soul. Or it may not even be in our neighborhood. It may be blocks away in a poorer one. It doesn't matter. Each loud or violent incident is premonition. *Our* Negroes are different. But who knows who will follow them?

Sometimes, like a thunderbolt, the violence does strike next door, or near enough to frighten us. Four doors away an elderly white widow is raped by a Negro burglar. It does not reassure my neighbors to read about a white suburban burglar who perpetrates the same crime upon his victim.

Live for the moment, I tell my wife. The trick is to learn to live with the Negro family next door to you (as yet, there is none). You simply cannot keep your reason if you try to live next door to every Negro in the neighborhood and next to everyone who may move in throughout the years we live here. It is good advice, but neither one of us can quite accept it.

There are two things, among others, that we white families fear: overcrowding—two or three families, evacuees, as a rule, from the city's redevelopment projects, friends, cousins, sisters, aunts, pooling their meager salaries in order to move into one of our modest one-family houses; and profanity and violence on our quiet streets.

Yet a friend of ours, in a section of the city whose white complexion is still unchanged, tells us with composure that in the big old houses on her block retired white couples have begun, illegally, to take in boarders. But they are all one color there and no one reports anybody or moves away because of the proliferation of unlicensed rooming houses.

Another friend, who lives in a fashionable suburb, tells us with helpless amusement of the old bachelor who bought the house next door to hers and installed his mistress. Nothing stirs in there till after sundown. Then there are quarrels, curses, screaming all night long. But he is a well-known roue, scion of an old Virginia family, whose pranks have furnished the neighborhood with gossip for many years. My friend tells the story as a dinner joke, perhaps even with a touch of pride at having a local celebrity for her neighbor. She does not plan to move.

In our city it has become fashionable to live in the mid-city slums. Young professional couples, often with a child or two, buy a tiny cramped row house in the oldest section of town and proceed to remodel at great expense. They furnish it with the skimpy, compact furniture that is one of the triumphs of contemporary living, scatter a pound of grass seed on the tiny plots out front and back, and settle down contentedly across the street from the still unregenerate lairs of Negro drunkards, thieves and prostitutes.

In our neighborhood the houses were built by generous hands. The rooms are generally lofty and well-proportioned. We have porches and fireplaces. The kitchens are light and large enough to eat in. The yards are big and seldom without old trees. Yet it is a rare young white couple that will consider moving into one of these houses. And when a Negro moves in—usually a government worker, a pharmacist or a teacher—consternation grips white families for blocks around and For Sale signs sprout on the front lawns.

If a strange man walked up to you on a public street and spit in your face and yelled, "I hate your guts!" you and everyone around would have a right to think he was insane. Yet white people do the equivalent of that to Negro families in my neighborhood every day and no one pays any attention to it.

Why? Surely you know why! Behind the appearance of middle-class respectability is the specter of Porgy and Bess, Catfish Row and sex. Intermarriage is the abruptly blurted fear. We white people think it and sometimes voice it in our attempts to fathom the situation we are in. Beneath those clerky, neat exteriors the untamed African nature may still be lurking. Or it may not lurk at all. We are caught either way. Either intermarriage is wrong because of racial traits and racial inferiority, or it is wrong—but there we stop; and reason evaporates in thin air.

"It is all right for them to go to school together, but they should not play together," a white teacher in my daughter's school says firmly.

"Why not?" asks my wife.

"Because then they'll grow up thinking there is no difference."

Well, noise and sex aside, aren't there other reasons for moving? Like calls out to like. "You know they would rather be with their own kind," a Jewish woman who is moving said to me. Graciously. Magnanimously. And what could I say to her? You shouldn't have to tell a Jew what's wrong with ghettos.

I'm Jewish and sometimes I feel as if I'm standing on my head. We, the people of the Book, who have been oppressed by quotas, wish, if only there were quotas! We who profess to hate hatred now find cause to hate.

Whose fault is it? Who is to blame for racially changing neighborhoods? The Negroes who precipitate the change? But they come because they desperately need houses and there are very few open to them and it is our communal will to herd them into one neighborhood at a time rather than let them move freely wherever they please. The real estate dealers who find the houses for them? Some of them try to scare us into selling our homes. But they say they only carry out our wishes for homogeneous neighborhoods. They want to make money and if white people allow rumor, panic and causeless hatred to override their common sense, the dealers can't be held entirely responsible. The white families, then, who run without waiting to meet their new neighbors? But their animus was bred into them as children; they flee not out of prejudice alone but to escape the terrible tension of living with an unknown people. The city that does nothing? The school that does nothing? The church that does nothing? Blameless, blameless, we are all to blame.

Sometimes I wonder why any Negro wants to live among us. I asked a Negro neighbor, "Would Negroes be happier in an all-Negro neighborhood?" He thought they would, for he at least did not welcome the strain created by the presence of white people. But, he said, if there are no whites around, the police will begin to think of our neighborhood as a Negro district, the real estate dealers will think so, the teachers and the trash man. And gradually the experienced teachers will ask for transfers. The policemen will appear more rarely. The broken street lamp will go unrepaired. The gutters will be unswept. And the awful stench of the slum ghetto that Negroes are trying to escape will begin to haunt our streets. And even if physically nothing in our neighborhood should change except the skin color of the homeowners, still the Negroes there will know they have failed again; they approach the center of the American community as one goes toward fool's fire in deep woods or toward the mirage in the desert only to find no warmth, no drink and nothing but the limbo they have always known.

Of every thoughtless, frightened white person who moves from this street I should like to ask one question: What will you do when the first Negro family appears in your new neighborhood? For, of course, that family will appear. Those of us who run from integration run in a circle. The time we gain by our evasion is only the time it takes to run off and around until we come suddenly face to face with the problem once again.

Having asked my question, where am I then? With the best will in the world, how can we stay? The neighborhood is "tipped," as real estate dealers like to say. Even though there is a larger number of white than Negro families here, few white families will move in; only Negro families will come readily and it seems to us, in our moments of despair, that we are only a few years away from living in a Negro neighborhood. "Yes, yes," a liberal suburban friend says to my wife. "I understand. It isn't that you're prejudiced. It's just that you don't want to be the last white family on the block."

How reasonably she puts it. Who can dispute the soundness of what she says? Yet even as she speaks an old question nags me. Is it skin that matters? What about personal worth? If Mahatma Gandhi were alive today and moved onto my block, some of my white neighbors would take one look at those sheets, those bare feet and those ragtag disciples and their homes would be up for sale by nightfall.

Still the questions keep flooding back, addressed to me personally. Do I believe in brotherhood? Do I believe we are all born free and equal? Do I believe in the sacredness of the individual? Suddenly I am pushed beyond easy platitudes into that difficult and stony place where we are forced to take a stand for our professed convictions or abandon them. I can't abandon them. Governor Almond is right. Integration can depend upon a single person. And if I am sick of prejudice, if, as a Jew, I know in my blood and bones what it means to be stamped "Refuse" and thrown out on the garbage heap, I have no choice. I must remain.

11

Embattled

The final sentences of my *Atlantic Monthly* article, as originally submitted, were: "I must remain—or try to. For even with the firmest resolve, my wife and I face many of the doubts and conflicts our departing neighbors did. We hope we have the will to resist the forces that erode conviction." With a few strokes of blue pencil an editor eliminated all our qualms.

He or she struck out everything after "I must remain," leaving Naomi and me seemingly more committed than we really were. The truth is that for the first year or two in our new neighborhood and even afterwards, with almost each new crisis our family faced, Naomi and I debated the wisdom of staying on and subjecting our three children to the fight we found ourselves engaged in.

What we quickly discovered, as we sought to enjoy the placid greenery of Manor Park, was that we had moved onto a battlefield. The peaceful aspect of the streets belied the fight going on virtually block by block and house by house. In our racially changing neighborhood, the enemy was not "the Negro," who was often unconscionably victimized, but a horde of real estate brokers. The year was 1957, and the brokers had most of the weapons. There were no federal fair-housing laws in those days, and there was no city fair-housing ordinance or agency we could appeal to. Racially segregated housing was accepted as the normal order of things.

For most Americans outside the South, the civil rights struggle at that time was something going on many miles away, in Montgomery, Alabama, involving such heroic figures as Rosa Parks and Martin Luther King, Jr. But to Naomi and me the struggle seemed a great deal closer than that. On a much less hazardous and epic scale, it seemed to be going on right on our own front porch at 6405 Third Street, N.W.

The battle began almost as soon as we moved in; the real estate brokers descended on us at once. They aimed their missiles at us through the mail: letters and postcards, in almost every delivery, offered us ready cash for our house. Many nights, sometimes as late as 9 or 10 P.M., the phone would ring and a dealer, in a voice full of sure presumption, would say, "Mr. Caplan? Hi. Due to the changing nature of your neighborhood, wouldn't you like to sell your house?" We had moved in in March. As the weather warmed, we got house calls; salesmen appeared on our doorstep, often Negroes, smiling and advising us that they had just sold the house down the street, or the house behind us, to a colored family and wouldn't we . . . ? In our anxiety, we came to recognize every For Sale sign as a banner posted by an advancing army; every Sold sign pasted over it as a victory for their side.

How had we blundered into this mess? We knew the answer once we realized that the classified-housing-ad section in the daily papers was still another weapon in the agents' arsenal. Real estate ads in those days carried racial designations. We had bought our house without benefit of agent, directly from the owners, an elderly white spinster and her brother. They had run a "white ad," as the brokers called them, one that made no mention of race. If a real estate speculator had been handling the property, even though the block was still predominantly white, he would surely have inserted "col." or "colored" in the ad. The effect would have been to turn away potential white buyers, even whites like us who would not have minded living on a racially mixed block; instead, only black homeseekers were steered to the house. The ads were one more potent trick the dealers used as they plied their craft, known brutally in the real estate profession as "blockbusting."

The elite of the trade, the "realtors" (the trademark name of members of the National Association of Real Estate Brokers), professed nothing but disdain for the rough tactics of the speculators. But actually blockbusting was possible only through the tacit collusion of all the brokers who handled residential property in the metropolitan Washington area.

Good housing was still scarce in those postwar years. Much scarcer for blacks than for whites. Most of the new suburban subdivisions were intended for whites only. The salesmen, unrestricted by any law or regulation, told black homeseekers outright, "Sorry. We don't sell to colored."

Inside the District, Rock Creek Park became the dividing line for real estate sales in the desirable Northwest sector. The realtors who handled the fashionable—and exclusive—areas west of the park would sell only to whites. Blacks were directed to the east side of Rock Creek. And there the speculators lay in wait for them.

Now, as I recall those days, I realize upon reflection that many of the real estate dealers whom I accusingly brand "speculators" and "blockbusters" would react to that in angry protest. We had subsequent encounters at community meetings in which they argued that I defamed them. What I called "blockbusting," they insisted, was actually a public service. Unlike their colleagues west of Rock Creek Park, they welcomed colored customers. They took them in hand, showed them what was on the market, helped them buy decent places to live. To some extent, I must agree. Unquestionably, they did open housing opportunities for blacks. But it was the way most of them went about opening those opportunities that aroused my opposition.

Most of the neighborhoods east of Rock Creek were modest ones, inhabited mainly by native Washingtonians, low-grade government workers in a company town. When a house in an all-white section came on the market, the dealer who bought it and resold it to a black home-buyer would often use the transaction as the opening gambit in a campaign to "bust" the neighborhood. For then, by mail and phone and door-to-door solicitation, he would announce the sale and try to panic the remaining white homeowners into selling.

The warning such dealers issued to whites, that the entrance of black families into the neighborhood would bring property values down and make their home investments worthless, became what students of blockbusting called a "self-fulfilling prophecy." For once whites panicked and dumped their houses on the market, the speculators could reap the harvest. They would buy up the places cheap and turn around and resell them to desperate black homeseekers at inflated prices.

On our side of Rock Creek, the postwar blockbusting campaign began in the neighborhoods south of Manor Park. The speculators advanced like a conquering army. Once a neighborhood was "tipped," as they liked to say, and turning by what seemed an irrevocable process from white to black, they would move on to the white neighborhood north of it. Washingtonians' penchant for living in self-contained, distinctively designated sections—Petworth,

Brightwood, Takoma, and the many "Parks"—played right into the speculators' hands.

When they began their assault on Manor Park, they established a beachhead along Kennedy Street, the major commercial strip and one of the area's boundaries. By the time we moved into the neighborhood, about twenty-one speculative brokers had opened offices along the six and a half blocks of Kennedy that lay between Third Street and Georgia Avenue. It only fueled my indignation to discover that most of the brokers were Jews.

White neighbors on our block told us later, when we got to know them, that they were astonished to see us move in. Pleased, but astonished. "I watched them unloading you and your furniture," said Rose Greenbaum, who lived two doors up from us and had lived there for something like twelve years, "and I wondered, Don't they know what they're getting into?" We didn't. It was as if, out on a picnic, we had found a pretty spot and spread our blanket, unaware that we were sitting down to eat under crossfire. A few years after Rose Greenbaum and Naomi had become friendly and Rose had confided her feelings about us to my wife, a few years after Freya, our eldest, then six or seven, had become enamored of the Greenbaums' son Allan, a lively nine-year-old given to puns and outrageous mugging, the Greenbaums moved away. Out to an all-white, Jewish neighborhood in Montgomery County.

And a black couple, a schoolteacher and an accountant with two teenaged sons, moved into their house.

In search of allies who might be as ready as Naomi and I to combat blockbusting, I joined the Manor Park Citizens Association.

The association, in existence since developers first laid out the neighborhood during the 1920s, met once a month, just up the street from us, at the John Greenleaf Whittier Elementary School. Like its counterparts in neighborhoods throughout the city, the association filled an important gap in District politics.

D.C. had no self-government then.[1] Its citizens were as powerless and disenfranchised as the early American colonists under British rule. Although its residents paid federal and district taxes, they had nothing to say about how they were governed. They had no elected city officials; no elected representatives in Congress. The District's government was administered by three commissioners appointed by the president. Its laws were enacted by the District

---

1. I would agree that even with an elected mayor and an elected city council, the District of Columbia today still has no self-government. But that's another matter.

committees of the House and Senate. Since the members of those congressional committees came from all over the country and very few of them lived in the District itself, the capital's problems were of little personal concern to them. D.C. residents often called their city, bitterly and accurately, "the Last Colony."

The Federation of Citizens Associations sought to fill the political vacuum. Its chapters, of which Manor Park Citizens Association was one, brought homeowners together to lobby Congress and the district government for badly needed facilities and services. Forty-five associations belonged to the federation, representing—or so its president claimed in a speech I heard him give—43,000 homeowners.

During its early, vigorous years, the Manor Park Citizens Association had campaigned successfully for neighborhood schools: Whittier Elementary and Calvin Coolidge High were impressive evidence of that. We also had the association to thank for the pleasant recreation center across the street from our house, where our family got to enjoy the children's playground, the concrete tennis courts, and the free outdoor Olympic-size swimming pool.

By the time I joined the association, though, its best days were behind it. I found myself in the company of about a dozen survivors, mostly elderly retirees and a few middle-aged government workers and shopkeepers. A conference table in one corner of Whittier's commodious gym-auditorium was enough to accommodate all of us. The majority of the members were Christians. The only other Jews I could discern in the group were a government economist and a fairly prominent District jeweler. (World citizen, egalitarian that I am, I find I do take notice of such things.)

I was a rarity, a new recruit to their dwindling ranks, a mere youngster of thirty-seven. They welcomed me warmly. The monthly meetings became a tranquil refuge from the battle I felt raging outside the auditorium in which we gathered. Blockbusting and panic-peddling were simply not on the agenda. The association's major concerns, I discovered, were threefold: to seek protection from the pigeons that nested on our roofs ("such dirty birds"); to get the District to replace with oaks and maples the many ginkgo trees that lined our downtown sidewalks ("the fruit has such an offensive odor"); and to exempt all D.C. residents seventy-five or older from payment of the D.C. income tax. The foremost advocate of these proposals was the association treasurer, Ernest Pullman, a retired government worker who happened to have just turned seventy-five; he was greatly venerated in the association, since he had been its first president and was the sole surviving founding member of our chapter.

A dumb persistence kept me coming to the meetings; that and Mrs. Carrie

Seaquist's marvelous home-baked cookies, which were served with tea and coffee during the refreshment and social hour that followed the business meeting.

After three meetings I grew restive. I had discovered, upon reading the by-laws, that membership in the association was restricted to white homeowners. (Black homeowners, in black and changing neighborhoods, had organized a Federation of Civic Associations, I found out later.)

One evening, during new business, I got up and moved that the bylaws be amended to admit our Negro neighbors into membership. A cold silence followed my motion. No one seconded it. I spoke to it nevertheless, saying that as a newcomer to Manor Park it seemed to me blockbusting was the most important and destructive problem our neighborhood faced. If we were to deal with it, I said, we needed the help of every homeowner ready to join us. I sought to stress general self-interest, not principle. Although I didn't say so, my own personal self-interest was certainly involved. Naomi and I had borrowed $1,000 from my father for a down payment, and we couldn't possibly repay him anytime soon. We had bought the house for $15,650; if we tried to sell it in Manor Park's jittery market, we would surely get a great deal less.

When I finished speaking, there was no further discussion. Mr. Pullman scrambled to his feet, painfully, as if he were being gouged out of his folding chair. My motion, he shouted, was out of order. An amendment to the bylaws had to be submitted in writing to the full membership at least six months before a vote could be taken on it; and it had to be approved by two-thirds of the members present. Thereupon he moved for adjournment, and my rebellion was promptly quashed.

To my surprise, two association members approached me as I stood apart, consoling myself with a couple of Carrie Seaquist's walnut clusters. They wanted to thank me for raising the "white only" issue. What's more, they agreed with me. One of my new friends was the jeweler; the other was a local architect, a true, native Washingtonian, born and raised in Manor Park.

I was encouraged to find sympathizers in the chapter. But in the face of the speculators' onslaught, I did not see how we could wait idly for six months before raising the issue again.

Two old friends from Richmond gave us an idea of what we could do in the meantime. The Bakers came to visit us: Helen, Brownie Lee Jones's one Negro staff member at the Southern School for Workers; and Bunny, the genetics professor at Virginia State. They had left Virginia shortly before we did, after Brownie had been forced to close the Southern School for lack of funds. Bunny resigned from the Virginia State faculty, and they had gone to work for the American Friends Service Committee, directing various community projects for the Quakers in Richmond, California, and in Chicago and Philadelphia. But Bunny missed the academic life and his research with fruit flies. So he accepted a professorship at Morgan State, and now they were living in Baltimore.

After listening to our woeful tale of life on the Manor Park battlefront, Helen had the answer to our problem.

"What you need here," she said briskly, "is a neighborhood stabilization project."

Blockbusting was not unique to our area. Homeowners in urban neighborhoods throughout the country were confronted by the tactic, and some of them were beginning to develop techniques for dealing with it. The Bakers told us of their own experiences with blockbusting when they lived for a time in the Hyde Park section of Chicago. There, black and white neighbors had organized themselves to fight the speculators, to quell panic, and to "stabilize" the neighborhood and keep its racially integrated character. And were the neighbors ever vigilant! Soon after the Bakers moved in, they left their empty trash cans in the alley overnight. The next morning there was a friendly note taped to one of the can lids welcoming them to the neighborhood and urging them to help keep Hyde Park clean and neat.

In the Germantown section of Philadelphia, a white friend of theirs was directing a neighborhood stabilization project for the Quakers, seeking to stem white flight and black resegregation. If we were interested, the Bakers said, they would be glad to put us in touch with that woman, and perhaps she would be willing to come to Washington and advise us.

I broached the Bakers' suggestion in phone conversations with my new confederates, Mel Foer, the jeweler, and Homer Smith, the architect. When both of them expressed an interest in pursuing this prospect, I called the Bakers' friend in Philadelphia and was pleased to hear that if we would pay her train fare, she would be glad to accept our invitation.

So we brought Jane Reinheimer Motz to Washington and drew guidance from her sensible advice. But her coming was preceded by one stormy confrontation, and her speech touched off another.

The first explosion occurred when I proposed inviting her. That was at a meeting of the Manor Park Citizens Association, first chance I got, and Ernest Pullman struggled to his feet at once, objecting. Mel Foer, Homer Smith, and I were able to quiet him, however, when we offered to pay all the costs of her visit. I then proposed that we not limit our meeting with Mrs. Motz to association members only but instead open it to the entire community and publicize it widely with a leaflet distribution throughout Manor Park.

And let the colored in? To a meeting of the association? I had Pullman and two friends of his shouting at me on that one.

Mel Foer came to my assistance and proceeded, by quiet threat, to lower the temperatures of my antagonists. Yes, he said, if we opened the Motz meeting to everyone, Negroes might very well attend. He hoped they would. He intended to invite some of his own new Negro neighbors. And if anyone in the association tried to keep them out, he, personally, would go down to Franklin School (the D.C. Board of Education's headquarters) and demand to know why, since the District schools were now desegregated by order of the U.S. Supreme Court, the board still permitted racially segregated groups like the Manor Park Citizens Association to meet on public property.

On the night that Mrs. Motz addressed us (sometime early in 1958), the association regulars held a business meeting first, in closed session. Then they unlocked the auditorium doors and departed, ten or eleven of them, leaving me to chair the rest of the evening.

The public response to our invitation was gratifying. A racially mixed audience of about a hundred people filled the rows of folding chairs. Mrs. Motz's speech was a dispassionate account of how one goes about organizing residents in a racially changing neighborhood. She might have been instructing us in kitchen remodeling or lawn care. I thought it was all the more effective for her calm, factual, didactic tone. I was unprepared for the reaction she evoked.

For when I thanked her for her presentation and opened the floor for questions, no one had any questions. Not for Jane Reinheimer Motz, anyway. Instead they opened up on me.

A black man stood up, stated his name, Tracy Dunn, and with a broad grin and in an almost taunting tone said, "Now what I've heard here tonight sounds good to me. I think we all ought to work together. I'm ready to pay my dues right now. How much does it cost to join this Manor Park Citizens Association?"

"Mr. Dunn," I said, "I'm sorry to tell you, you can't join. The association's bylaws limit membership to whites only. But I want you to know several of us are working to change the bylaws and open the association to all the residents of this neighborhood." (Dunn, when we became acquainted, confessed to me that he knew he couldn't join that night. He was merely trying to provoke some frank discussion. If so, he succeeded.)

An angry murmur went scattering through the audience. From the floor, a furious black woman called out, "Then what are you wasting our time for? What's all this who-struck-John about an integrated community? You know we'll never have one in this Jim Crow town!"

The meeting was clearly getting out of hand. An elderly white woman arose and tried to come to my defense. She was sure, she said, that I was only trying to help us get to know each other better. She was too late. Blacks and whites insisted in rancor that they already knew each other well enough.

The Manor Park they knew was a grim and hostile place. This was a neighborhood where white and black neighbors shunned or insulted each other; where black parents, new to the PTA, could sense a chilly resentment to their presence; where seasoned white collectors for the annual United Givers Fund often found they couldn't extract a penny from the black newcomers; where white parents were afraid to let their children go trick-or-treating on Halloween; where people were afraid to walk their dogs at night; and where an old tradition of sending carolers out in the Christmas season, to wander the snowy streets singing, had to be abandoned because of fear and lack of interest.

Two black men in the audience helped moderate the ugly temper of the evening.

A portly gentleman took the floor. Clad in formal tie and jacket, skin the color of a pecan, he offered, smilingly, his reaction to the black mother who complained with a shiver of distaste of the icy reception she got at her first Whittier PTA meeting ("It was like walking into a refrigerator. Brrr!").

"Yes," he said, "I have to agree. You *can* get the cold shoulder at those PTAs. I went back a couple of times, though, and at the end of an evening I went up to the principal and introduced myself. 'Mrs. Shugrue,' I said, 'I'm Warren Van Hook. I'm new to the neighborhood and my daughter Allegra is in third grade here. I just want you to know I'm ready to volunteer my services in any way that you think will help Whittier.' And guess what?" he asked, touching off one of the evening's few genuine bursts of laughter, "I've been appointed chairman, starting next month, of the newspaper-collection drive."

Another conciliator was brought to his feet by the old-time resident's lament for the demise of Christmas caroling. This was a handsome chap, of black-coffee complexion and with a bristling moustache and an easygoing manner. He was sorry to hear that there were no more carols. "My wife and I love to sing," he said. "And we love Christmas. We moved here, over on North Dakota Avenue in late November, right after Thanksgiving, and we were looking forward to celebrating Christmas in our new house." They were the first black family on the block and the rash of For Sale signs that broke out on their neighbors' lawns was, he admitted, rather upsetting. But nevertheless he and his son David, a Whittier second-grader, went door to door to the houses on both sides of the street and deposited in mailboxes holiday notes of his wife's design, inviting everyone to an open house on Christmas Day. Four of their white neighbors dropped by to exchange holiday greetings, and afterwards, one woman, a widow, even took her house off the market.

A murmur of approval greeted this recital, and Jane Reinheimer Motz exclaimed, "There! Good! That's *exactly* the sort of thing you have to do to stabilize the neighborhood!"

But such bright moments in the course of the meeting were rare. Most of those assembled preferred to grumble.

At precisely ten o'clock the emotional bloodletting came to a halt. It had to. The janitor appeared and announced that under school board regulations he was required to close the building.

Yet Naomi and I considered the meeting a success. I had asked each person who addressed us to identify himself or herself. Each time someone with a constructive or thoughtful point of view—like Warren Van Hook, or Sam Grant of the Christmas open house—got up to speak, Naomi jotted down the name. We ended up with a list of four or five prospects for another meeting, a smaller and more productive one perhaps, where a group of us could gather in our living room over coffee and discuss Manor Park's problems informally and try to figure out what, if anything, we could do about them.

12

Neighbors, Incorporated

In April of 1958, members having been duly notified six months earlier, the proposal to eliminate the whites-only restriction from its bylaws came before the Manor Park Citizens Association. Those of us who supported the motion lost. Of the twenty-four members who showed up, thirteen voted for the change and two abstained. (Mel Foer confided to me afterwards that it made him uncomfortable to notice that most of the "for" votes were cast by Jews.) We were unable, however, to muster the necessary two-thirds vote of those present to get the amendment adopted.

After the vote Ernest Pullman took the floor triumphant. Seeing him smile was like watching wrinkles creep into a prune. He hoped Mr. Caplan knew, he said, that the issue could not be raised again for another six months. Mr. Caplan did know, but by then Mr. Caplan didn't care.

Naomi and I had decided, long before the vote, that it was a waste of time to try to work through the citizens association. Homer Smith only confirmed our conviction when he observed to me, as we walked out after our defeat, "You'll never change these hardheads."

Fortunately, we had an alternative course of action under way. Soon after Jane Reinheimer Motz's appearance, Naomi and I invited about eight of our black and white neighbors to drop in for an evening and discuss her suggestions for community action. Both Homer Smith and Mel Foer came. By the end of the get-together, we all agreed that we ought to continue such informal meetings on a regular basis.

We had already met about three times before the Manor Park Citizens Association considered changing its bylaws. When that effort failed, we decided not to pursue the matter any further. Instead, we talked about forming a new organization, integrated from the start. Our little group drew up a list of neighborhood problems we wanted to address. Two of us, Warren Van Hook and I, were assigned the task of drafting a statement of principles. By then we were calling each other "Van" and "Marvin" and I knew his profession. He was a pharmacist who operated his own drugstore.

When the group felt ready to present our proposals to the residents of Manor Park, the question of where to meet came up. We couldn't meet at Whittier Elementary. We would have needed special permission from the school board and the principal, and we would have had to pay a rental fee.

Homer Smith had a suggestion. "Call Reverend Tom Ehlers at Brightwood Park Methodist Church. Only don't tell him I told you to call. My dad was a big churchman there, but I'm not. You might say I'm a better Mason than I am a Methodist."

So I called the Reverend Mr. Ehlers one afternoon while I was out on my beat, appropriately enough from a phone booth in the U.S. Supreme Court pressroom.

Although Ehlers and I had never met, I knew from Homer Smith something important about the man. Soon after he took over as pastor of Brightwood Park Church, Ehlers became aware of the steady advance of racial change in the neighborhood. One Sunday morning he took the pulpit and declared that he could not in conscience continue to minister to an all-white church in a racially mixed neighborhood; he was serving notice, therefore, that it was his intention to go around and knock on doors and invite black neighbors into membership. The announcement split the congregation. A loyal faction supported Ehlers in his determination; a substantial number departed.

It was in this troubled time for the church that I phoned him. I was only halfway into my spiel when he interrupted me. "Mr. Caplan," he said, "if this is an attempt to keep colored people from moving into our neighborhood, I'll have nothing to do with it." I pressed on with my explanation, and once he grasped what our little integrated group was trying to do, he said, "Mr. Caplan, the church is yours."

About fifty people, white and black, responded to our leaflet invitations. We met on a June night in the basement of the church. It was a much calmer meeting than the one we had held at Whittier. We showed a filmstrip on neighbor-hood stabilization that Jane Reinheimer Motz had sent us from Philadelphia. Warren Van Hook and I, as co-chairmen, presented our statement of princi-ples. In it we invited everyone to join us in exploring a new experience: "living in an integrated neighborhood." The statement was unanimously adopted. And in another resounding vote, those assembled approved the formation of a new organization to pursue our goals. I, as acting chairman, was authorized to call another meeting, once a committee of us had drawn up bylaws and agreed on a name for our group.

Those were exuberant days. The speculators had already launched their spring sales drive, but our sense of organizing to meet them head-on heartened many of us. And yet, in hindsight, I make a sad confession here: I took each sale of a house to a black family as a setback for our side. Each sale became a goad. If I had stopped in the course of action and looked deeply into myself—and I did not want to—I am sure I would have had to confront racial impulses and a racial bias that would have distressed me.

Our planning committee began a round of weekly meetings. Tom Ehlers, an energetic and pragmatic man in his mid-sixties, threw himself into our de-liberations. So did several of his most active church members, both white and black. Confronted by the upheaval in their congregation, they welcomed out-siders like us as newfound allies. "We just leaned on each other," Naomi used to say, when she recalled those early days.

One of the hardest questions we faced was what to call ourselves. Appropri-ately, it was Ehlers who christened us. He broke the impasse by declaring, in his snappy, no-nonsense way, "Why not call ourselves Neighbors, Incorpo-rated? Isn't that what we're all about?"

A month or so after our first assembly, we convened another general meeting, again in the basement of Brightwood Park Church. It was a session instructive in helping us discover our resources.

As the only designated officer, I chaired the meeting.

"But who will be secretary?" I asked. Dead silence.

"No volunteers?"

No volunteers.

"Well, I'm sorry," I said, folding my arms. "We can't continue without a secretary."

So we sat a while, as members of the audience tittered, whispered, and ex-changed self-conscious glances.

At last a young white woman, a high-spirited-looking brunette, flung her hand up.

"Oh, I'll be secretary!" she exclaimed, confirming what soon became evident, that whenever we faced a crisis, small as this one, or larger, someone in our emerging group was ready to respond.

The new secretary was Adele Hutchins, daughter of Lucille and Lester Reese, two of Tom Ehlers's most faithful supporters. Born and raised in Manor Park, she was the first of our emerging assets. Adele was by profession a high-school teacher of sociology. That night marked the beginning of a long, sustaining friendship between the Hutchins and Caplan families.

The meeting continued in high good humor after that. The membership enthusiastically endorsed the name Tom Ehlers had suggested for the organization. The goals and course of action our planning committee proposed were readily accepted. The members departed, leaving implementation to a handful of us.

Privately, Naomi and I agreed we faced a formidable task. House-bound and job-bound, we felt that the kind of organizing campaign called for was beyond us. What we needed was a skilled professional, someone like Jane Reinheimer Motz, to help us address our problems on a day-to-day basis.

My calls from the Supreme Court phone booth to organizations like the NAACP and the Friends Service Committee and the Anti-Defamation League drew words of commendation for what Neighbors, Inc., was trying to do but no concrete offers of help. It was summer and some of the groups I spoke to suggested I get back in touch with them after Labor Day, when they were operating on full schedules.

Then Naomi had an inspiration. She was reading the *Washington Post* one morning after I had gone off to work, and ran across an item describing the grants made to a number of local community organizations by the Eugene and Agnes E. Meyer Foundation, a fund endowed by the publisher of the paper and his wife. If them, she asked herself, why not us?

She looked up the foundation's phone number, called them cold, and spoke to one of the top staff people, Mrs. Wayne Coy, wife of the crusading chairman of the Federal Communications Commission. Mrs. Coy was quite taken with Naomi's description of Neighbors, Inc., and what we were trying to do. "It sounds intriguing," she said. "Why don't you come down here and tell us more about it?"

A racially mixed half dozen of us accepted her invitation. We met with Mrs. Coy and the foundation's secretary, James Kunen. The Reverend Tom Ehlers and Warren Van Hook, I remember, were prominent and vocal in the discussion. When we finished talking, the two foundation officials encouraged us to submit a grant application.

In January 1959, the Meyer Foundation awarded Neighbors, Inc., $10,000 for one year. Mrs. Coy could not make a commitment, but she intimated that if our efforts to fight blockbusting and our experiments in fostering an integrated community showed promise, the foundation would consider renewing our grant. With that, NI, as we had taken to calling ourselves, became one of the richest as well as one of the smallest and newest citizen organizations in the District of Columbia.

We could not engage the services of Jane Reinheimer Motz. But we found for our executive secretary another remarkable and committed woman in the person of Margery T. Ware.

In a way, Margery Ware had already been working for us. I had happened upon her the previous summer when I was phoning around to see if one of the national civil rights or community welfare organizations could give us some professional help. I called the Washington branch of the National Urban League and was referred to their housing specialist, Margery Ware. After listening for a while to my account of Neighbors, Inc., and our ambitions for the new organization, she asked, "When's your next meeting? I'd like to come."

Mrs. Ware began attending NI meetings and soon made herself a valuable resource. She was familiar with the city's housing laws and real estate regulations, however confusing or sketchy they might be. And she had connections with housing officials down at the District building. She had many useful suggestions for us as we struggled to define the course of action we should take to thwart the blockbusters.

Margery Ware was that rarity, a white person employed by a predominantly black organization. She reminded me of Jane Motz in that she, too, was someone whose sober, understated manner only barely suggested the depth of her dedication to the cause of civil rights. Her orientation, like Jane Motz's, was essentially religious, not political. Her persuasion was Unitarian.

Born in Manlius, New York, she was the daughter of an Episcopalian minister who espoused the Social Gospel. This was a movement in American Protestantism that saw a concern for social issues as the highest manifestation of religious belief. It was a movement, incidentally, whose adherents exerted a strong influence on Martin Luther King, Jr., when he was a student at Crozier Theological Seminary.

Suiting action to belief, Margery Ware's father, Albert Taylor, once delivered a Sunday sermon on venereal disease, a bold step in the 1920s. The following Sunday a church official announced during service that the Reverend Mr. Taylor was being replaced by another minister.

Since she was raised in a family that took its religious convictions seriously, it is not surprising that Mrs. Ware evinced an early interest in social concerns, even as she pursued a college career that found her majoring in zoology. Athletics was her greatest skill, and upon graduation she became a coach and an instructor in physical education.

An energetic and adventurous person, she also took up flying as an avocation. During World War II she became one of a cadre of women who relieved male pilots of a lot of routine work by ferrying transport planes and other aircraft to fields all over the country.

She came to Washington in 1945 to teach physical education at George Washington University but quickly involved herself in the burgeoning civil rights movement. In 1948, she went to work for the Washington Urban League and within eight years had become executive director of the Washington bureau. But she was only acting director; the director's job, she was told, would have to go to someone black. "Nothing," she recalls, "upset me more than that."

It was at this critical moment in her career that NI was able to offer her the directorship of the office we planned to open with the Meyer Foundation money.

Margery was not the only candidate for our job. Another top contender was a black man, Walter Bendy Lewis, who had helped write the housing code for the District. He made a strong impression on our executive committee—so strong that our first impulse was to try to hire both him and Margery. But our treasurer, Warren Van Hook, assured us that such a notion was well beyond the limits of our budget. So after several evenings of agonizing debate we chose Margery. Race, mainly, dictated that choice. One of our staff executive's major activities, we had agreed, was to go into blocks that the speculators were trying to bust and arrange block parties, where we would attempt to introduce resident white homeowners to some of the new black families moving in and try to stem panic. That task, we reasoned, could best be done by a white person; a white woman ringing a harassed resident's doorbell would gain readier access, we felt, than a black man. I think, too, that on some unspoken, unconscious level we were trying to find someone as much like Jane Reinheimer Motz as possible.

It was my uncomfortable assignment to phone Walter Bendy Lewis and inform him of our decision and the reasons for it. To my great relief, he took the news graciously. And yet, although nothing was said, I'm sure the irony that found a group of us who espoused racial equality and a color-blind society denying a job to a man because of his race was not lost on Lewis or me.

Margery Ware promptly rented a little one-room office, a second-floor walk-up over a florist shop on Georgia Avenue. By coincidence it was close by "speculators row" on Kennedy Street. Here, with a part-time secretary and a few sticks of second-hand furniture, she undertook prodigies of labor that finally got our stabilization campaign under way.

And so, as the *Atlantic Monthly* predicted, Naomi and I remained.

Uneasily. For the other side of our militancy was anguish. There was something inexorable about the way whites moved out of the neighborhood and blacks moved in. Departing white families took some of our hopes for stabilization along with them, particularly families with evident commitment to our cause, like the Mel Foers. Whenever Freya, Anne, or Bennett made a white friend in school, our hearts sank; in a short time, we knew, and we were rarely wrong, the friend would leave. (Months later I was to learn the corollary of that: a black doctor who had moved to Manor Park when "a rough element" started coming into his old downtown neighborhood told me it saddened his young son to find that nearly every time he made a white friend at Whittier, that friend moved away.)

Although Naomi and I were all for integrated schools, we had never intended to let our children be token whites in nearly all black classes. Bennett, our youngest, was well advanced in Whittier—third or fourth grade—before he realized that the overwhelming majority of Americans were white. Everything in his experience till then suggested otherwise.

And yet there were signs that encouraged us. Whenever Naomi recalled those early years she would say, "Every time I'd think, 'Enough! I've had it! We've got to move!' someone would give Marvin another award."

And so it was. The favorable recognition Neighbors, Inc., brought us was a sustaining factor in our darkest moments. It even upgraded our social life.

One memorable evening, in March of 1960, Naomi and I, through Margery Ware's conniving, were the guests of honor at a private dinner party in Georgetown at the home of Mrs. Gifford Pinchot, widow of a former governor of Pennsylvania. It was a small, gracious affair, designed to introduce us to about twenty of her influential friends and, in a tasteful, understated way, help raise money for our organization.

Among the guests that night were Mr. and Mrs. Michael Straight, he the publisher of the *New Republic,* whom I had not seen since we had both been delegates to the American Veterans Committee convention in Milwaukee, back in 1947.

Another guest was a prominent businessman by the name of Harold Freudberg, who remarked to me in a perfectly friendly way, "I've met some crazy guys in my time, but you take the cake!"

More to my liking, and Naomi's, too, were the observations of one of the most distinguished persons there, Dr. Mordecai Johnson, president of Howard University. In a splendid little speech, he declared that what Neighbors, Inc., was doing was "absolutely determinative of the future of integration in Washington."

So there we were. For once, we found ourselves in the vanguard of a popular movement. By a wonderful stroke of luck we had helped inaugurate Neighbors, Inc., when the civil rights struggle had begun to gather momentum and capture national attention. Young idealists and even idealists of our own generation were drawn to it.

John F. Kennedy's election in 1960 gave a powerful impetus to the cause. No matter how JFK himself may have vacillated, juggling the complicated politics of the issue, his administration attracted to federal service young men and women committed to advancing racial equality. For many of them, the idea of living in an integrated neighborhood had considerable appeal. Integration was a new and shining goal. Neighbors, Inc., was catching on, even among members of the stolid, non-activist middle class. Old, established District organizations began to call upon me to speak. I was invited to appear on panels and TV discussion programs. The awards Naomi spoke of—bronze plaques and parchment citations from Jewish and Christian congregations, black sororities and fraternities, organizations like the ADA and the AVC—began to appear on the walls of the office I had made for myself out of the little sun parlor beyond the dining room.

Typical, as I sit and look up at it now, is the bronze plaque awarded to me by the Men's Club of B'nai Israel, a large synagogue just south of Manor Park. It was given IN RECOGNITION OF HIS DEVOTED AND COURAGEOUS SERVICE TO PROMOTE AND IMPROVE INTERGROUP RELATIONSHIP IN OUR RAPIDLY INTERGRATING [sic] COMMUNITY. It is dated January 22, 1961. Four years later B'nai Israel sold its building to a black congregation and moved on to reestablish itself outside the District, in overwhelmingly white Montgomery County.

But by then Naomi and I had come to accept such developments with equanimity. For a new NI community seemed to be growing up all around us. Many young white Kennedy administration officials and their families began to seek us out. Naomi played a crucial role in attracting them. A few years earlier she had begun to question NI's direction. It was foolish and wasteful of our efforts, she argued, to spend so much time trying to soothe the resident whites, to try to keep them from panicking and persuade them to stay. She proposed establishing a Housing Information Service, which she offered to chair, whose main purpose would be to advertise the NI neighborhoods and encourage white families who shared our convictions to move into them. It was an idea born, she once remarked, of her "creative anxiety."

By then NI was active in three other neighborhoods besides Manor Park, which was more or less a lower-middle-income area. We were engaged in working with neighbors in Brightwood, the area that surrounded Tom Ehlers's church and extended to the borders of that great divide, Rock Creek Park; and in two of Washington's more prestigious residential neighborhoods, Takoma and Shepherd Park. Takoma, established near the end of the nineteenth century by a number of Department of Agriculture executives, was noted for its large Victorian-style houses and their vast gardens. Shepherd Park was a relatively new, upper-middle-income neighborhood, developed shortly after World War I and distinguished by many substantial structures of brick and stone, often custom-built. By our time, Shepherd Park was known as the neighborhood to which wealthy Jews aspired (since the Christians who had first settled there fled at their coming). The four neighborhoods together constituted an area of about 250 city blocks and a population of some 40,000. The Housing Information Service could offer homeseekers a broad range of dwelling-places to choose from; even more important, it offered them, free of charge, the personal, solicitous attention (perhaps even too much attention) of NI members anxious to get them settled in our area.

What Naomi sought to demonstrate to skeptical real estate dealers—for some of them had begun to take notice of us and had even evinced an interest in working with us—was that there were white as well as black customers for their properties. In the three or four years she chaired the Housing Information Service it grew into one of NI's most active projects. Starting as a tyro at real estate, Naomi became such a knowledgeable practitioner in the field that a couple of dealers tried to get her to join their sales staffs. She declined all such offers.

Psychology was her profession. She continued to practice it through all our vicissitudes. Two days a week, when the children were small, she drove a great distance across the District into northern Virginia to work at the Alexandria Community Mental Health Center. Luckily for us, she became a full-time staff member at the center when the children reached high school and we faced the fearsome prospect of college tuitions.

In the four neighborhoods, blacks eventually came to outnumber whites. The 1990 census estimated the four areas to be about 63 percent black. But as long as Neighbors, Inc., was integrated and growing, racial percentages were not intimidating. The young families, white and black, that were drawn to NI in its early years and became active in it brought such skill and imagination to the organization that we attracted national attention.

You can see these changes taking place if you examine NI's annual reports.

Our first publications were crude mimeograph affairs with a Neighbors, Inc., logo (drawn for us by a sympathetic but unimaginative calligrapher), whose loops and curlicues, an irreverent new member said, made us look like an old-fashioned ice-cream parlor.

By our third year, 1961, we were publishing reports whose covers featured the superb prints of a *Washington Post* photographer, Douglas Chevalier, who had moved into Takoma. A professional graphics artist redesigned our letterhead. The starkly simple logo she devised for us was accompanied by an arresting semi-abstract design of a small black and a small white figure, side by side, hands joined. That sketch was the work of another newcomer, Peter Masters, a man who arranged many of the Smithsonian's exhibitions. An advertising copywriter for Hecht's, Marge Brockman, produced a slogan for the four NI neighborhoods—"The IN Community: INtown. INtegrated. INteresting."

I believe we *were* interesting. We were a neighborhood rich in residents with inventive minds and ingenious ideas. That was evident in a number of projects that began to emanate from the NI area.

One of the first events to make a big splash and help establish the NI area's reputation throughout metropolitan Washington as a lively place to live was our 1961 reception for the diplomatic families of the newly emerging African nations. This was the brainchild of a newcomer to the neighborhood, Dr. Robert Good. Bob Good was a State Department specialist in Africa, who succeeded me as president of NI and went on to become the first U.S. ambassador to Zambia. The long day of festivities, conducted in Shepherd Elementary School and in a dozen host homes, brought many diplomats and high government officials to the area and drew wide press coverage. My speech and the speeches of our dignitaries, including the president of the D.C. Board of Commissioners, were recorded and broadcast by the Voice of America.

Nancy Good, Bob's wife, developed a project of her own. At Paul Junior High she instituted a program she called "Democracy in Action." It sought to instruct students in the art of government through extensive field trips to Capitol Hill, the federal courts, and federal agencies. Her skillful use of the resources of the nation's capital as educational tools was greatly admired—and copied by other District schools.

Naomi's Housing Information Service profited from the fresh thoughts of new recruits. The new assistants she acquired inaugurated an annual home and garden tour that always got good press in the society columns of the daily papers and brought droves of curiosity seekers and prospective home buyers to the area.

A music-loving physician and his organist wife formed a children's chorus that specialized in singing the songs of many countries in the native languages. One of the group's soloists was a youngster who went on to become the highly regarded baritone Ben Holt.[1]

Encouraged by fellow NI members to turn their talents to the benefit of the neighborhood, one woman organized a cadre of tutors to work with slow learners at Paul Junior High; another founded the city's first integrated Girl Scout troop.

Still another new homeowner made an important financial and cultural contribution to NI. Dr. Samuel Halperin, who served as congressional liaison for the Department of Health, Education, and Welfare, conceived an annual art and book festival that not only brought us wide media attention but proved to be lucrative as well. For several years it raised at least a quarter of our annual budget. Robert Kennedy, then U.S. attorney general, upon opening the first festival on June 8, 1963, declared, "What is so impressive about what you have done here is that you have shown the way, that it can be done, that it is possible." He was referring, our annual report went on to note, "to our continuing effort to establish in this racially changing section of Northwest Washington, a genuinely integrated community."

NI emulated the old-line citizens associations, to some extent, by sponsoring more conventional activities: a garden club; an annual clean-up campaign that began with a big parade down Georgia Avenue; a monthly open house at different neighbors' homes for an evening of socializing.

And we revived an old tradition. On Christmas Eve a choral group toured the streets singing not only carols but, true to our heterogeneous nature, Chanukah songs, African American songs like "Michael Row the Boat Ashore," and others.

---

1. A singer of prodigious gifts, Ben Holt made his debut with the Metropolitan Opera in 1985 and sang the title role in the New York City Opera's production of *Malcolm X* in 1987. Tragically, he died at the age of thirty-four, on May 5, 1990.

More and more, our work carried us beyond the boundaries of our four neighborhoods. When my *Atlantic Monthly* article appeared in July 1960, the Hyde Park–Kenwood neighborhood in Chicago, whose activities as related to us by Helen Baker had helped inspire our own stabilization effort, invited me to come out there and give them an account of our experiences. (Fairchild Publications, incidentally, was so impressed by my appearance in such a distinguished magazine that they gave me a major assignment—a three-month tour of eleven sub-Saharan countries, to report on business and investment opportunities in the newly emerging African nations.)

We declined invitations to form other NI chapters in the Washington metropolitan area because we had neither the staff nor the energy to undertake such an expansion. However, Margery Ware and I did accept many speaking engagements and helped set up new groups that we felt furthered and complemented the work of NI. Most notably, we stimulated the organization of Suburban Maryland Fair Housing, a committee of Montgomery County residents whose purpose was practically the obverse of NI's: to help Negro families find homes in the suburbs and to facilitate their entrance into previously all-white areas. We also offered guidance to the American Friends Service Committee in projects it undertook to further suburban integrated housing.

One of our most essential campaigns was our effort to persuade the three daily newspapers to stop using racial designations in their real estate ads. The AVC and the ADA joined us in this fight. After numerous visits to the editors and after we'd persuaded several friendly representatives and senators to introduce bills to prohibit such advertising, the papers capitulated. Sometime in 1960, quietly and without informing us, all three papers notified real estate dealers that they would no longer allow them to run ads by race.

By the early 1960s NI was an established organization, and thanks to subsequent grants from the Meyer Foundation and other foundations like the Taconic in New York, and thanks to the revenue from our art and book festivals, we were reasonably sound financially. An important contribution to our economic health was our tax exemption, negotiated for us as a public service by Al Arent, one of Washington's foremost tax attorneys and a leader in the Jewish community. Our membership increased from a nucleus of 175 in 1958 to 1,400 by 1965. By then, our annual budget was $25,000, and Margery Ware moved to a larger office and acquired a full-time office secretary and an assistant.

But I have drawn too bright a picture, which I now must darken. By 1968, the year of Martin Luther King's assassination and the urban riots it provoked, there was growing nation-wide disenchantment with integration as an attainable or even a desirable goal. The rise of the Black Power movement aroused deeply atavistic white fears. Many whites came to resent black advancement when they counted the cost to themselves in inconveniences like school busing and in lost job opportunities due, they felt, to affirmative action. Many blacks were disillusioned, ready to abandon their efforts to move into the mainstream of our society, when it became apparent that even as federal civil rights laws and federal enforcement programs opened new opportunities to them, they still faced discrimination; they still encountered segregation and prejudice. *Racism* became the widely used term to describe what they were suffering.

These murky currents were manifest in our four neighborhoods.

Although NI was not impervious to these conflicts, one thing eased our task of racial reconciliation. We did not, to any great extent, have to contend with class differences. Most of the blacks moving in were economically and educationally the equals and often the superiors of the whites whose homes they bought. They found friendship and ready acceptance among the young white professionals active in Neighbors, Inc. Indeed, class was a stronger bond than race. In more instances than I like to think about, our black and white neighbors could make common middle-class cause against the poor. An instance of this, early in NI's history, came when the residents—new and old, white and black—on a Manor Park block banded together against a poor black woman who had turned her house into a neighborhood nuisance by operating an illegal day nursery, crowding her rooms with boarders, and filling her backyard with mounds of garbage and three wildly barking German shepherds.

The hostility she aroused became a unifying force. Even Carrie Seaquist, the Manor Park Citizens Association's creative cookie maker, who lived two doors away from the old woman, came to several mixed-race strategy sessions we arranged for block residents. She even paid her NI dues (though to my memory, she never attended an organizational meeting).

In the end we prevailed. The old woman was ordered by a municipal court to comply with the neighborhood regulations or lose her home.

However, this story of class conflict has a sequel, in which the old woman, without knowing it, got a measure of revenge on me. The instrument of her revenge was her grandson, Al, a skinny little tough of six or seven. One of my black neighbors, Ernie Wilson, comptroller at Howard University, took one look at Al and said, "I'd never let my Chico play with that kid." I was vexed with Ernie and told him so. Bennett, who was around Al's age, became friendly with the little boy, and I, the sanctimonious liberal, was not about to forbid the friendship. I let Bennett play with Al. But after they were both apprehended by the police and hauled into the Fourth District station house for stealing candy in a Safeway store, and after I caught them breaking into mailboxes on Al's block, looking for cash enclosures, I did what any sensible black, middle-class father would do. I told Bennett outright, once and for all, he was *never ever* to play with Al again.

I can think of at least two other occasions when class self-interest united us without regard to race. When a newcomer to Manor Park, a white minister who directed a community center in a slum neighborhood, proposed at a general meeting that NI sponsor a refuge for the homeless, he was promptly hooted down. And when Marjorie Webster Junior College, a posh girls' finishing school in Shepherd Park, went bankrupt, and Miss Webster's heirs, in 1971, sought to sell the handsome institution to a psychiatrist who wanted to reopen it as a lab school for youngsters with learning difficulties, and use it, so rumor said, as a halfway house for drug addicts, the NI members who lived nearby rose up in arms. The campaign against these proposed changes was led by one of NI's celebrities, Patricia Roberts Harris. She had been President Johnson's ambassador to Luxembourg (the first black woman ever to assume such a post). She had also served as both housing secretary and health secretary in the Carter administration. NI hired an attorney for the fight, and Mrs. Harris's forces successfully blocked the sale.

Class homogeneity helped keep us together. But as alike as we were, racial tensions cropped up among us from time to time. Black NI members were acutely and uncomfortably aware that while the Housing Information Service was available to homeseekers of their race, Naomi and her assistants were primarily interested in attracting white families to the area. Each white newcomer got a red-carpet welcome that was not always extended to a new black family.

"You have to have a very tough skin to be a Negro in Neighbors," one homeowner confided to Haynes Johnson, at that time a reporter for the *Washington Star,* who in 1965 wrote a long front-page feature on our activities. Johnson, a skeptical, clear-minded journalist, encountered other notes of disharmony; but even so, he was persuaded in the end of the worth of our efforts. Members of NI, he concluded, "have become, whether they want to or not, a model."

Naomi and I were both convinced of the importance of the work we were doing. It was demanding, though. Almost everything we did was connected to NI. When out-of-town friends passed through Washington and stopped by to say hello and ask, "What's new?" Naomi, in an ironic gesture, would just hand them the latest copy of *Neighbors, Ink,* our monthly newsletter.

We were uneasily aware of the toll our activities took on our family life. I sometimes felt as if I were on call twenty-four hours a day. My week was crammed with meetings—parlor get-togethers on blocks the speculators were trying to break, committee meetings, special project meetings, mail-stuffing parties, meetings of the full NI membership. I was often invited to speak before other organizations or to take part in panel discussions or make guest appearances on TV and radio talk shows. My schedule became so overwhelming that Naomi finally rebelled. To appease her, I agreed to limit myself to no more than three nights out a week.

In desperation, we sought refuge in religion. We began to observe the Sabbath every Friday night. It was, at first, nothing more than expediency. Neither Naomi nor I was particularly observant. We had joined a local synagogue, one attended by cousins of ours who still lived in what was, after all, the remains of a heavily Jewish neighborhood. But we showed up at shul only on Purim and the High Holy Days. Now, when I was asked to take part in a Friday night meeting, I begged off on grounds that a higher duty called. Yet what began as a subterfuge gradually took possession of us. We came to look forward to the ceremony, to the candle-lighting and the blessings over bread and wine and the Shabbes songs, and to the blissful relaxation of a night at home without business encounters or phone calls.

Still, if you attached any importance to your family, these brief respites weren't enough. We came to recognize at last what a spot we had put the children in. Our eldest child, Freya, made us aware of that.

In 1968, when she was seventeen, she graduated from Calvin Coolidge High. She had attended all the neighborhood schools: Whittier Elementary, only a block away; Paul Junior High, a ten-block walk from the house; and Coolidge, directly across the street from us, five minutes from our front porch if you took the shortcut over the playing fields. Freya graduated with distinction: top of her class, editor of the *Coolidge Courier,* a participant in an enrichment program for gifted students that the District schools arranged with a consortium of area colleges. She scored high on her SATs and was readily accepted by Barnard, the first college she applied to.

Naomi and I were elated. Freya was triumphant proof that we had been right not to run but to stay, resist the white flight to the suburbs and fight for integration. True, Coolidge High, by Freya's time, was 90 percent black; but integration, to a zealot of my persuasion, was a state of mind. Freya was one of only twenty or thirty white students, but she had a circle of white and black friends; she even had a white boyfriend, an estimable young man, a Quaker, a good student and a good athlete.

If she had been our only child, Naomi and I could have sighed with relief and felt our cause vindicated. But we had two other children: Anne, who by then was fourteen, and Bennett, who was twelve. And right after graduation Freya took Naomi and me aside and said firmly, "I don't think it's right or fair to make Ben and Annie go through what I've gone through."

So now Naomi and I had to confront what we had chosen to ignore. Or rather what *I* had chosen to ignore. For Naomi had always been beset by doubt and apprehension during the ten years we had been living in the NI area. Once Freya had spoken, Naomi, as a practicing psychologist, called a colleague of hers for an appointment and rushed the five of us into family therapy.

Blinders fell—no, blinders were torn from my eyes during the six months we went for weekly consultations. Both Anne and Bennett were attending Paul. The junior high not only was 90 percent black but, because of the District's open enrollment policy for secondary schools, had a social-class mix as well, with a large contingent of tough kids from low-income families. They were older and bigger and crueler than the well-bred, middle-class black youngsters Ben and Anne were used to in elementary school.

Our children's black elementary-school classmates were as scared of the tough blacks as Ben and Anne were. But our kids' white skins made them easy to pick out and easy to pick on. Anne, resilient and committed to her parents' ideals, had to admit as we talked in the doctor's office that she was unhappy and socially isolated at Paul. She had no girlfriends. "Sure, they'll wave and say 'hi!' But after school they go their way and you go yours." On Monday mornings she had to endure the happy chatter about weekend events to which she had not been invited. But there were worse things than being slighted. She was teased, too. Chosen from her class to appear in a photograph of the school library, evidently to help integrate the picture, she was waylaid afterwards by two girls who pulled her pigtails out of envy. During lunch a group of girls and boys brought her to tears by following her around and chanting, "Chicken in a biscuit with a white cracker."

When an insensitive black teacher told her class one day about a group of white teenagers who were terrorizing the black families on her block, a boy came up to Anne afterwards and said, "See? You white people hate us."

Bennett had an even harder time. Although he was solidly built and tall for a twelve-year-old, the boys he was afraid of were taller and tougher than he. When I drove him to Paul in warm weather, with the car windows down and the radio on, he would reach over as we approached the school and switch stations from one for rock music, which he loved, to one for soul. He knew the black kids would poke fun at him if they heard him listening to rock.

If he was walking home alone, some of the big black kids would come up behind him, step on his heels, call him "honky," and punch him and shout, "Say, 'sir,' you shit. Say 'sir.' " At lunchtime, he admitted at our family sessions, he often hid in a corner of the yard or under the hallway stairs to escape being noticed by his regular tormentors. Sometimes he didn't dare go to the toilet when he badly needed to because he knew that was where the big kids hung out, smoking cigarettes and just waiting for a honky to come in so they could put the muscle on him.

Bennett said enough to persuade me that we could not let him stay in Paul. Eight years later I got other insights into how much he had suffered. In 1976, a writer for the *Washingtonian* magazine came to the house to interview me for an article he was writing on race relations in D.C., and since Ben was home from college, we invited him to take part in the discussion. Under the writer's questioning Ben admitted he had been "petrified" most of the time. His stay at Paul, he said laughing, "was a lesson in survival." Part of surviving, he said, was learning to adapt to black behavior. So he developed a knack for black street lingo and a loose-gaited stride he copied from his classmates. With perverse pride he said, "Even today I can pass for black."

We were still in therapy when Martin Luther King was assassinated. Our family's grief at that tragedy was complicated by bitter personal experience. King was murdered on a Thursday. The riots that erupted in Washington the ensuing weekend brought federal troops to our neighborhood, even though we were several miles from the downtown fires and lootings. That shook us. We were even more shaken, though, when Paul's principal, a black woman, phoned us Sunday night to say she was calling the parents of all the white students in the school and advising them to keep their children home for the next few days.

That incident and the substance of our talks under the supervision of a sympathetic psychiatrist plunged me, for the moment, into a spell of self-doubt and self-reproach. It occurred to me that Neighbors, Inc.—a thousand or so dedicated souls in a community of forty thousand—might not be a vanguard but a coterie. At that time of crisis, I was ready to concede that integration had as few adherents among blacks as it did among whites.

I was surely troubled then, and profoundly self-questioning. But today as I look back on that time, I believe Naomi and I did only what we felt we had to. Not only out of self-interest, but out of commitment to our goal—a society in which the preeminent measure of any member of it is personal worth.

I had invested quite a lot of myself in Paul. For two years I was president of the Home and School Association. I had helped Nancy Good establish her Democracy in Action program. After 1965, when Bob Good became the first U.S. ambassador to Zambia and the whole Good family moved to Africa, I redoubled my efforts to help keep that program alive. I chaired the Institute for Educational Development (IED), an ambitious project based at Paul that was funded by a Department of Education grant of $100,000. An NI activist, an expert on education, had gotten us into that endeavor. The institute paired our neighborhood schools with the University of Maryland, where our resident educator was a member of the faculty. In exchange for making practice teaching posts available in our schools and making ourselves and our children available for study projects, we were to enjoy enriched classroom experiences and an opportunity to send our brightest students to university classrooms for advanced instruction.

But when I was faced with the evidence, in our family sessions, of what our children were enduring, I could not go on. Naomi and I arranged to have Anne and Bennett transferred to Alice Deal Junior High, on the other side of Rock Creek Park. That school had more white students than black and drew most of its student body from the affluent families in Chevy Chase.

One bleak morning I had to face the IED board and tender my resignation as chairman. I told the members why I was resigning, and the teachers and my fellow parents, both white and black, assured me they understood.

Did I regret what I had done in consigning our children to neighborhood schools? Freya asked me that question not long ago, and I said no. Selfish as it may sound, I told her, I did what I felt I had to do if I were to live with my conscience.

It's a truthful answer—as far as it goes. What it omits is guilt.

In synagogue, on Rosh Hashanah, the Jewish New Year, I read the Akedah, the story of how our patriarch Abraham, at God's command, is ready to sacrifice his beloved and only son, and how at the last minute, as he lifts the knife, an angel stays his hand and Isaac's life is spared.

I contend that our children were spared, too. All three of them have gone on to fashion useful careers and fulfilling lives for themselves. And yet I cannot read the old biblical tale without reflecting upon my own actions as a parent. When I do, I am kin, for a time, with Abraham, with every father who finds himself stubbornly and blindly ready to sacrifice a child for his beliefs.

Part IV

The Leadership Conference on Civil Rights
1963–1981

13

A Crucial Change

In the summer of 1963 I was offered what sounded to me like the opportunity of a lifetime. Yet for a while I was reluctant to take it.

This is what happened.

Joseph L. Rauh, Jr., called me up at Fairchild one morning and invited me to meet him for lunch at the Democratic Club in the Carlton Hotel. The invitation puzzled me.

I scarcely knew Joe Rauh. I had heard of him largely by reputation. I knew him to be a founder and president of the militantly anti-Communist group of liberals, the Americans for Democratic Action, ADA. He was also, I knew, a power in the liberal wing of the Democratic Party. Reportedly, he was one of the authors of the forthright civil rights plank in the platform the party adopted at its 1948 national convention. It was that plank that infuriated southern Democrats and caused serious rifts in the party. But I applauded its adoption. It was that plank, after Truman's election, that drew me back to the party and away from the moribund Progressives.

Rauh and I, so far as I could recall, had met on only two occasions. Once, when I had addressed an ADA meeting on the work of Neighbors, Inc.; and the other time, when I had been one of five panelists at an ADA civil rights symposium that he was chairing.

I was not a member of the ADA. I was put off at first by its strident anti-Communism. But even when that changed and I came to know and respect and work with several ADAers, somehow I never got around to joining. Was Rauh, I wondered facetiously, going to try a membership recruitment on me?

Joe Rauh erect was an imposing figure: over six feet tall, broad-shouldered and muscular, still imbued with the energy of his years at Harvard, when he had been a star player on what he would be the first to say was a hapless basketball team. (His penchant for bow ties, I thought, lent a certain collegiate jauntiness to his appearance.)

But Joe Rauh seated was impressive, too. He was already waiting for me at a table when I came out of the June heat and into the club's cool, dim, cavernous interior. With a massive head crowned by a thatch of wheat-white hair, and with a ruddy face defined by stark, black-framed glasses, he was a looming presence among the other diners as he smiled and beckoned to me with a broad sweep of his arm.

He was already well along into a martini when I sat down. Once I declined, with thanks, to join him in another, and once we had placed our orders, he came right to the point.

"I have you in mind for a job that's opening up soon," he said. "You're aware, I suppose, of that new civil rights bill that Kennedy's just sent up to Congress?"

Yes, I said, and from the news stories it sounded like a good one.

"Good? Yes, it's good. I've read it. Oh, of course it's still short of what we want. But if Congress ever passes it, it'll be a major breakthrough. It's so important, the Leadership Conference on Civil Rights is planning to open a Washington office to do nothing but carry on a day-to-day lobbying operation for it. They're going to need someone to help manage the office. And I thought of you."

I was surprised. And pleased. And told him so.

Rauh brushed that aside. He felt I had the right commitment, from what he knew about my work with Neighbors, Inc. And since I covered Congress for Fairchild, he figured I knew my way around Capitol Hill. Those were the essential qualifications. If I was interested, he was ready to recommend me. But first he had a question.

"How much do you know about the Leadership Conference?"

"Not much," I admitted.

What little I knew about the Leadership Conference on Civil Rights, or LCCR, and what Rauh told me as we ate and talked, suggested to me an organization of a rather informal, ad hoc nature. In recollection now, I'm sure I add more than I learned that afternoon and even in the next two weeks as I struggled to make up my mind.

The Leadership Conference was founded in 1950 by three men. Two of them were among the country's foremost civil rights leaders. The older of the two, A. Philip Randolph, then sixty-one, was one of the movement's most venerated pioneers. He gained national recognition as the organizer and president of the Brotherhood of Sleeping Car Porters, the country's first black labor union. In 1941, Phil Randolph's threat of a national march on Washington to protest the denial of jobs to blacks in the rapidly expanding defense industries alarmed President Roosevelt. It prompted the president to issue the first executive order on fair employment rather than face an embarrassing demonstration on the very eve of America's battle to save democracy.

The younger man, Roy Wilkins, forty-nine in 1950, was the executive secretary of the NAACP, and in that office was emerging as one of the most adroit and effective civil rights advocates of his generation.

The third and youngest of the Conference founders was Arnold Aronson. Aronson, thirty-nine, a trained social worker, headed the Bureau on Jewish Employment Problems, a Chicago-based, one-man operation financed by the American Jewish Committee, the American Jewish Congress, the Anti-Defamation League of B'nai B'rith, and the Jewish Labor Committee. Although he was the least well known of the Leadership Conference's originators, within the civil rights movement he had gained a reputation as a skillful strategist. His wholehearted engagement in the fight for full employment had won him Phil Randolph's trust and friendship.

It was Randolph who set things in motion. Aware in 1943 that the president's executive order on fair employment would expire with the end of World War II, he organized the National Council for a Permanent FEPC. This was a coalition of national civil rights, labor, religious, and civic organizations that undertook a campaign to write fair employment into federal law.

Unfortunately, Randolph soon ran into organizational difficulties.

"In a revolution," he once remarked to Arnold Aronson, "never worry about details." But it was precisely his inattention to details that threatened to wreck the National Council. In 1943, he opened headquarters in Washington, and since he chose not to oversee operations himself, he engaged Anna Arnold Hedgeman, a prominent churchwoman, to run the office.

It proved to be an unhappy choice. Considerable friction developed between Anna Hedgeman and Randolph and grew worse as the campaign progressed. The breakup came in 1946, when in her preparation for an FEPC rally she took an unwise step. Directing an organization that was financially precarious to begin with, she ordered, Arnold Aronson recalls, an enormous number of FEPC buttons—a million of them.

In a flurry of recrimination on both sides, Anna Hedgeman and her staff resigned. Desperate to salvage the National Council, Randolph sought the help of two good friends, Roy Wilkins and Arnold Aronson.

Wilkins agreed to chair the council's executive committee, and Aronson took over as secretary. Under their direction, the organization soon began functioning more efficiently. However, both of them felt the concentration on a single issue was too restrictive. A coalition, they thought, should address the whole range of civil rights issues.

The opportunity to broaden the scope of the National Council's concerns came in 1949, when shortly after his inauguration President Truman sent to Congress a substantial package of civil rights proposals. Besides calling for a permanent FEPC, Truman also urged enactment of an anti-lynching law, repeal of the poll tax, and a prohibition against discrimination in all places of public accommodation.

These proposals, ambitious and broad-scale for their time, came before an unreceptive Congress. The key Senate and House committees to which the president's bills were referred were either chaired or dominated by hostile southerners. Although the situation was unpromising—perhaps *because* it was unpromising—Wilkins and Aronson were bent on doing what they could to back the president. To that end, they summoned member organizations of the National Council and other sympathetic groups to a national rally in support of the Truman package.

Under a new name, the National Emergency Civil Rights Mobilization, Wilkins and Aronson invited everyone to come to Washington on January 15, 1950, for three days of lobbying. In response to the call, 4,269 delegates from 33 states (including 291 brave souls from the South), representing 58 national organizations, converged on the capital. Although the mobilization was modest in comparison with later civil rights events of a similar nature, it was described in one press report as "the greatest mass lobby in point of numbers and geographical distribution that had ever come to Washington in behalf of any legislation."

To the importunings of rally delegates and the president, congressional members generally turned a deaf ear. If there was a national emergency, Congress didn't or wouldn't recognize it. No federal civil rights law had been enacted since 1875. The rules of the House and Senate appeared designed to foreclose the possibility that any civil rights law could ever pass again. In both bodies the rules of seniority left southerners entrenched and in control of key committees. In the Senate, Rule 22, the rule for ending debate on a bill, became, in the phrase of *New York Times* columnist Arthur Krock, "the gravedigger of civil rights."

Under that rule in 1950 it took sixty-four votes, two-thirds of the entire Senate, to break a filibuster. In consequence, anti-lynching legislation pledged in both Republican and Democratic platforms had come before every Congress since 1922, only to be blocked in the Senate by filibuster. Bills to repeal the poll tax passed the House five times only to be talked to death in the Senate. By 1950, a bill to establish a permanent FEPC had been reported favorably out of Senate committees in four Congresses. Each time it was throttled on the Senate floor.

The Emergency Mobilization produced no concrete results. Nevertheless, Wilkins and Aronson were not discouraged. Indeed they counted the event a great success. Although it was meant to be a one-time effort, the enthusiastic response of the national organizations and the wide favorable publicity it received encouraged both men to try to hold on to the Emergency Mobilization name and concept.

Not the least of their accomplishments, Wilkins and Aronson agreed, was that they had been able through a rigorous screening process to keep Communist and Communist-front groups from taking part in the conclave. Back in those days any hint of Communist involvement was almost certain death for a civil rights campaign. The Emergency Mobilization had avoided that taint. The cohesion and trust the event engendered among its participants was something to build on. At the same time, in deference to Phil Randolph, both men did not want to establish anything that might seem to compete with his National Council.

Since pretty much the same groups were members of both the National Council and the Mobilization, it was decided to proceed under a joint letterhead: "National Council for a Permanent FEPC in Cooperation with the National Emergency Civil Rights Mobilization." It was soon evident, however, that the double name was cumbersome and served no useful purpose.

On December 17, 1951, Arnold Aronson, as secretary of both the National Council and the Mobilization, called representatives of the cooperating organizations together to plan another Washington meeting: a "Leadership Conference on Civil Rights," to be held in February of the following year. The purpose of the new campaign was to seek a revision of Rule 22. The Senate would be urged to limit and close debate on a bill by a simple majority vote.

It was under the Leadership Conference name that the National Council–Mobilization coalition continued from then on.

By 1951, Arnold Aronson had already made, so far as the Leadership Conference was concerned, a serendipitous change in jobs. He had moved from Chicago to Manhattan. He was program director of the National Community Relations Advisory Council (NCRAC—or "Nak-Rak," as its members took to calling it), a coalition of local and national Jewish organizations. His office was only a short walk away from the NAACP headquarters on West Fortieth Street, where Roy Wilkins was located.

Both men considered such physical proximity a valuable factor in carrying on the work of the Leadership Conference. There were no funds for the LCCR in either the NAACP or the NCRAC budget. For the next thirteen years, the Leadership Conference operated out of a desk drawer and filing cabinet in Arnold Aronson's office.

But then, from its inception till almost 1963, the LCCR was essentially committed to a narrow purpose: to reform procedures in the House and Senate that blocked the enactment of effective civil rights legislation.

Every four years a group of LCCR organizational heads, led by Roy Wilkins, came before the Democratic and Republican national conventions to call for the inclusion of a strong civil rights plank in the party platform. Throughout that decade, given a resistant Congress, the major civil rights imperatives urged upon both parties were little different from those Truman had advocated in 1950. LCCR spokesmen (women had yet to emerge within its leadership ranks) often took to Capitol Hill, too. Whenever a civil rights bill was introduced, they testified gamely before congressional committees, no matter how futile an exercise that was. At the very top of the LCCR's legislative agenda was its call for fundamental change in Senate Rule 22.

It was in the course of the Rule 22 campaigns that Joe Rauh became involved in the Leadership Conference. He was general counsel for the United Auto Workers, one of the LCCR's staunchest supporters. As a UAW representative to the Conference, Rauh devised a strategy for changing Rule 22 at the start of a new Congress, and the LCCR adopted the proposal as the one it sought to advance.

But since the proposal was highly legalistic, Rauh recalled in one of my later conversations with him, "the Conference sort of adopted me, too. I was the only person who thoroughly understood the argument for the change, so I was the de facto counsel in the filibuster rule fight." In the easy way such things were arranged in the Conference, which operated then without a constitution or bylaws, Rauh was designated as LCCR's general counsel.

He held that position for the next forty-one years, Conference leaders insisting he was "indispensable," even when after his eightieth birthday his health began to deteriorate seriously. In March of 1991, however, Joe Rauh, ever the realist, declared his indispensability was "nonsense," that the job needed a younger, more vigorous man. And so, indifferent to attempts to persuade him to reconsider, he resigned. He died in 1992.

Testimony before national conventions and congressional committees and lobbying sorties on Capitol Hill were only one phase of the Conference's work.

Protest and advocacy were other aspects of the Conference's activities. In the aftermath of the Supreme Court's *Brown* school desegregation decision in 1954, it agitated for government intervention to protect black students from harassment when those seeking to enter the Little Rock, Arkansas, Central High were attacked. The LCCR urged President Eisenhower to condemn the virtual anarchy that was the Deep South's response to *Brown*—the southern governors' declaration of "massive resistance" to the decision, and the "Southern Manifesto" of 1956, signed by 101 members of Congress including every southern senator except three, Lyndon Johnson, Estes Kefauver, and Albert Gore. That extraordinary statement deplored the court's ruling for "destroying the amicable relations between the white and Negro races" and pledged a campaign to overturn it.

Whenever it could, the Conference staged events to call national attention to the sufferings of black Americans. In 1955, it organized Bill of Rights Day rallies in twelve states to protest the denial of constitutional guarantees. In 1956, in the vast Interdepartmental Auditorium in Washington, the LCCR convened a "court of inquiry." There, under the scrutiny of network cameras and the questioning of prominent civil rights attorneys, Joe Rauh among them, a national audience could see and hear the harrowing testimony of some of the victims of southern bigotry: a South Carolina contractor forced out of business by economic reprisal and KKK threats because he petitioned his school board to integrate the public schools; a Mississippi NAACP official who was shot and almost killed because he registered to vote; the Reverend Ralph Abernathy, a participant in the Montgomery, Alabama, bus boycott; and Autherine Lucy, the young black woman who came to national attention after she was insulted and pelted with eggs and stones when she tried to enroll in the University of Alabama.

That "court of inquiry" is an event I remember well. It was my first encounter with the Leadership Conference. I was there as a reporter on special assignment.

In the course of covering the U.S. Supreme Court for Fairchild, I had become acquainted with the nationally known journalist I. F. Stone. In journalistic circles he was considered to be one of the best newspapermen in America. But in the 1950s, at the height of the anti-Communist hysteria, given the fearful, cowed nature of the media, there was not a major newspaper in the country that would have dared hire Stone, owing to his leftist orientation. To earn a livelihood, he launched his own newsletter, *I. F. Stone's Weekly*. It quickly won a large, loyal following, counting Albert Einstein, Bertrand Russell, and Eleanor Roosevelt among its readers.

But meeting a deadline every week was an exhausting job, even when the publication was a mere four-page journal. Stone was on the lookout for an assistant. I am happy to say he liked the way I wrote and invited me to become a contributor to the *Weekly*. In the course of the next few years, I moonlighted for the letter, submitting about a piece a month on civil rights issues and congressional matters of no interest to Fairchild.

I even edited the *Weekly* for a month, when Izzy Stone decided that he, as a Socialist and philosophical Marxist, should take time off and visit the Soviet Union. And here, in indignation, I feel I must digress and rise in I. F. Stone's defense. For in recent years, Stone, who died in 1989, has been accused of being a Communist agent and even a spy for the Russians. I believe such charges are slanderous. Stone, as I remember, came back from the Soviet Union bitterly disillusioned by what he found there. He said so in subsequent issues of the *Weekly*—a declaration that provoked a rash of subscription cancellations by a goodly number of his far-left readers.

While he and I had occasional ideological disagreements, I admired the man and enjoyed writing for the *Weekly*. I particularly welcomed the assignment to cover the Leadership Conference's "court of inquiry," for I was deeply moved by the witnesses. I would have been amazed to know that within seven years of that night I would be offered a chance to work for the LCCR.

In hindsight, it was perhaps inevitable that the Leadership Conference would eventually outgrow the confines of Arnold Aronson's desk and filing-cabinet drawers. For in the 1950s, the upsurge of dramatic nonviolent demonstration—Rosa Parks's refusal to move from her seat when the bus driver ordered her to; little black children trudging stolidly past jeering crowds on their way to schools newly opened to them; black citizens refusing to respond to unprovoked attacks as they marched peacefully to assert their right to register and vote—began to rouse the nation from lethargy and indifference. Even a glacial Congress began to respond to the changing temper of the times.

In 1957, in what Leadership Conference officials considered a significant breakthrough, Congress finally enacted a civil rights law. A weak one, but a civil rights law nevertheless.

The main provisions of the Civil Rights Act of 1957 were drawn from recommendations set forth some ten years earlier in *To Secure These Rights,* the landmark report of the Truman Committee on Civil Rights. A key section of the bill, Part III, sought to empower the U.S. attorney general to seek injunctions against those who would deprive any citizens of their civil rights. Other sections would protect the right to vote and establish both a Civil Rights Division in the Department of Justice, headed by a U.S. assistant attorney general, and a six-member Commission on Civil Rights, appointed by the president, to investigate deprivations of rights and to collect and study data of such violations.

The bill made it through the House in reasonably good shape. But in the Senate, majority leader Lyndon Johnson, in order to avoid a filibuster and get the measure passed, cut it back drastically. In the course of the Senate maneuvers, most of the new empowerments the House bill would have given the U.S. attorney general were eliminated, and enforcement of the voting rights provisions was weakened. The sections authorizing the Civil Rights Division and the new Civil Rights Commission survived.

Some members of the LCCR were so disappointed at the final version that they were ready to denounce the bill. The American Civil Liberties Union rejected it outright. But Roy Wilkins, Arnold Aronson, Joe Rauh, and, perhaps most persuasive of all, Clarence M. Mitchell, Jr., director of the Washington office of the NAACP, argued that getting any civil rights bill through Congress after eighty-two years of stalling was a significant achievement. Its surviving provisions, they felt, were better than nothing. In the end, sixteen national organizations in the Leadership Conference—the NAACP, the UAW, and the ADA in the forefront—came out in support of the measure.

In 1960, liberal members of Congress who felt that the 1957 act had done little to enfranchise black citizens brought forth another bill. With Johnson in charge of Senate considerations, however, not much was expected to come of it. Yet the bill that was finally enacted did register small gains for civil rights. For one thing, it broadened the U.S. attorney general's powers in voting-rights cases. And it provided a bit more authority to the Civil Rights Commission, which in its brief lifetime gave evidence of becoming a useful agency—in a sense, the federal conscience in civil rights matters.

Nineteen-sixty was also the year in which John F. Kennedy was elected president. Hopes were high in the civil rights community that his ascension to office would made a difference. Hopes were too high, however. Wilkins, Rauh, and Aronson all got a taste of what was in store in brief post-election meetings with Kennedy.

Majority leader Johnson had scheduled a special session of the Senate in the wake of the November elections. Since both the Republican and the Democratic conventions had come out with platforms strongly in support of a federal fair employment program, Rauh and Aronson approached Kennedy in his Capitol Hill office and suggested that since he was still a Senate member, he ought to push for the enactment of an FEPC bill.

Kennedy, Aronson recalls, exploded, saying in substance, Are you two out of your minds? It was evident that he had no intention of moving that fast on civil rights.

He made his reluctance clear again in a subsequent meeting that Wilkins and Aronson had with him while he was still president-elect. They met with him at his suite in the Hotel Carlyle in New York City. The two advocates sought to enlist his support in the next campaign to modify Rule 22, when the new Senate convened. They got a negative response. When they persisted and urged him to use his influence with the new Senate majority leader, Mike Mansfield of Montana, Kennedy said he didn't think he could help there, and added, musingly, "I don't know what Mike Mansfield wants." They pressed him for his views on future civil rights legislation; Kennedy argued that he could advance their cause more readily by executive order. A fair-housing order, he maintained, could end discrimination in that area "with the stroke of a pen."[1] At the end of their conversation, he invited their advice on what could be done to end discrimination in federal programs.

Arnold Aronson's most vivid recollection of that disappointing encounter is of the physical circumstances of the meeting. It was noon, so Kennedy ordered lunch while they sat and talked. But he ordered lunch only for himself. And when the meal arrived, he sat and ate it in front of his two guests. "The son of a bitch," Aronson said, "didn't even offer us a cup of coffee."

Nevertheless, they responded to his request for suggestions. Their reply was one of the LCCR's most important studies. The report, *Federally-Supported Discrimination,* which Wilkins and Aronson delivered to the White House in 1961, documented how federal funds were being used to subsidize racial ineq-

---

1. On November 22, 1962, after much importuning from civil rights forces, Kennedy made good on his promise and issued an executive order on housing. It had little substantive effect.

uities in housing, employment, education, and an array of government services. The authors of the report outlined a course of executive action that could be taken to eliminate racial discrimination in any federally supported program. Notwithstanding Kennedy's expressed reluctance to take the legislative route, they outlined in a footnote the kinds of civil rights bills they felt were sorely needed.

The report became the basis for President Kennedy's Executive Order on Fair Housing and, ultimately, for an important section of the Civil Rights Act of 1964. That was Title VI, which prohibited discrimination in any federally funded program or activity. In Arnold Aronson's opinion, this has become one of the most effective portions of the law, since it blocks discriminatory acts "wherever the federal dollar goes."

It is useful, in light of future concerns of the Leadership Conference, to consider what the report did not say. The discriminations it documented were those directed against Negroes. It noted, moreover, that such discriminations are "suffered by other Americans as well, solely because of their race, religion, nationality or ethnic background." But "sex," "age," "physical disability," "sexual orientation" had not yet entered the civil rights movement's vocabulary when its leaders spoke of discrimination.

Initially, civil rights was low on President Kennedy's agenda—understandably, since he had no wish to antagonize Congress as he pursued what he felt were more important legislative goals. Events, however, finally compelled him to reconsider his priorities.

By 1963, the South was in turmoil. Throughout the region every assertion by blacks and their supporters of the simple rights of citizenship became a provocation. Lunch-counter sit-ins, Freedom Rides, orderly demonstrations, attempts to register and vote were being turned into bloody confrontations by enraged and frightened whites. A nation was outraged by nightly scenes on TV of unarmed, unresistant men, women, and children being knocked to the ground by firehose water jets, beaten with clubs, and set upon by dogs.

Faced with mounting civil disorder, Kennedy was forced to act. On June 11, in a nation-wide broadcast, he urged the country and Congress to face "a moral issue," to see "that race has no place in American life or law." On June 19 he sent to Capitol Hill the most sweeping civil rights bill that had ever come before Congress. And on June 22, in response to his summons, the country's major civil rights leaders came to Washington to discuss the crisis and advise the president as to what they could do to help him deal with it.

Prominent among the men who assembled that morning in the Cabinet

Room of the White House, were Martin Luther King, Jr., who had commanded national attention with the demonstrations he organized and led; Roy Wilkins and the NAACP Washington bureau chief, Clarence Mitchell; Phil Randolph; two labor movement representatives, Walter Reuther, president of the United Auto Workers, and UAW counsel Joe Rauh; and Arnold Aronson.

All of those in attendance applauded Kennedy's actions, convinced that the terrible upheavals in the South offered a historic opportunity for legislative advance. The president was less enthusiastic. He felt he had nothing to gain politically from what he had done, and much to lose. A recent poll, he told the group, showed his popularity dropping below 50 percent for the first time in his presidency. He thought he might even be endangering his chances for a second term. Nevertheless, he was determined to stay the course. Now, he wanted to know, what could they do for him?

The president was no doubt unaware that the answer to that question involved a bit of fancy footwork. A strong sense of rivalry and wariness of each other existed among the members of the group. Although their organizations all belonged to the Leadership Conference, each one felt inclined to act primarily in his own self-interest.

Walter Reuther, who, it was suspected, had a fairly low regard for Roy Wilkins's capabilities, was already jockeying to take the lead in public interest lobbying for the president's civil rights bill. He had invited at least a dozen of the men present to join him for lunch at the Statler Hotel on K Street after the White House meeting. There he was expected to propose a lobbying effort that he would subsidize and lead, independent of the Leadership Conference, even though the UAW was a member of the coalition.

But Wilkins was aware of Reuther's ploy. Arnold Aronson had gotten wind of it, probably from Joe Rauh. So Wilkins now preempted Walter Reuther. Before anyone else could reply to Kennedy, he advised the president that the LCCR was opening an office in Washington immediately, to coordinate a day-to-day campaign by its members on behalf of the new civil rights bill.

After that announcement, the president was considerably less pleased to hear from Phil Randolph that he and several others were planning a march on Washington in the next month or so, to keep the nation aware of black America's problems. Kennedy feared such a march could touch off civil disruption right there in Washington and provoke congressional backlash at the very start of debate on the bill. He declared, "We want success in Congress, not just a show on the Capitol." But he recognized there was nothing he could do to stop the event, and the meeting concluded amicably enough.

Joe Rauh carried away one more significant impression. Vice President

Lyndon Johnson was at the meeting; as a senator he had been unpopular among the activists for his seeming opposition to civil rights legislation. Yet when Rauh expressed his opinion that the president's bill didn't go far enough, and wondered how the administration would feel if the LCCR pushed for an FEPC provision and other extensions, Johnson, to Rauh's surprise, said in substance to go ahead: "It'll be good to have someone to the left of us."

Appropriately, it remained for Phil Randolph to suggest an unofficial name for the bill. "It is," he declared sonorously, "a Magna Carta for Civil Rights."

By the time Joe Rauh and I met in the Democratic Club, plans were already under way to carry out Roy Wilkins's pledge of an LCCR campaign for the Civil Rights Act of 1963.

Rauh proceeded to fill me in on the essentials. Walter Reuther, deferring to Wilkins, had agreed to underwrite most of the lobbying effort, not as president of the UAW but in his other capacity as president of the Industrial Union Department, AFL-CIO. I was familiar enough with labor union politics to be aware of what was involved in this arrangement.

When the country's two major labor coalitions, the American Federation of Labor (AFL) and the Congress of Industrial Organizations (CIO), merged in 1955 with George Meany of the AFL heading the new amalgamation, the constitution established the Industrial Union Department, presumably to offer the CIO unions special services but actually to preserve them as a distinct entity—in short, to give Walter Reuther his own domain.

The IUD, as I came to know, prided itself on maintaining the old CIO's progressive spirit, its readiness to move beyond labor's own self-interest and address a broad range of social issues. Where George Meany was reluctant to involve the federation in joint action with non-labor groups, even though he was not unsympathetic to the struggle for civil rights, the IUD with Reuther at its head made common cause with many organizations outside the labor movement.

The IUD was already in the process of finding office space in downtown Washington for the LCCR campaign. Logically, Arnold Aronson was the one to head that office, but he could not suspend his duties as NCRAC's program director and relocate in the capital. So they were scouting for someone else, and that brought Rauh to me.

I was elated at the prospect of devoting all my energies to a civil rights issue. But as we got into the particulars of the job, Rauh brought me down to earth with a bump. The IUD would pay my salary, of course; but as Rauh saw it, the lobbying campaign was a short-term, one-time affair, an intensive effort that by his estimate would take about three months. Was it possible for me to get a leave of absence from Fairchild for so short a period? Somewhat deflated, I agreed to get back to him with a quick reply.

I put the question to Fairchild's bureau chief, Jack Norman. (Harry Ressiguie, who'd hired me, had retired by then, and Norman, as senior member of our staff, was his successor.)

"A leave of absence?" Norman pondered the matter in his reticent, deliberate way. "I'll ask New York for you, but I'll tell you now. The answer will be no."

He was right. If I left Fairchild for no matter how short a time, the New York bosses said, I had to know I'd be leaving for good.

I took the sad news back to Rauh. But Joe was not one to give up. After consultation with Reuther's assistant, Jack Conway, who ran the IUD operation, he came back with another offer. The IUD would put me on its payroll as a full-time employee—salary, benefits, the whole works—and assign me to the LCCR office.

And after three months? I wondered. What happened then?

"Oh," Rauh said airily, "I'm sure IUD will find something else for you to do."

So I went back to Jack Norman, and Jack, recognizing the gravity of the choices I was facing, saw the need for extreme measures. He took me out to lunch.

"Marv," he said, "Fairchild would be sorry to lose you. But let me speak to you, now, as a friend. Let me tell you something. I've had experience with labor unions, and I've got to say the unions are the worst employers there are. Sure, they'll take you on, use you for their needs, and when they're through with you—zip. You'll get the old heave-ho."

That gave me pause. More than a week had gone by, and I still could not give Rauh a final answer.

At home, needless to say, Naomi and I talked of nothing else but Joe Rauh's offer—whenever, that is, we found a moment of quiet away from the kids. Freya was twelve then, Annie nine, and Bennett seven. Never had they seemed more tender and vulnerable to me than at that moment when I was pondering what to do with my life.

I vacillated, confronted by considerations of principle—and practicality.

Never before had I been paid for anything I'd done in the cause of civil rights. As a matter of principle, I wouldn't dream of asking to be paid. That was a basic assumption with me: it guaranteed my dedication—and my independence. I could always walk away from an enterprise if I found I disagreed with it—my experience with the Progressive Party being a good example. But could I quit a campaign if I were tied to it by a paycheck? What happened then to my self-respect? Such was the nature of my high-minded reluctance.

As I mulled the matter over, I began to have practical worries, too—job security, for one thing. I was troubled by Jack Norman's warning. No doubt the IUD would give me a substantial raise in pay—at first. But suppose after three months, the bill enacted, the IUD decided it had no more use for my services and laid me off? What then? Was it fair to my family to run that risk?

These were the sort of questions I addressed to my wife, time and time again. And she, trained in the psychologist's art of nonjudgmental listening, smiled, shrugged, shook her head, and said, "Oh, honey. That's something only you can decide."

And so I tossed and turned, in bed and out of it, until one night in the middle of a midnight wrangle with myself I sat up. I shook Naomi's shoulder gently. "I've made my mind up," I said. "I'm going to try for the job. What the hell? I'll never get a chance like this again."

"Oh good," my dear wife mumbled, rolling away from me. "Maybe now we'll get some sleep."

Early the next day I called Joe Rauh and told him. He was glad, but cautioning. "I'll put your name right in. My recommendation'll carry weight, of course. But remember, I don't have the final say."

As it turned out, though, he did. Once he passed the word along to Jack Conway, things resolved themselves quickly. Conway invited me up to his office for an interview, and since it was almost noon when I got there, he took me along with him to a big labor-conference luncheon in the Lafayette Hotel, next door to the AFL-CIO building on Sixteenth Street. He asked me perfunctory questions from time to time even as he conversed with eight other people at our table. Afterwards, as we stood outside on the sidewalk shaking hands, he said, "Joe recommends you very highly. Come by Monday morning, if you can, and we'll begin arranging to take you on."

I returned to the Fairchild office in a tumult of feeling. Harry Ressiguie had hired me on a Friday morning. On a Friday afternoon, I asked Jack Norman for a private conference and told him, to his head-shaking disapproval, that I was giving notice.

About once a month, most often on a Saturday night, Neighbors, Inc., held an open house. Naomi and I went to one less than forty-eight hours after I had told Jack Norman I was leaving Fairchild. Keyed up and agitated at the bright but uncertain prospect before me, I could not keep it secret. I told several NI members I felt close to about the momentous change I was about to make in my career.

One of my confidants was Walter Hanula, a sculptor, whose family had been drawn to the neighborhood because it was racially integrated and because of NI's purposes.

"Ah," he said cruelly, after listening to me. "I see how it is, Marvin. What heretofore you've done out of hot passion, now you'll do for cold cash!"

14

The Fight for the 1963 Act Begins

On the morning of July 2, 1963, I met Arnold Aronson for the first time; our years of collaboration began that day. Of even more consequence to me, however, was the realization as we worked together that I had gained a wonderful mentor and friend.

The occasion for our meeting was a hastily convened follow-up assembly, in New York City, of organizations eager to respond to President Kennedy's call for help in getting his civil rights bill through Congress.

Although I was not yet officially off Fairchild's payroll and on the IUD's, the transition was so far under way that I had no trouble getting Jack Norman's permission to go. Jack Conway and I took an early shuttle up to La Guardia and a taxi to the National Community Relations Advisory Council offices on West Forty-second Street.

Joe Rauh was already there. He and Arnold were engrossed in talk of agenda and tactic. I had time for just a fleeting impression of Aronson—of a slender, wiry man of middle height and trim appearance, of close-cropped grey hair, shrewd eyes behind steel-rimmed glasses, speech flavored with the broad *a*'s of his native Boston. (Back in D.C., I got used to phone calls from New York that began: "Mahv? Ahnie.") Then I was pressed into service.

A brief Leadership Conference opening statement was needed for the meeting and for a press release. Since I, as Joe Rauh pointed out, was a writer, I was assigned the task of composing it. A reporter still, I jotted down notes as Joe and Arnold sketched out for me what was wanted. Then I was led to a vacant typewriter. I cannot remember now what I wrote. But after twenty minutes of cogitation and rapid keyboard work, I brought the first draft back to the three of them, for Conway was now engaged in the preparations, too. They examined what I'd written, and Aronson, mainly, had changes to suggest. The re-draft passed muster and was handed over to Arnold's secretary to be retyped.

From the sidelines, idle, I could observe Aronson more closely. He struck me as someone quick-witted and skilled at repartee, remarkably adept at shuffling papers even as he puffed on a cigarette. And yet in brief moments of repose, that thin, white face had a profoundly pensive look.

The statement I wrote was the first of countless LCCR statements, papers, flyers, memos that Joe and I and Arnold worked on. Usually, Joe and I, in Washington, would draft the copy, and for run-of-the-mill matters what we came up with was usually good enough. But when we were engaged on an important document—congressional testimony, for example, or a position paper—even after the two of us were satisfied with it, Joe would usually say, "Now let's let Arnold cast a cold eye over this." And more often than not, after Arnold Aronson's inspection, we would end up with suggested changes that Joe and I agreed improved and sharpened what we had to say.

The gathering at the Roosevelt Hotel in downtown Manhattan consisted mainly of representatives from Leadership Conference member organizations. Their number was augmented by representatives of unaffiliated groups, the National Council of Churches chief among them, who were eager to bring their organizations into the lobbying campaign.

Joe Rauh briefed the assemblage on the administration's bill. The representatives unanimously endorsed it as well as Rauh's suggestions for strengthening the measure. Martin Luther King then took the floor to announce Phil Randolph's call for a march on Washington. Randolph, as chairman of the event, designated his close associate, Bayard Rustin, to be his deputy and chief organizer. The date of the march was to be Wednesday, August 28, only seven weeks away. Although some questions were raised about whether it was possible to organize a mobilization on such short notice and whether it was feasible to hold it on a working day, the march, too, received unanimous approval.

Delegates to the meeting reacted enthusiastically, I was glad to hear, to one more announcement—that the Leadership Conference planned to open a

Washington office to coordinate full-time lobbying for the Civil Rights Act of 1963.

Since it was the general expectation that Congress would dispose of the bill in a few months, the IUD looked for something it could acquire quickly and cheaply. It settled on a suite in the Mills Building, a worn-out structure only a block from the White House, on the corner of Seventeenth Street and Pennsylvania Avenue. Desks and chairs, tables and filing cabinets were bought from an association that was closing up shop in the same building. The IUD sent a batch of typewriters over on loan.

As Arnold Aronson's newly hired assistant, I soon found myself in charge, seated at an old battle-scarred desk in a shabby office, still furnished with the previous tenant's dusty brown-and-white swag draperies, and cooled by several old but operable air-conditioning units chugging away on the broad, chipped sills of our three high-ceiling rooms.

The rest of the staff was assembled as hastily as I and the office furniture. *My* assistant was one of Joe Rauh's old associates, Violet Gunther, former executive director of Americans for Democratic Action. Our secretary, whom I acquired after numerous turndowns by applicants who were put off by the temporary nature of the job, was a newcomer from the South, a young black woman, Geraldine Boykin.

A churchwoman representative to the Leadership Conference who knew how desperate we were for office help put me in touch with Geraldine. ("You'll like her," the representative said. "She's a *dear* girl.")

Recently up from North Carolina, Geraldine Boykin had a pleasant, good-natured demeanor that gave no hint of her strong convictions on matters of racial equality. A government agency had hired her as a secretary, but she was so upset by the discrimination she encountered ("I saw black lawyers working as mail clerks") that she quit. When I caught up with her, she was working as an unpaid volunteer in an office that the National Urban League had made available to local organizers of the march on Washington. We met at an Urban League reception late one afternoon, leaning against a wall, facing each other as we talked.

Unfazed by the shortcomings of what I had to offer—the modest pay, the prospect of long hours, the chance that she might be out of work again in a few months—she responded instead to what I was able to convey to her of the importance of what we were about to undertake.

Yes, she said, she'd come and work for me. And she gave me a broad, dazzling, gap-toothed smile. "It sounds real interesting."

So far as I was concerned, there was one more person who was a member of the LCCR's Washington office force—someone unacknowledged officially, and physically not even on the premises. This was Howard Holman, the IUD's controller. A strong union man and a devout Catholic who sought to live his religious beliefs, Holman was attracted to the goals of the Leadership Conference. It was he who found and rented and equipped the LCCR office before I came on board. It was Holman I turned to in any early office emergency. Until I finally found Geraldine Boykin, he somehow managed to send a succession of IUD secretaries over as temporaries. Whenever I needed large-scale duplications, whenever I had a mailing to get out, Howard Holman was on hand, ready to stay on after office hours to do a runoff for me in the IUD's well-equipped mailroom.

As time went on, he found a printer for us and added the Leadership Conference's bookkeeping to his heavy IUD schedule.

Today, in retirement, we are still good friends.

Leadership of the lobbying campaign on Capitol Hill was assumed by Clarence M. Mitchell, Jr., director of the NAACP's Washington bureau. That, I later learned from Arnold Aronson, was something of a coup for the Conference. Although the NAACP was one of the founding members of the LCCR and Roy Wilkins its chairman, Mitchell had always been somewhat skeptical of the importance or effectiveness of the coalition. He and Roy were not on the best of terms, and there was a strong sense of rivalry between them. Even so, Mitchell agreed to become our legislative chairman and direct the lobbying by representatives of the fifty-two participating organizations.

At fifty-two, Clarence Mitchell was a seasoned lobbyist. He had directed the NAACP's bureau since 1950 and represented it in all legislative matters.

A large, heavy-set, powerful black man, Mitchell carried with him the physique and confidence of the amateur boxer he had been in his youth, when he fought under the name of "the Shamrock Kid." Impeccably dressed, stately, slow and thoughtful of speech, he had the air of a tribal chieftain.

But Mitchell brought more than just a courtly, dignified presence to his work. He was unique among lobbyists for public interest groups. He was one of the few who had mastered the rules and procedures of the House and Senate. In later years, when honors for his life's work were rained upon him, many members of Congress took to calling him "the 101st Senator." It was more than just a sobriquet. It was recognition of the fact that he inhabited the Hill and its atmosphere as much as any member of Congress. When representatives and senators met with him, it was often as though they met with a colleague. He was a careful analyst who knew the details of the bill under consideration as well or even better than they, a good parliamentarian, and—most important of all—a good vote counter.

Besides presence and high technical competence, Mitchell brought other resources to his job: patience, a feel for the deliberate pace of Congress, and a realistic idea of what it was possible to accomplish. These qualities sometimes subjected him to the scorn of young, militant members of the NAACP and other black civil rights organizations, who saw him as a temporizer and compromiser. A lot of this criticism was unfair. If he compromised, it was because circumstances convinced him there was no other course. If he held his temper, it was because he knew losing it could lose the battle. It took a while, sometimes, to know when Clarence Mitchell was angry and struggling to control himself. A certain steeliness would creep into his eyes; his lips would curl into a slight, sardonic smile. If he were in the ring and looked like that, you'd realize that the fight would be over soon.

Mitchell brought one conspicuous failing to his work with the Leadership Conference. It was a tendency to carry on a lobbying campaign by himself or with the aid of only a few trusted allies, Joe Rauh first among them, and after that perhaps Andrew Biemiller, legislative director of the AFL-CIO, a former Wisconsin congressman and a seasoned lobbyist himself. Biemiller shared Clarence's notion that the most effective lobbying could be done in small meetings, personal encounters, and private deals. Both men chafed under the restraints of coalition effort; professionals, they became impatient when they had to accommodate their pace and their instinctive tactics to the floundering efforts of newcomers and slow learners.

The Washington office of the NAACP reflected Mitchell's reluctance to share his authority and responsibilities with others. That was evident in the smallness of the staff: it consisted of one assistant, J. Francis Pohlhaus, a very able white attorney, as devoutly Catholic as Howard Holman and a modest, self-effacing man who readily left the limelight to Clarence; and two young black women who did all the secretarial work and mundane office chores.

Representatives of some of the less prestigious or powerful organizations in the Leadership Conference were sometimes alienated by Mitchell's disposition to go it alone. Rauh and Aronson, however, had a strong feeling for the importance of concerted action; they fought constantly, and with considerable success, to keep the lobbying from being confined to a small circle. They firmly believed the Leadership Conference's effectiveness grew from the number of people it involved in its lobbying, particularly representatives of the religious groups.

The bill that the Kennedy administration sent up to Congress on June 19, 1963, was, as Joe Rauh attested in our first meeting, a pretty good one. It was designed to prohibit racial discrimination in most places of public accommodation and in the granting of federal contracts; it authorized the government to withhold funds from school districts that refused to desegregate; it made a start, at least, toward removing barriers to voting.

But the Conference found the bill seriously deficient in at least three respects: the public accommodations section left the way open to exempt many businesses from coverage; the power of the attorney general to seek an injunction in dealing with civil rights violations would be limited to cases involving school desegregation; and omitted entirely was any prohibition against discrimination in employment—for the Leadership Conference, at least, the greatest shortcoming.

On this last issue, the administration was particularly obdurate. Its strategists felt that adding a fair employment practices (FEP) provision was too drastic a step to take. They were convinced it would sink the bill.

A delegation from the Leadership Conference, Clarence Mitchell, Joe Rauh, Andy Biemiller, James Hamilton (Washington representative of the National Council of Churches), and the Reverend Walter Fauntroy, Martin Luther King's Washington representative, met with White House and Justice Department officials and tried to negotiate the addition of what they considered to be three essential provisions: an all-inclusive public accommodations section; a federal FEP program; and what in lobbyist shorthand came to be called "across the board Part III," authorization to the Justice Department to seek injunctive relief in all instances of civil rights violation. When these negotiations failed they turned to Congress, where they found ready allies.

Like most bills that come before Congress, H.R. 7152 (the number assigned to the omnibus bill) originated in the House. It went first to the House Judiciary Committee, whose chairman, the septuagenarian New York Democrat Emanuel Celler, was fully committed to the cause of civil rights. By another stroke of good fortune, the ranking Republican on the committee, a rather prim-looking, unassuming little man, William McCulloch, from the rural town of Piqua, Ohio, shared his chairman's sympathy for the legislation. Although there were occasional flare-ups and misunderstandings and interparty tension between them, the two men for the most part worked in harmony. They were the chief framers of the bill that finally cleared the House.

For the initial hearings, Celler assigned the bill to Subcommittee No. 5, which was also chaired by him. Celler readily agreed to add an FEP section, and other subcommittee members agreed to strengthen the public accommodations and Part III provisions. The subcommittee Democrats were ready to act despite the administration's objections and despite Attorney General Robert Kennedy's assertion that what the Leadership Conference wanted in pressing for an FEP provision was "an issue, not a bill."

A remark like that seemed to encapsulate the reluctance the Kennedy administration brought to the fight for civil rights. We thought we understood why the Kennedys resisted our appeals to enlarge the bill. Jack Kennedy had won the presidency by the smallest margin in American history. Since he was already campaigning for reelection, he felt he could ill afford to antagonize Southern Democrats further and solidify their opposition to his entire legislative program and to his efforts to win a second term.

In an acute analysis of the situation, Joe Rauh once wrote of Kennedy that rather than moving to implement the Democratic platform promises that had helped him win the Negro vote in 1960, the president was content "to limit himself to patchwork improvement." Rauh was of the opinion that in 1964 Kennedy would be ready to run "on his unprecedented record of Negro appointments and aggressive Executive action."

What that meant for us was that opposition to our efforts to broaden and strengthen the administration's measure was not going to come from just the southern members of Congress. Robert Kennedy's intemperate accusation was evidence of that.

The LCCR soon established a mode of operation that it adhered to throughout the long months of lobbying for H.R. 7152.

Once a week, usually on Wednesday, at 2 p.m., representatives of the participating organizations would crowd into the conference room on the third floor of the Mills Building. Once settled in the rows of folding chairs or on the windowsills, or leaning against the back wall, they would be briefed on the latest legislative situation. They would go on to compare notes on what they were doing to mobilize the support of their memberships. Then they would take assignments—representatives and senators who needed to be checked out to determine their positions on whatever was the critical issue of the moment.

Clarence Mitchell presided at these sessions with Joe Rauh at his side.

Rauh and Mitchell had begun teaming up as lobbyists years before the LCCR Washington office opened. On any civil rights issue they were often inseparable. Rauh's proudest moment in the course of their alliance occurred, he often said, during the Senate debate on the Civil Rights Act of 1957. Mitchell and he were sitting together in the gallery, as they often did, when Senator Harry Flood Byrd, Jr., singled them out for special attention. Pointing up at them, the reactionary Virginia Democrat exclaimed, "There they are! The Gold Dust Twins!"[1]

Arnold Aronson came down by train from New York for almost every one of the weekly meetings.

After the legislative briefing session was over, he, Vi Gunther, and I would meet to discuss what the office needed to do by way of support and follow-up. I was impressed by his flair for PR and his gift for devising ways to dramatize an issue. Aronson proposed the *Memo,* which the Conference sent out to members almost every week during the lobbying campaign for H.R. 7152. As a report on the progress of the bill and a call for specific action, it quickly became a mainstay of the lobbying effort.

It was Aronson who suggested that when we listed House Judiciary Committee members, whose votes were critical in the early consideration of the bill, our *Memo*s give not only their parties and districts but also their religious affiliations, the national organizations they belonged to, and the names of their largest contributors. Such information was often extremely useful to any Conference group planning to visit a member's Capitol Hill or home office.

Aronson was the one who usually picked up on incidents and news stories that could be spread about to illustrate the issues embodied in the bill.

Joe and Clarence often lingered on after the weekly meeting to discuss strategy with Arnold and me. And when Arnold was in New York, he stayed in touch with us by phone almost every day.

From the beginning of the campaign it was recognized in the Conference that religious organizations could become a powerful force in our lobbying. Civil rights had been a concern of several prominent national religious groups for some time, and the major faiths were at least represented in the Leadership Conference when it first began. But racial segregation was endemic in many denominations. It was not until the late fifties that church groups underwent critical self-examination. By the early sixties, religious organizational membership in the Conference increased significantly, and the groups began to take a more active part in the work of the LCCR. That Martin Luther King was a minister was no doubt an important factor in their determination to join the legislative battle.

The emphasis on a moral or religious obligation may have obscured other

1. "The Gold Dust Twins" referred to the logo of a popular scouring powder. It depicted two identical siblings—African, from their black bodies and kinky hair. It was another of the insensitive stereotypes of black Americans current at the time.

imperatives in the civil rights struggle. The great demonstration of the summer of 1963, the August 28 March on Washington, was officially a "March for Jobs and Freedom." But the economic component was often ignored. Moral principle appeared to be the overriding consideration. Although ten national figures representing civil rights, labor, and religious groups led the march, it is remembered today as Dr. King's march, and the one speech that remains in the public memory out of the dozen or so delivered is perhaps the most eloquent, King's "I Have a Dream" speech.

King himself had little to do with organizing the march. The Leadership Conference took no part in the organizational logistics, either. However, the focus of the march was on the passage of the civil rights bill, and the Conference was actively engaged in mustering support for that objective. The organizers and speakers represented groups that were Leadership Conference affiliates. The LCCR briefed marchers on the legislation and arranged meetings between the march leaders and key House and Senate members.

As the principal organizer of the march, Bayard Rustin deserves a major share of the credit for its success. Yet that success was as much a surprise to him as it was to both its supporters and its critics. Although it was widely publicized and extraordinary effort was expended on its behalf, a good deal of the organizing was hastily done. If you had asked him the night before, Rustin would have been hard put to estimate how many people would show up.

Those critical of the march raised objections that could not be lightly dismissed. The Kennedy administration shared the widespread public fear that the march might provoke a riot and result in a serious setback to the campaign for the bill. Alternatively, if the march drew a sparse crowd, that could be taken as a sign of a lack of public interest, and the bill's chances with a volatile and timorous Congress might be hurt.

Even organizations participating in the march had doubts about it. Although major Catholic organizations backed it, Washington's Archbishop Patrick A. O'Boyle, for one, feared violence and sent word out that nuns were not to take part in the event. It is not known how many disobeyed his order, but there were surely nuns in plentiful evidence.

Although many labor unions took part in the march and the IUD was deeply involved in it, George Meany, to his subsequent regret, would not let the AFL-CIO participate as an official body.

Since the Leadership Conference took no part in the march as an entity, I had to decide which organization I would march with. The IUD was the logical choice. But many Neighbors, Inc., members were eager to be there, choosing to ignore all dire predictions of violence. So about forty of us, including the entire Caplan family, rallied by previous arrangement in front of the National Theater on F Street and strolled over to the Ellipse and marched together in the parade to the Lincoln Memorial.

Whatever doubts and apprehensions there may have been about the march vanished before the event itself. It was, as everyone knows today, an immense success. In the middle of a workweek, in the middle of a Washington summer, at least 250,000 people took time off from their jobs and daily routines to convene in the nation's capital. The number exceeded Bayard Rustin's most optimistic expectations.

Instead of a riot atmosphere, the day was marked by a spirit of almost idyllic calm. The marching and the speeches from the steps of the Lincoln Memorial were stirring and militant. But the event might well have been occurring in the Forest of Arden. If you looked about on that bright August day you saw people lounging on the grass, picnicking in the shade of old trees, or sitting directly below the Memorial along the rim of the reflecting pool, soaking their hot, tired feet in its waters.

The impact of the march on the nation and Congress was considerable. Senators and representatives who attended the event were faced with an enormous crowd chanting, "Pass the Bill! Pass the Bill!" And House Speaker John W. McCormack, Democrat of Massachusetts, after visiting the Lincoln Memorial area and meeting with leaders of the march, said he thought a fair-employment practices provision could win approval in the lower chamber.

Only after the event did I learn from Arnold Aronson of a crisis behind the scenes that threatened to turn the march into a public relations disaster.

The leaders of the civil rights movement were scheduled to address the marchers, and so the night before the event the texts of their speeches were released to the press. Since it was assumed that all the orators were committed to call for passage of the civil rights bill before the House, consternation gripped the participants when they discovered that one of their number, a black man, was going to speak out against it. This was the youngest speaker, twenty-five-year-old John Lewis, chair of the Student Nonviolent Coordinating Committee. He was going to pronounce the bill worthless and urge that it be rejected. What's more, he was going to call for militant protest.

Randolph, Wilkins, Reuther, Aronson—all his seniors took the young renegade aside and urged him to reconsider. It was a tense interlude. The whole intention of a peaceful demonstration seemed endangered. Word of Lewis's dissent leaked out, and a thrill of fear ran through some of the key supporters of the march. Several of them threatened to quit.

Out of deference to Randolph, Lewis finally allowed himself to be persuaded to back down and drop offensive passages from his speech.

The march went off without incident. And Lewis went on to become one of the most highly regarded graduates of the civil rights demonstrations of the sixties. In 1981, he won election to the House as representative of Georgia's Fifth District (including the city of Atlanta). He has emerged, in the opinion of many of us, as a wise and generous-spirited member. Evidently his colleagues think so too, for in 1991 he was chosen to be Democratic chief deputy whip, the third-highest position in the House Democratic leadership.

Moving evidence of his evolution from youthful firebrand to responsible lawmaker was displayed not long ago. On March 11, 1997, he took the House floor to pay tribute to someone with whom he had had differences at that critical moment in the March on Washington. The occasion was Arnold Aronson's eighty-sixth birthday.

John Lewis said, in part: "As Americans, we owe a debt of gratitude to Arnold Aronson. We live in a better country, a better society, and a better world because of the work of this civil rights pioneer. I would not be here, I would not be a Member of Congress, but for the hard work, dedication and commitment by Arnold Aronson and others like him." After Lewis finished speaking, he left the well of the House and went up to the gallery, where Aronson sat among friends and members of his family. And there the two men embraced.

All through the summer and into early fall the House Judiciary subcommittee worked on the bill. The deliberations of its members were influenced not only by the lobbying of Leadership Conference representatives but also by events outside of Washington. Most affecting and shocking for members of Congress— and for the entire nation—was the bombing of the Sixteenth Street Baptist Church in Birmingham, Alabama. On Sunday morning, September 15, 1963, four little black girls were killed when a bomb went off under the church steps. Twenty other youngsters were injured. When the police responded with tanks and shotguns to the riot that followed, two more youngsters lost their lives.

Geraldine Boykin recalls her reaction to the bombing. "To hell with the legislation," she remembers thinking. "Let's take to the streets!"

The concentration of the LCCR strategists on the bill and on how to use these terrible, senseless murders to advance its prospects struck her as "crazy." But then any alternative to legislation was, for those of us in the Conference, beyond consideration. En route to Birmingham for the funerals, Roy Wilkins stopped off in Washington and stated the issue with his customary quiet eloquence:

"This outrage," he told the press, "demonstrates the need for going beyond the present bill and enacting legislation that will eradicate the consuming poisons of racial discrimination. . . . In the face of these murders it is obscene to talk about compromise."

In the South itself, the blast stung others into speaking out. National attention was given to a speech by a young Birmingham attorney, Charles Morgan, Jr., who in an address to the Chamber of Commerce asked, "Who did it? Who threw that bomb? We all did it." And on the House floor a young southern freshman, Charles Weltner, Democrat from Atlanta, said he knew why the Birmingham bombing occurred. "It happened because those chosen to lead have failed to lead. Those whose task it is to speak have stood mute."

Before the end of September the House Judiciary Subcommittee No. 5 reported out a version of the bill that was broader and, in the opinion of the Leadership Conference, much better than the measure the administration originally sent to the Hill. It incorporated a number of Conference suggestions, and most important of all, it contained a provision establishing a federal Fair Employment Practices Commission (FEPC). Now H.R. 7152 was sent on to the full House Judiciary Committee, a less friendly venue.

Attorney General Robert Kennedy began at once to attack the subcommittee bill publicly, calling it "impractical," even "extreme," and its supporters (i.e., the LCCR) "extremists." The administration chose to ignore the fact that the provisions it found objectionable did not, as the Leadership Conference pointed out, go beyond anything in the civil rights plank of the platform the Democratic Party had adopted at its 1960 convention.

The attorney general then undertook a campaign to moderate—in the Conference's view, to weaken—the subcommittee bill. Insisting that a scaled-down bill was necessary to win Republican support, he met in private with the full Judiciary Committee and in informal caucus with Chairman Celler and other committee members, forcing delays in committee consideration of the bill until he felt he had collected enough support for his point of view.

His efforts met with some success. On October 29, the full committee by a vote of 19 to 15 defeated a motion to report out the subcommittee bill intact. Then by a vote of 20 to 14 (later amended to 23 to 11), it approved a compromise version that had been worked out by the administration and the Republican leadership.

It was still broader than the original administration bill, but considerably weaker than the version the subcommittee had approved. The FEPC provision was weakened. A commission would be established, but with reduced powers:

for one thing, the commission would not be able to issue final orders once it found a party guilty of discrimination. It would be left to the courts to issue such orders. The bill omitted the broad authority the subcommittee measure would have given the attorney general: to institute civil suits on behalf of any citizens who were denied their constitutional rights. The public accommodations section contained significant exemptions. It didn't cover retail stores, beauty parlors, barber shops, swimming pools, or bowling alleys.

Joe Rauh found it "repugnant."

"If you're a Negro," he observed, "you can eat, sleep, and watch, but you can't participate." In other words, he said, integration in places of public accommodation would be required "except in those places where our bodies touch."

Clarence Mitchell was in the corridor when the full committee broke and announced the bill it had approved. Reporters crowded around him. Furious, struggling to control his temper, he called the administration's conduct in the matter "reprehensible." The tactic of getting the full committee to delay meetings until the administration had enough votes to defeat the motion to accept the subcommittee bill was, he said, "a filibuster."

Deputy Attorney General Nicholas deB. Katzenbach, chief architect of the latest version of the bill, had established himself in Celler's office during the full committee meeting. Now he came over to Clarence and a bit sheepishly shook Clarence's hand and asked him what he thought of the compromise. Clarence expressed his dissatisfaction, particularly with the FEPC provision. Katzenbach said, "Well, Mr. Mitchell, all the other provisions are in there—subpoena power, right of investigation."

"Yes, but the commission cannot issue final orders. Only the courts can, after review," Mitchell said. "You gave us a gun, but you say you can't shoot it." Katzenbach, a large, bald-headed man, with a tie perpetually awry, said, "Yes, but the gun's loaded, Mr. Mitchell."

One of the reporters asked Clarence if half a loaf wasn't better than none.

"I want to be sure it's half a loaf," Clarence replied, "and not a painted one. I want to be able to slice it and eat it."

As we walked down the corridor of the Longworth House Office Building, we encountered Manny Celler and Bess Dick, a tiny, round-shouldered woman with heavy glasses, the chairman's personal secretary and his closest working associate.

"Well, Clarence," Celler asked, "is your tail between your legs?"

"No, Mr. Celler. I wish my teeth were in somebody's pants. I'm not the kind of dog that keeps its tail between its legs."

But Clarence," Celler remonstrated, "we could never have gotten the sub-committee bill through. There would have been a motion to recommit when it reached the House floor, and that would have been the end. We had polls that showed it, Clarence. Polls you don't know of."

"No, Mr. Celler. I only know we had 214 votes in the House for that [sub-committee] bill."

"Clarence, you only talk about the bad things in the bill. What about the good things? Why don't you say something about them?"

"Mr. Celler," Clarence said, "all I know is, you take Part III. A Negro has to institute his own suit before the Justice Department will intervene. That's a terrible burden on colored people, Mr. Celler. The only way you could ever know that would be if you had a black face and lived in the South. That's the tragedy."

Bess Dick, always the arbitrator, a woman divided at that moment between her loyalty to the chairman and her genuine affection for Clarence, approached him and said, "Mr. Mitchell, you come to the office sometime soon. You and the chairman can sit down and talk this over more calmly."

In the taxi on the way back to the NAACP office Clarence slumped back on the seat, easing the strain he was under. With a wry smile he said, "I resent being treated like a fool."

Yet, afterwards, when we looked at the compromise bill more closely, we had to agree it improved significantly on what the administration had originally proposed. The *New York Times* came close to the mark when it observed in an editorial on October 30, "It [the committee bill] is a compromise in the right direction, in the direction of a stronger—not a weaker—bill than the White House had apparently believed was susceptible of committee approval, or even desirable."

Now the bill faced its next hurdle. It was a forbidding one: the House Rules Committee, to which the bill was sent to schedule the time and terms of the House floor debate. The committee's octogenarian, implacably segregationist chairman (Judge) Howard Smith of Virginia, a powerful figure in the Byrd machine, was determined to try to bury the bill.

Time already seemed to be working in his favor. The days it took to get the bill from the Judiciary to the Rules Committee seemed interminable. H.R. 7152 didn't even come before Rules until well into the month of November. It was evident that the full House would not be able to act on the bill before the end of the first session of the Eighty-eighth Congress. Consideration of the measure would have to be carried over to the second session, in 1964.

15

An Unexpected Ally

Most Americans who were alive and aware on Friday, November 22, 1963, re-member the circumstances in which they first heard the news of President John F. Kennedy's assassination.

I had just come back from a quick lunch in the cafeteria around the corner from the Mills Building. The building's sole elevator was waiting, door open, as I entered the lobby. I dashed into the cage, and as we began our ascent the operator, a young black woman, said in a voice of great agitation, "President Kennedy was shot."

"What!" I jerked my head up in disbelief, banging the back of it against the ornate metal grill. "No! Where?"

"Down in Dallas. They say he's hurt bad."

They already knew about it in the office. Geraldine Boykin was standing at her desk, tears streaming down her face. She ran over to me, hugged me, and cried: "They shot the president!"

The office had no TV set or radio. I was of a mind to lock up and go some-place where we could follow the news. But just then the phone rang. It was a cousin of Rita's, the young black woman Geraldine had hired to help with the typing. Her TV set was on. She turned up the volume so that by holding their ears to the receivers Rita and Geraldine could hear the announcer and repeat aloud fragments of what he was saying.

The president and Governor Tom Connally had been shot by an unknown assassin as their motorcade drove through downtown Dallas, the president perhaps fatally. A Secret Service agent was reported as saying, "My God! He's dead!" However, the president was not officially dead, and I kept telling Geraldine and Rita (and myself, privately) over and over that we were not to believe he was.

While they went on repeating bits of whatever they were hearing, I went through my office and into the conference room beyond. Two of its windows were at the front of the building, overlooking the intersection of Seventeenth Street and Pennsylvania Avenue. Outside, the sky was clear and bright. People who had not yet heard the news were strolling about in the mild sunshine. Traffic flowed at a normal rate along the street and the avenue. The broad sidewalk in front of the White House was empty of loiterers. All the flags I could see were flying at full mast. But even as I watched, the scene below began to change. When cars stopped for the light, windows were rolled down and motorists called out to each other. A little knot of people formed outside the White House gate on Pennsylvania Avenue. It quickly grew in size.

There was no mistaking when the end came. At 2 P.M. Rita repeated in a sober tone what the announcer was saying, "The word is official. The president of the United States is dead." We heard a faint, wild, despairing scream.

"My cousin's crying," Rita said.

I was supposed to fly to Cleveland that afternoon to speak at a convention of the National Association of Intergroup Relations Officials, one of our participating organizations. At 3 P.M. I called Cleveland. They said they were still going ahead with the convention and hoped I would come. If I couldn't make it, they said, they would understand. But on reflection, I realized I had no reason not to go. Washington would manage quite well without me.

That evening in the Pick-Carter Hotel, I addressed a grieving assembly on the situation confronting H.R. 7152. I praised the lobbying efforts of many Ohioans in the audience and the work of Congressman William McCulloch; I urged my audience to zero in on Ohio congressman Clarence Brown, the ranking Republican on the House Rules Committee, and to begin, even then, to call on the senators to pass the bill, particularly Senator Frank Lausche, a notoriously unstable vote.

I spent the next day at the convention. Late Saturday night I sat in my hotel room watching TV the way it ought to be, in somber black and white, without commercials; I sat and watched and wept as I listened to the Philadelphia Orchestra, under Eugene Ormandy, play Brahms's "A German Requiem."

The immediate question before the Leadership Conference was this: what could we expect from President Lyndon B. Johnson? Our expectations were low. As Senate majority leader, Johnson had hardly been a friend. He had engineered the compromise that sharply reduced the effectiveness of the Civil Rights Act of 1957. We believed we had him to thank, too, for weakening the Civil Rights Act of 1960. And it was hard to imagine that Johnson, a man known to nourish slights, would not remember that vivid TV image of the LCCR's general counsel, Joe Rauh, jumping to his feet on the floor of the 1960 Democratic convention, when Kennedy announced his running mate and shouting, for the whole nation to hear:

"Jack! Don't do it, Jack!"

And yet what a mass of contradictions Johnson was.

In his memoir, *Breaking Barriers,*[1] journalist Carl T. Rowan gave a concise sketch of the incoming president: "Lyndon Baines Johnson was egocentric, domineering, imperious, mean, insecure, cornpone, unfaithful, crude. He was also generous, brave, a fighter for the little guy, loyal to friends and causes— and damned effective."

It was our good fortune to find ourselves in alliance with the Johnson of Rowan's second sentence.

We surely didn't expect it. We approached his first public appearance with dread. On November 27, a group of us sat together in the LCCR office conference room watching his address to a joint session of Congress as it came to us on a tiny portable TV set we had somehow acquired. We whooped with surprised delight when we heard him say, in his flat-tone Texas drawl, "First, no memorial oration or eulogy could more eloquently honor President Kennedy's memory than the earliest possible passage of the civil rights bill for which he fought so long. We have talked long enough in this country about equal rights. We have talked for one hundred years or more. It is time now to write the next chapter—and to write it in books of law."

Johnson followed rhetoric with action. About ten days after the assassination he placed a call to Joe Rauh and asked Joe to go with him to the funeral of former New York senator and governor Herbert Lehman, an invitation so remarkable that the *Washington Post* ran a front-page story about it. In the course of that journey, Johnson said, "I want to talk to you about civil rights."

1. Carl T. Rowan, *Breaking Barriers* (Boston: Little, Brown, 1991), 236.

Rauh remembered the subsequent meeting with Johnson in the White House as an astonishing encounter. "There was the president of the United States apologizing to me for our past differences." Rauh let the president know that meeting with him was not enough. The Leadership Conference, Rauh said, operated as a group, and Johnson would have to meet with Clarence Mitchell, too. Johnson readily agreed. Mitchell approached the meeting with considerable skepticism. After their fights over the 1957 and 1960 laws, he had no reason to trust the president. He felt, too, that Johnson had been snubbing him. But he was soon persuaded of Johnson's sincerity. In the course of the campaign for the Civil Rights Act of 1964 and in the years after its passage, the two men became close friends. It was a friendship that extended to members of the Johnson family, so that at the memorial service for Clarence Mitchell in Baltimore in 1984, Lynda Johnson Robb was present at her own request to eulogize "Uncle Clarence." In spite of that unfortunate choice of a title, there was no mistaking the genuine fondness she felt for him.

The Leadership Conference now addressed itself to mobilizing grassroots support for the next battle: getting H.R. 7152 through the House Rules Committee. An emergency meeting was convened in the Mayflower Hotel in Washington on December 4, 1963. More than two hundred delegates from around the country attended.

The grassroots effort was already under way. Labor unions were bringing delegations in to meet with members of Congress whose election campaigns they had supported. The National Council of Churches, meeting in triennial session in Philadelphia, urged its four thousand delegates to go home by way of Washington and visit their representatives. Back from an ecumenical council in Rome, Catholic bishops sought to rouse the dioceses.

The support of church groups manifested itself in other ways. Joe Rauh recalled the first time he was aware of the full extent of that support. "I date it from the day Clarence and I were standing outside the House Judiciary Committee waiting for a session to break up so that we could buttonhole members. Twenty-one Episcopalian ministers in full regalia came up and joined us. For me that was the realization of a great shift. When those guys stood up and took their places beside us—that was a watershed for me."

When the bill came before the House Rules Committee, Judge Smith, that ancient tyrant, threw down the gauntlet by announcing bluntly that he would do what he could to keep the bill bottled up in committee. That was a mistake by a man who seldom made mistakes. Representative Richard Bolling, the liberal Missouri Democrat and a member of the Rules Committee, took the announcement as a cue for action. Smith, he told us, "must be losing his flex."

Bolling proposed to file a discharge petition. If a majority of the House, 218 of its 435 members, signed the petition, the Rules Committee would be discharged from further consideration of the bill and it could be brought directly to the floor.

Representative Manny Celler took up Bolling's suggestion. At noon on December 5, before a gallery crowd running heavily to clergymen wearing what the Reverend Robert Spike of the National Council of Churches called their "dog collars," Celler introduced the discharge petition and invited members to come forward and sign it. The petition became the Conference's new rallying cry. Organizations, by mail and phone call, began urging their House members to add their names.

The discharge petition failed. Smith took some of the steam out of the campaign by agreeing to hold hearings on the bill "reasonably soon in January." And congressional courtesy—a greater degree of automatic deference to a committee chairman than ever seemed necessary to me—and congressional apathy finished off the drive. But the campaign for signatures was not a wasted effort. It helped build the national pressure on Congress to act on the civil rights bill. A majority of the Rules Committee's fifteen members, Republicans and Democrats, let Smith know that they were ready at some committee meeting soon to take the bill away from him if he continued to delay. Smith announced that he was scheduling hearings on the bill for January 9, saying, "I know something about the facts of life around here."

Playing possum is an old southern trick. Even as he seemingly gave in to the irresistible tide that was carrying the bill forward—the bombardment of the Hill by mail and delegation, President Johnson's renewed call for speedy action in his State of the Union address—Smith was biding his time until he could launch a new assault. The Rules Committee hearings went off with dispatch. In its last *Memo* for January 1964, the Conference urged everyone to come to Washington for the week of February 3, when the House was scheduled to debate the bill.

The LCCR also announced that it was moving its headquarters to Capitol Hill. It had rented a couple of rooms in the Congressional Hotel, and all visitors were welcome. Major organizations in the Conference began gearing up. The NAACP and the National Urban League were bringing in large delegations. The AFL-CIO was inviting 50 to 60 top union leaders from around the country. The Union of American Hebrew Congregations was bringing in 20

Reform rabbis, some from as far off as California and Hawaii. Six hundred students from the D.C. area and 50 Quaker pastors were going to be on hand. And the American Civil Liberties Union's Art Division, led by such celebrities as Burt Lancaster and Rod Serling, issued a call for the enactment of H.R. 7152.

That week a new harbinger of hope arrived from the South: the *Atlanta Constitution* gave editorial endorsement to the public accommodations section of the bill.

House members were of two minds about the LCCR delegations that came to Capitol Hill once the floor debate on H.R. 7152 got under way on Friday, January 31. Representative Frank Thompson, a New Jersey Democrat, an ardent supporter of the bill, praised this show of public interest during his appearance on a TV newscast. Representative William Colmer, a Mississippi Democrat on the same program, grumbled about "galleries and corridors filled with representatives of organized pressure groups." And James A. Haley, a Florida Democrat, in a floor attack on the legislation declared that if you took away the "vultures in the spectators galleries, who were controlling votes in the House, or at least calling the turn on them . . . I do not think you would have 25 votes for this monstrous bill."

The "vultures" were hundreds of representatives of Conference organizations, who took turns sitting in the House spectator galleries throughout the entire debate, checking on whether or not their members were present for quorum calls and how they were voting on amendments.

In 1964, long before the electronic tally system that the House uses today, voting on bills was a rather primitive and often secretive affair. There were no recorded roll calls on amendments, a situation that some members could use to their advantage in dealing with a bill that many of their constituents liked and they didn't—the civil rights bill, for one. They could vote for weakening amendments, reasonably confident that how they voted would never be known to voters back home. Afterwards, if and when amendments had harmed the bill, they could vote for the measure on final passage when votes did become a matter of public record.

Even if you sat and watched them from the gallery, it wasn't easy to tell how members were voting on amendments. Such votes were conducted in three stages. The chair would first ask for a voice vote on the amendment. If the shouted ayes and nays didn't sound conclusive, the chair or any member could then ask for a vote by "division": members would be asked to stand in turn for or against the amendment, and the chair would count them. A quorum of the Committee of the Whole, as the House designated itself during these deliberations, was 100 members. If the total count on division was less than 100, any member could "note the absence of a quorum."

Bells would then ring all over the House side of Capitol Hill, and all 435 House members would be summoned to the chamber. The chair would designate "tellers," one for the amendment and one against. All the members would then troop up the center aisle ("looks like a sheep's run," one of our gallery watchers once remarked) while the tellers, standing opposite each other, would clap and count each shoulder as it passed under their hands and, in the end, call out the totals to the chair.

Confronted by the rapid and chaotic movement on the floor, forced to view proceedings from above at a considerable height and distance, the "vultures" would sit and crane their necks, trying to recognize members as they came up the center aisle and see whose hand they gave their shoulders to. Note-taking is forbidden in the spectators' galleries, so the observers had to keep mental track of several votes. In spite of such obstacles, the Conference cadre was able to arrive at surprisingly accurate tallies.

Each morning before the House resumed debate, the spotters crowded into the Conference suite in the Congressional Hotel to report their observations, discuss the legislative situation, and determine which members needed visits to shore up their votes.

Once this group moved out to the House galleries, a second group came in for a briefing session. This was "O'Grady's Raiders." "O'Grady" was Jane O'Grady, the young, blond, vivacious legislative representative for the Amalgamated Clothing Workers. Under her direction, about a dozen or so men and women were assigned to cover all floors of the two House office buildings, the Cannon and the Longworth, named after historic Speakers.

Each day, O'Grady's Raiders would take up their posts in the offices of the bill's managers and champions. As soon as an alert was phoned in from the Capitol that a vote on an amendment was coming up, the Raiders sprang into action. They dashed off to canvass the offices of all the members on their floor presumed to be in favor of the bill. The Raiders' task was to make certain that supportive members were aware of the vote and able to take part in it. Members were frequently escorted from their offices to the elevators; members absent or on business off the Hill were urged, through their staffs, to get to the House at once. "We were the original beeper system," Jane O'Grady recalls.

The first day of the debate, everyone in the offices the Raiders visited was intrigued by the novelty of the operation. "By the third or fourth day," O'Grady says, "you'd poke your head in, smile, and say, 'Just checking.' And the secretaries would yell, 'He's all right! You don't have to come in here!'"

But the Raiders *did* have to. It was disillusioning, these vote herders agreed afterwards, to find that practically no House member could be taken for granted. The most devoted supporter of the bill could easily be distracted by other business. The president of a black sorority, in her first experience on the Hill, was "shocked," she said, to find that even Congressman Adam Clayton Powell, a Harlem Democrat, the most widely known black member in the House, was sometimes laggard and sometimes even away on an errand just when a critical vote was coming up. Hill veterans smiled when they heard her complaint, aware of how capricious Powell could be.

The House debate lasted until Monday, February 10, an unprecedented nine legislative days. One hundred thirty-four amendments were offered, and most of them, including most of the substantial changes proposed, were defeated. But one substantive amendment that was adopted illustrates vividly the guile of the southern opposition and the state of the civil rights movement at that time.

The sponsor of the amendment was Representative Howard Smith, the possum revivified. Peering up at his colleagues from the lectern in the well of the House, the old Virginian proposed that Title VII, the equal employment opportunity section, be amended by adding "sex" to the list of discriminations in the workplace that it would already prohibit—those based on race, creed, color, or national origin. "Now what harm can you do to this bill that was so perfect yesterday and so imperfect today?" he asked his colleagues with feigned innocence.

Clarence Mitchell, who was against the amendment, said afterwards, "It was an apple of discord." For the moment it achieved its purpose. Celler, as chief manager of the bill, was on his feet at once, announcing his opposition. Although he had at least one seemingly valid reason—it would strike down state laws specifically designed to protect the health and safety of working women—his principal, unspoken reason was more important: he feared Smith would achieve his purpose of setting the bill up for defeat by adding a highly controversial feature to it. Also Celler, at seventy-one, was an unregenerate male chauvinist who later fought against the effort of militant women's organizations to add the Equal Rights Amendment to the Constitution. It is not unlikely that he was viscerally against Smith's proposal.

William McCulloch, as chief Republican sponsor of the bill, said nothing, perhaps recognizing a lost cause when he saw one. Even women House members were split on the Smith amendment. Five immediately announced their support; one, a Democrat, spoke against it. In the ranks of the Leadership Conference, the amendment caused alarm and much soul-searching.

The Conference was geared to fight discrimination based on race. Religion, too, and national origin. It was still several years away from squarely facing the issue of discrimination against women. There were about eight or nine national women's groups among the LCCR's members, but none represented the new breed of feminists that was soon to make its appearance on the national scene. The National Organization for Women (NOW) was founded in 1966 and did not become a member of the Leadership Conference until a year or two later.

The Conference's unawareness of the sex issue is evident in the *Memos* it issued at that time. They speak of writing to and contacting one's "Congressmen." They urge any participating organization with a Washington representative to "let us have his name and address so that we can invite him to future legislative meetings."

The Smith amendment was adopted by a teller vote of 168 to 133, profiting from an ad hoc alliance of opponents of the bill and some of its most militant backers. In the gallery, as the final vote was announced, a woman spectator stood up and cried, "We've won! We've won!" and was promptly hustled out by a couple of male doorkeepers.

The Leadership Conference was in something of a quandary. If it wanted the bill, it had to accept the "sex" amendment. Mitchell, Rauh, and I shared Celler's fear, that it could doom the bill, but we had no choice. Needless to say, this fear was groundless, as subsequent events proved. If anything, I now believe the "sex" amendment eventually strengthened support for the measure. The *Memo* reporting House passage of H.R. 7152 and our support of it noted, with a superciliousness that makes me cringe today, that Smith's amendment was "adopted in what almost seemed like an excess of gallantry toward lady House members."

The House passed the bill on February 10, 1964, by a vote of 290 to 130.

Jane O'Grady, who often observes that "nagging counts," sought to soothe any irritation Leadership Conference allies in the House might have had from the Raiders' attentions. "After ten days of being a pain in the neck," she recalls, she and Peggy Roach, the National Catholic Conference's representative, stayed up most of the night baking sugar cookies decorated with the equal sign that had become the civil rights movement's symbol of equality. The next day they took their confections around to the offices of cooperating House members.

16

Walls Come Tumbling Down

Even before the House passed H.R. 7152, the Leadership Conference, anticipating that victory, sent a *Memo* out to all its member organizations urging them to begin approaching senators.

Since it was February, the *Memo* noted, many senators would be home for the holidays. It went on to observe that February was "a month that includes the birthdays of our two most famous Presidents, Race Relations Sunday, Brotherhood Week, Negro History Week, and Purim, the Jewish Feast of Lots, when the overthrow of the terrible tyrant Haman is celebrated, [and] is precisely the month that supporters of civil rights legislation can turn to good advantage. There will be countless celebrations in civic, social and labor groups and in churches and temples. If brotherhood and freedom are to receive more than token celebration, these holiday festivities should be used to build support for the bill."

The Leadership Conference was not the only one gearing up for the Senate fight. More than a month before the bill came to the House floor, President Johnson had begun consolidating his position with the black community by calling in black leaders one at a time to discuss civil rights and racial problems. He saw Roy Wilkins on Friday; Whitney Young, director of the National Urban League, on Monday; Martin Luther King, Jr., on Tuesday; James

Farmer of CORE on Wednesday; and so on. Someone close to the situation in the White House told Joe Rauh they were calling the whole procedure "the Negro of the Day."

Early on, Johnson stressed the urgency of passage with other elements in the Conference coalition, particularly the labor movement. He made personal appeals for support to George Meany, president of the AFL-CIO, and, in a Rose Garden meeting, to twenty members of the federation's executive council.

Within the hour after the House passed the bill, Joe Rauh remembered, he and Clarence, upon returning to LCCR temporary headquarters in the Congressional Hotel, found messages asking them to call the White House. It was the president. "What are you fellas doing about the Senate?" Johnson wanted to know. He urged them to get over there and get to work.

"This guy is always ahead of us," Rauh said, impressed.

On Monday, March 9, the Senate turned its attention to the Civil Rights Act of 1964.

Senators in support of the bill faced three tasks: to hold the House-passed bill, H.R. 7152, at the desk and keep it from being referred to the Senate Judiciary Committee, whose chairman, James O. Eastland, a Mississippi Democrat, boasted that he had a special place for civil rights bills—his hip pocket; to keep a quorum of the Senate—51 of its 100 members—available at all times to answer roll calls and thus keep the body from being forced to adjourn; and to begin at once to line up the 67 senators (two-thirds of the Senate membership) needed to break the filibuster that opponents of the bill were determined to mount against it.

Fortunately, the bill could not have had better floor managers than the ones designated for those posts by the two Senate leaders. The two Senate leaders themselves, however, were somewhat unknown quantities.

The Democrat, majority leader Mike Mansfield of Montana, was a man of great integrity and greatly praised for that. It was safe to assume he was for the bill. But Mansfield was not much given to exchanging confidences with his colleagues or with his president. And, it hardly needs to be said, he was impervious to lobbying. An aloof and chilly man, he was not about to meet or consult with any representatives of the Leadership Conference.

However, the Democrat whom Mansfield appointed to be the floor manager for the bill was the majority whip, Hubert H. Humphrey of Minnesota. Humphrey had led the celebrated floor fight at the 1948 Democratic convention in which the addition of a strong civil rights plank to the platform had prompted a sizable number of Southern Democrats to bolt the party in that election year. He was a friend, even a crony, of such Conference leaders as Clarence Mitchell, Joe Rauh, and Andy Biemiller. It was at Humphrey's suggestion that regular strategy meetings were held throughout the Senate floor fight. Every Monday and Thursday, Senators and their staff members, representatives of the Justice Department, and several of us from the Leadership Conference would gather for assessment and consultation a half hour before the Senate convened.

On the Republican side, minority leader Everett McKinley Dirksen, an Illinois conservative, was not expected to be of much help. It was recognized that he was crucial to any effort to line up the Republican votes that eventually would be needed to break a filibuster. But the Leadership Conference had little access to him. His chief lieutenant, however, and the man he designated to be his party's floor manager, was Tommy Kuchel of California, an affable, liberal Republican, easily available to many of us in the Leadership Conference and generally looked upon as a comrade-in-arms.

Once again the battle of the mailboxes began. Every Conference *Memo* exhorted our readers to write to senators urging their support, for the letters against the bill were now outnumbering the letters for it. Mississippi organized and financed a group called the Coordinating Committee for Fundamental American Freedoms, whose purpose was to rally the country in opposition to the extension of freedoms the bill contained. Robert Welch, president of the extreme right-wing John Birch Society, jumped into the fray, calling upon his members to mount "the most massive protest that we have ever undertaken with regard to legislation."

"Q and A" was Arnold Aronson's idea.

Although the regular *Memo*s kept our coalition members and our supporters abreast of how H.R. 7152 was progressing through Congress and when and where pressure needed to be applied, we soon recognized that something more was needed—a "backgrounder" that could be put into the hands of anyone who wanted to lobby for the bill, something that would set forth what its eleven titles contained and provide arguments in support of our position.

Arnold proposed a simple question-and-answer format. We worked on a pamphlet all the while the bill was making its way through the House, revising our draft to reflect the changes the amendments made. But when the bill finally reached the Senate and Senator Mansfield predicted a long debate, one that might very well go on for months, we sent our manuscript to the printer, certain it would be timely for many weeks to come.

Soon after the Senate debate got under way a copy of "Some Questions and

Answers on the Civil Rights Bill," a twenty-four page pamphlet, was sent out with a cover letter to the three thousand or so people on our mailing list. Copies could be ordered for $10 a hundred, $90 a thousand. Individual copies were free. That single mailing generated an enormous demand. Orders from national organizations and local groups came pouring in. Before long, sorting, packaging, and mailing "Q and A" became the principal task of the Conference's tiny staff and the volunteers who came to the office almost every day to help us.

In the course of the Senate debate, 250,000 copies were sent out. Not every request that came in was a bulk order. A remarkable one came from Rockland, Delaware. Handwritten, on stationery bearing the letterhead of "Pierre S. Du Pont IV, The White House," and signed by that gentleman, it asked for two copies of "Q and A" and noted, frugally, "It is my understanding that there is no charge for this material."

Mississippi's Coordinating Committee for Fundamental American Freedoms was busy with its own publications. It ran a full-page ad in two hundred newspapers, vehemently attacking the bill. It was an extraordinarily long and detailed diatribe. But the flavor of its arguments can be grasped, I think, from its banner headlines:

ONE-HUNDRED-BILLION-DOLLAR BLACKJACK:

THE CIVIL RIGHTS BILL——THE BILL IS NOT A MODERATE BILL AND IT HAS

NOT BEEN WATERED DOWN——IT CONSTITUTES THE GREATEST GRASP

FOR EXECUTIVE POWER CONCEIVED IN THE 20TH CENTURY

THE SOCIALISTS' OMNIBUS BILL OF 1963 NOW BEFORE THE SENATE

In much the same vein, the first paragraph went on to say: "The American people are being set up for a blow that would destroy their right to determine for themselves how they will live."

Some papers said they ran the ad as a matter of principle, but then went on to express, editorially, their displeasure with it. The *Kansas City Times* called the ad a "fantastically distorted interpretation of the civil rights proposals currently before Congress" and urged the Senate to pass the bill. Two New Hampshire papers ran the ad but sent the full amount they received for it to the NAACP as a contribution. And a third paper in the state offered the NAACP a free full-page ad in rebuttal. The Coordinating Committee's ad was strongly criticized on the Senate floor—and not by liberals only. Senator Gordon Allott, a conservative Colorado Republican, said he was not sure he could vote for all the sections of the bill, but the ad, he admitted, made him "uneasy."

* * *

The desultory floor debate that now ensued was a matter of secondary importance in these early weeks. The Senate leadership's main concern was still procedural: to keep the bill away from the Judiciary Committee graveyard and to try to maintain a quorum.

Although his record on civil rights was exemplary, Senator Wayne Morse, an Oregon Democrat, moved to refer the bill to the Judiciary Committee. Morse, the maverick, insisted on following what he considered to be proper procedure no matter what risk it posed to the legislation. The first victory for the Senate leadership was the defeat of the Morse motion, 50 to 34.

That victory also suggested that LCCR's efforts were having some effect. It is extremely difficult to pinpoint specific members of Congress who were influenced by our lobbying. But at least two senators appear to have voted against Morse because of us. Joe Rauh, in his essay on the LCCR campaign, wrote jubilantly, "The crusade of the religious groups in behalf of the bill was beginning to pay off. Two of the most conservative members of the Senate—Republicans Karl Mundt of South Dakota and Roman Hruska of Nebraska—voted with the civil rights forces against the Morse motion amid mutterings about pressure from the ministers back home."

There is independent evidence to support Joe's assertion. Father John J. Cronin of the U.S. Catholic Conference, who came often to LCCR's legislative briefings, recalled later that he got a bishop in South Dakota to lobby Mundt. After the vote on Morse, Mundt emerged from the Senate chamber and grumbled, "I hope that satisfied those two goddamned bishops that called me last night."[1]

Maintaining a quorum, a majority of the one-hundred-member body, was one of the most difficult jobs confronting the floor managers of our side of the debate. Senators have many claims on their time, particularly in an election year. It was no easy matter to keep fifty-one of them on the alert, ready to answer a roll call, whenever an opponent of the bill demanded one, hoping to force the Senate to adjourn for lack of a quorum.

Adjournment would derail further consideration of the bill and force the leadership to begin, again, the whole cumbersome procedural process of making the measure the pending business.

Once there was a near disaster. On Saturday, April 4, one of the opponents

1. This both paraphrases and quotes from an account of the episode in Robert Mann's admirable book on civil rights legislative battles, *The Walls of Jericho: Lyndon Johnson, Hubert Humphrey, Richard Russell, and the Struggle for Civil Rights* (San Diego: Harcourt, Brace, 1996), 413.

of the bill arose and, glancing around the empty chamber, suggested the absence of a quorum. Only thirty-nine senators appeared in response to the bells. Quick parliamentary maneuvering by the Senate leadership staved off adjournment. Mansfield, who rarely displayed emotion, exploded, saying bitterly that "the high rate of absenteeism" made "a travesty of the legislative process." Humphrey warned that "the only way we can lose the civil rights fight is not to have a quorum when we need it."

From then on, the LCCR ran a "Quorum Boxscore" in every *Memo*. It noted which senators were answering the calls and which ones were absent. The Conference urged its supporters to congratulate those who were usually on hand and to express regret and disappointment to those who were not.

An uncommon aspect of the filibuster that developed was that most of the time it kept to the issues. The folklore surrounding filibusters as depicted in old movies like *Mr. Smith Goes to Washington* is that senators seeking to delay action on a bill will talk on any subject, however irrelevant, to hold the floor— read the telephone directory aloud, for instance, or offer recipes for corn "likker." There is some truth to the picture. But here, instead of letting the filibusterers ramble on, senators in support of the bill sought to engage them in meaningful debate, challenging them and confronting them with the injustices the bill was designed to correct.

Interesting information was sometimes elicited by this tactic. Senator Allen Ellender, Democrat of Louisiana, admitted that white people in some sections of his state were "scared to death" about letting too many Negroes vote. Senator Richard Russell, Democrat of Georgia, a southern conservative but essentially an honorable man, admitted under questioning that "in some counties in Southern states there has been rank discrimination against Negroes in voting." He recalled that in 1957 he had said any Negro in his state who wished to vote could do so, but, he added, "later I found to my embarrassment that there were two counties where this was not so."

Although there was a welcome absence of much of the blatant anti-black sentiment that cropped up frequently in congressional debates on civil rights, there were still manifestations of racial prejudice. Senator Russell commended the instinct of the white people of the South that "mixing the races in every activity of life would bring about the amalgamation and mongrelization of our people." Senator Russell Long, Democrat of Louisiana, attacked the Declaration of Independence for preaching such imported nonsense as the proposition that "all men are created equal." Senator Strom Thurmond, Republican of South Carolina, in a TV debate on the bill with Senator Humphrey, argued that if a masseuse in a hotel beauty salon were required to massage the face of everyone who came to her, including a black matron, she would be subjected to "involuntary servitude." It was at such moments, an LCCR *Memo* observed, that "the toga of the statesman slips and you glimpse the naked flank of the Southern Neanderthal."

LCCR organizations and individual supporters of the bill exhibited considerable ingenuity in trying to keep the issue before the public and their views before the Senate.

Letter-writing parties were commonplace. Many organizational meetings turned into correspondence sessions. Pens and paper were distributed, those in attendance wrote to their senators, and their letters were then collected, stamped, and mailed out.

Supporters of the bill who lived in southern states with hostile senators were advised to "adopt a senator" and write to sympathetic members asking them to represent their views.

Students in the seven universities in the D.C. area organized a week of speeches in support of the bill and delivered them at the base of the Washington Monument. Georgetown University sponsored an interfaith convocation in its gymnasium and attracted a record crowd of 6,500 people.

Yale University Law School sent to every member of the Senate a petition urging passage of H.R. 7152, signed by 80 percent of the faculty and more than 60 percent of the student body.

In April, several seminary students approached Arnold Aronson and asked him what he thought they could do to help the campaign. At his suggestion, they instituted a vigil in front of the Lincoln Memorial. For twenty-four hours a day, groups of three students, Protestant, Catholic, and Jewish, took turns standing in silent prayer before the monument. The vigil was maintained by students and teachers from seminaries throughout the country, unbroken throughout the long weeks of Senate debate.

Delegations of labor and civil rights leaders came in almost daily from different parts of the nation for visits the Leadership Conference arranged. The Anti-Defamation League of B'nai B'rith brought in 120 business and professional men and women, leaders in their communities; one member of the group was a senator's law partner; another a client of his senator's law firm.

Meanwhile, requests for the "Q & A" were coming in at the rate of one hundred a day. The colloquy was being reprinted in hometown newspapers and organizational bulletins. It was inserted in the *Congressional Record*. A radio commentator in Norfolk, Virginia, read it aloud on her program.

Organizational representatives to the Leadership Conference kept up a daily vigil of their own—in the Senate gallery, every legislative day. Foremost among the spectators was Clarence Mitchell, who rarely left the gallery—he seldom ate lunch anyway—and could be counted on to be sitting there almost every time a senator looked up: a formidable presence.

Off the Senate floor, meanwhile, the real battle was going on. Both the Republican and Democratic floor managers addressed themselves to the hardest task of all: gathering the sixty-seven votes we needed to invoke cloture and stop the filibuster. To this end, they and officials from the Department of Justice undertook to woo Everett McKinley Dirksen.

The minority leader was an enigmatic man. With his tousled grey-red locks, his mellifluous voice (almost a burlesque of senatorial oratorical tones), his bantering manner, he struck some people as a buffoon. He once described himself as a man of firm and unyielding principle, whose first principle was to be flexible at all times.

But under that clownish appearance was an astute politician. How did he stand on the bill? None of the Senate leaders of the floor fight who consulted regularly with those of us representing the Conference could say for sure. The Leadership Conference itself had no way of answering the question. Dirksen would not meet with Clarence Mitchell or with any other Conference officer. Religious leaders from his home state of Illinois who did get in to see him returned with discouraging reports. After a delegation of Illinois clergy met with him, Rabbi Rosenbaum of Chicago came back to a Conference caucus to say he had "no tidings of good cheer." Dirksen, he said, was impolite, angry, convinced he knew what was best for the country, and not ready to brook any arguments on that view.

"He was rude," Rabbi Rosenbaum said. "He told us his mail was running eleven to one against the bill and that clergymen did not represent his constituency. That he was rude to a rabbi is not particularly news. But he was rude to a monsignor of the Catholic Church as well." However, he felt that Dirksen was following the bill closely.

Evidence suggested that Dirksen was trying to obstruct the bill, offering at one point forty-nine crippling amendments, which he later reduced to eleven.

By early May it was apparent that the Justice Department and the Senate leadership were trying to come up with proposals that would meet Dirksen's objections and win his critical support. It was a given that without his help it would be impossible to obtain enough Republican votes to reach our goal of sixty-seven.

The LCCR was shut out of the negotiations with Dirksen. There was considerable fear in the Conference that his price for cooperation would amount to a sellout. By the end of May, however, whatever information we could gather suggested that the compromise that was emerging would not do serious violence to the House-passed bill. By May 25, the Conference *Memo* was able to report that Senator Dirksen was now preaching with the conviction of the newly converted. He rose on the Senate floor to quote Victor Hugo: "No army is stronger than an idea whose time has come." Civil rights, he declared to the press, was such an idea: "The challenge is here, it's inescapable and you've got to deal with it."

On Tuesday, May 26, Dirksen, on behalf of himself and Senator Mansfield and the whips of both parties, introduced the "package" on which they had been working for more than a month.

There was still preliminary maneuvering to be done before the cloture vote could come before the Senate; concessions had to be made on amendments that would do no appreciable harm to the bill. The fragility of the negotiations could be surmised from accidental occurrences. Dirksen was ill with a chest cold for two days, and for a while it looked as if the voting agreement was coming apart. "Around here," said one of Senator Mansfield's aides, "you've gotta keep bailing *all* the time."

On June 10, 1964, after an unprecedented seventy-five days of talking and for the first time in its history, the Senate of the United States voted to limit debate on a civil rights bill.

The galleries were packed and hushed as the vote began. Senators' wives were standing in the aisles, and high Justice Department officials crouched on the marble steps. Although only 67 of the 100 Senators were needed to invoke cloture, 71 ended up voting for it. All 100 senators voted. Senator Clare Engle, a California Democrat, provided what was perhaps the most dramatic moment of the afternoon. He was recuperating from brain surgery, yet he had himself wheeled into the chamber and, unable to speak, signaled his affirmative vote by pointing to his eye.

The galleries exploded into applause when the vote was announced. But the fight was not entirely over. Limited debate meant each senator still got an hour to talk.

The worst of the 119 amendments pending were beaten down. The LCCR *Memo* observed, "For days, like men rationing water in the desert, the Senators, particularly the Southerners, made sparing use of the 60 minutes each one had to speak on the bill and any of the pending amendments they chose to call up. In the end, when they no longer had any hope of weakening the bill, the Southerners simply poured out their anger. Much of the debate on the last day before the vote on final passage sounded like death scene arias of an interminable opera."

On the evening of June 19, one year to the day after President Kennedy had sent the bill to Congress, between 7 and 8 P.M. all debate ended, and H.R. 7152 was passed by a vote of 73 to 27. A few poignant moments, perhaps prophetic ones, awaited us outside the Senate chamber. A couple of us left the gallery with Clarence Mitchell. As soon as we emerged, the doorkeeper, a white Alabaman, insisted on shaking Clarence's hand. "No hard feelings," he said. "Some games you win. Some games you lose. And some are called on account of rain."

We took the elevator to the first floor. A Capitol guard, a southern white man, came up to Clarence in the corridor, shook hands with him, and said, "You deserved it. You worked hard for this one." Outside the Capitol, as we walked across the dark and silent plaza toward Clarence's office on Southwest Second Street where he was going to pick up his car and drive home to Baltimore, a handsome blond young man, one of the students who earned tuition by working on the Hill as a page or an elevator operator, came running after us. When he reached Clarence, he said, "May I shake hands with you? A word of congratulations from South Carolina."

Clarence thanked him and recalled that he was once arrested in South Carolina for sitting in a white waiting room and that afterwards a white newspaper editor came to escort him out of jail to show him there were no hard feelings.

This emboldened the young man to say he was a member of the Council of Concerned Citizens in Chapel Hill, North Carolina, Dr. Joseph Straley's group, and that he had been arrested twice for demonstrating.

It seemed as if the Old South was crumbling before our very eyes.

Each step, even after the Senate approved the Dirksen-Mansfield bill, was still a battle. When the bill was returned to the House for its concurrence in the changes the Senate had made, the southerners forced it back into the Rules Committee again by raising objections. But Representative Howard Smith knew better than to try to keep the measure bottled up. The bill was cleared for House action, and on June 30, 1964, the House agreed to a Celler resolution to concur in the Senate bill. The vote of approval on final passage was 289 to 126.

* * *

With seventy-two pens, each one a memento of the historic occasion, on Thursday, July 2, the evening of final passage, President Johnson signed the Civil Rights Act of 1964 into law. Johnson had hoped to sign it on July 4, but the holiday fell on a Saturday. Many senators had plans to be out of town.

Sad to say, after its triumphant passage, the signing of the bill was marred by pettiness, self-interest, and haste.

I spoke to Joe Rauh just before the ceremony, and he was somewhat bitter about the whole affair. "It's such an undignified way to end the fight. They had to scramble like that because the senators wanted a weekend."

Those of us in the Leadership Conference had reason enough to be un-happy. As late as Wednesday, the day before the bill-signing, we were unable to ascertain what the president's plans were. I called his assistant at the White House, Lee White, a neighbor of mine since he also lived in Shepherd Park and had moved there because of his own personal commitment to racial inte-gration. I couldn't reach him.

White called Vi Gunther back to say he didn't know when the ceremony would be. He doubted it would take place on the Fourth. That, he said, was newspaper talk. He thought it might even be put off to the following week be-cause of the mechanical problem of getting the bill engrossed.

I called George Reedy, President Johnson's press secretary. He, too, doubted that the signing would take place on Saturday. Thursday or Friday, he said, seemed more likely.

We heard nothing more from the White House. I had a luncheon appoint-ment on Thursday. When I got back to the Conference office, Vi Gunther had information at last. The signing was to be that evening, at 6:45 P.M. And I was not invited. Then she told me this story.

At 2 P.M. she got a call from "one of my spies," June Pickett, Andy Biemil-ler's secretary, who told Vi that Andy had been invited to the White House for the ceremony. Vi promptly called the man who had called Biemiller.

"I can't talk to you," he said. "I have two hundred people to call for the signing." He sounded, Vi said, nearly hysterical.

"Give me some names," Vi said, "and I'll help you." Then she checked some names with him. Joe and Arnold were not on his list. When she men-tioned that, he said, "Add them." Then she asked him, "Who gave you the list?"

He told her he had gotten it from Stephen Currier, head of the Taconic Foundation, a close friend of Bayard Rustin's and a philanthropist whose agency funded many civil rights projects, including Neighbors, Inc., for a time.

Currier, the man said, "is coming down with a planeload of people."

"See?" Vi said. "That's a millionaire for you. He must have given Johnson five thousand dollars for something or other."

As soon as she got off the line with the White House aide, she called Arnold. He said he would fly down. But his plane got hung up and he came to Washington too late for the ceremony. So he had to turn around and go back.

Joe made it and told us afterwards, "It was an exciting mishmash." With all kinds of people around who had had nothing whatever to do with the bill.

Hubert Humphrey publicly sought to put a better face on the occasion by observing that July 2 had its own symbolism. That was the day, he noted, that the Declaration of Independence had been ratified.

For the Leadership Conference, the date had another significance. Exactly one year earlier, at the meeting in the Roosevelt Hotel in New York, the decision to open an LCCR office in Washington had been ratified.

Clarence and Joe, our official representatives at the signing ceremony, each received a pen. Others of us received pens, too. As it turned out, there were a great many more than the seventy-two "official" pens. It was Johnson's style to be liberal with them. Eventually, I got one. We in the LCCR were also generous with pens. We had a batch struck off and gave them out to the many faithful volunteers who had been unable to obtain one from the president.

The new law that President Johnson signed into effect was a triumph for the kind of coordinated lobbying—between grass roots and Washington—that the Leadership Conference sought to exemplify.

The most immediate and evident effect of the Civil Rights Act of 1964 was in the area of public accommodation. A century of humiliation for black citizens—at least when they were traveling or out for the evening—was coming to an end. All places open to the general public—restaurants and hotels, gas stations, theaters, concert halls, arenas, and so forth—were now required to serve and admit everyone regardless of race, color, religion, or national origin. Exemptions were minor: genuine private clubs and small boardinghouses in which the owner lived and rented out five or fewer rooms (the "Mrs. Murphy exemption," they called it during the debate).

In regard to employment, the law forbade employers, unions, and employment agencies to discriminate on the basis of race, color, religion, nationality, or—thanks to that segregationist reprobate Representative Howard Smith of Virginia—sex. A new federal agency, the Equal Employment Opportunities Commission (EEOC), was to be established within the year to help enforce the law.

Federally financed programs—vocational training, crop loans and small business loans, hospital and highway construction, and so forth—had to be administered without discrimination or face a government cutoff of funds.

Where schools and colleges discriminated unlawfully, the U.S. attorney general was authorized to bring suit when he received a written and, in his opinion, justified complaint.

State-operated facilities—libraries, hospitals, museums, playgrounds, and the like—had to be open to everyone or face federal suit.

The life of the U.S. Civil Rights Commission, by then an agency of proven worth, was extended another four years. And a new agency, the Community Relations Service, was set up in the Department of Commerce to help local communities reach voluntary settlement of problems of discrimination and racial tension.

The law had its weaknesses and omissions. The most glaring fault was in the realm of voting rights. Although it sought to ban the use of such devices as discriminatory literacy tests and authorized speedy court action by the attorney general, what the act offered was no match for the kind of tricks and intimidation southern politicos and registrars customarily used to deny the franchise to black voters.

Another weakness lay in the area of employment. While the new EEOC was empowered to investigate job discrimination, when it found a violation there wasn't much it could do about it. It couldn't issue a final order; its only available remedy was persuasion.

Finally, the law had nothing to say about discrimination in the sale and rental of housing, a critical lack.

Still, it was well understood in the Leadership Conference that you cannot do everything in a single piece of legislation. Passage of the act demonstrated once and for all that despite southern and socially conservative opposition, you could now get meaningful civil rights laws through Congress. Enactment of the 1964 law heartened all of us in the Conference, and we soon marshaled our forces for new legislative battles.

The end of the 1964 campaign came none too soon. A few days after the bill-signing the Leadership Conference got a notice advising us to vacate the Mills Building by July 24. The last *Memo* on the 1964 bill observed, "It is peculiarly appropriate that the Mills Building, from which we waged our year-long campaign to destroy old forms of discrimination, will be demolished by the end of the month."

In retrospect, the demolition was symbolic in another way. The objectives in

1964, from a vantage point today, near the end of the twentieth century, were clear-cut: to put an end to racial segregation and racial discrimination. Our victory, though partial, seems almost tangible in its effects, exhilarating in its immediate results: Negroes could now eat and sleep in many places where they could not have done so before; schools once closed to them were open; when jobs were denied them because of race, they had a federal agency to turn to.

How inadequate our victory seems today! We went on to win other battles. The Voting Rights Act of 1965 was the first federal law to succeed in opening the ballot box to minorities; Roy Wilkins called it "one of the most effective pieces of civil rights legislation ever enacted," and he was right. The Housing Act of 1968 was more noteworthy for its intent than for its ability to open housing to minorities. But we are talking bedrock here. In the sixties we had established a basis for the enactment of other civil rights laws.

And yet, after 1964 everything becomes more complicated. In the decades that follow, victories that once seemed indisputable advances to us—affirmative action, racial integration, for instance—are often questioned by the very ones we thought would benefit from them. In the years that follow, rivalries and tensions among minority groups emerge that we barely anticipated in the full flush of the first major success that the Leadership Conference achieved.

This is a matter of such importance that it bears dwelling on. Passage of the 1964 act encouraged other groups in our society to seek full rights of citizenship. We were soon aware of that in the Leadership Conference. Those who considered themselves disadvantaged came knocking at our door. Those of us who directed the Conference, I regret to say, tended to admit some of these groups reluctantly.

Among the first of the awakened groups to apply for membership in the Leadership Conference were the new feminist organizations, notably NOW, the National Organization for Women. The LCCR executive committee considered the application with great misgiving. It was not a sentiment limited to committee males, either. Some of the representatives of old-line women's organizations were fearful of the issues NOW would bring before us. However, we could find no justification for keeping these new applicants out. They met our criteria.

So we let NOW in and its representatives soon confirmed our trepidation. The women they spoke for had as a major item on their agenda the addition of the Equal Rights Amendment to the Constitution. Many of LCCR's labor union members and a number of women's organizations opposed the amendment. They feared it would jeopardize the whole system of protective legislation for working women they had struggled so long and hard to get enacted.

Actually, though, the laws they sought to hold on to—limiting the hours and physical difficulties to which working women could be subjected—closed off much gainful employment for what was known then as "the weaker sex." For many of us it was not easy to come around to changing our point of view.

But almost every new incoming group forced us to reexamine basic assumptions: the Hispanic Americans, the Asian Americans, the aged, the physically disabled, gays and lesbians. We gave considerable thought to how we might keep some of them out. The application of the American Council of the Blind tied us up for weeks before we finally concluded we could not, in conscience, turn it down.

We did reject the first application we received from a gay rights group. Two of the most powerful members of the executive committee, Clarence M. Mitchell, Jr., and Andrew Biemiller, legislative director of the AFL-CIO, flexed their muscles and said we could not let gays in.

"We'll lose credibility on Capitol Hill," Clarence told the committee. "We'll become a laughingstock." So we turned them away. No one had the nerve to comment on an obvious irony: that the executive committee chairman (we had a way to go before we began using the term *chairperson*), the highly respected civil rights leader and chief organizer of the 1963 March on Washington, Bayard Rustin, was a known homosexual. A few years after Mitchell and Biemiller retired, however, the LCCR began admitting gay and lesbian groups.

But even groups we readily admitted to the Leadership Conference brought agendas with them that sometimes aroused angry debates within our alliance. The Hispanic Americans, as represented by the National Council of La Raza, set off several bitter confrontations. Among their goals were the institution of bilingual education programs in the public schools and their inclusion in the protections of the Voting Rights Act. The latter objective resulted in a head-on collision between La Raza representatives and Clarence Mitchell. In 1975, when renewal of the 1965 act came before Congress, the Hispanic Americans rightly sought to have the law amended to include themselves under its protections.

Clarence Mitchell objected. He was afraid that if the act were opened to add "national origins" to the list of prohibited discriminations—"race, color or creed"—extension of the law would be endangered. Things came to a head in an unforgettable and shocking moment when in a discussion of the proposed changes in the act, Clarence lost his temper while voicing his opposition to the issues being raised by the La Raza representatives, and shouted: "Blacks were dying for the right to vote when you people couldn't decide whether you were Caucasians."

It is testament to the inherent resiliency of the Leadership Conference, and to our awareness of how much we needed one another, that the coalition survived that encounter. Somehow our differences were patched up. Somehow we struggled on. The Leadership Conference with Joe Rauh in the forefront succeeded in getting the protections of the law extended to Hispanic American voters. But differences do erupt from time to time, and they simply underscore the uneasy suspicions and rivalries that underlie our alliance, no matter how effective it has been.

What we find in the Leadership Conference is nothing more than a reflection of the differences and occasional animosities that exist among various racial, ethnic, and social groups in American society as a whole.

We also find—and this is the moral of the tale—that such differences can be surmounted. Each new group, in our experience, adds its own strength to what we are trying to achieve. The LCCR is heartening evidence that people of varied natures and backgrounds can unite and work together in the pursuit of common goals.

The board of Neighbors, Inc., in 1959–60. NI's executive director, Margery Ware, is seated fourth from the left; its first president, Marvin Caplan, stands second from the right.
Photo by Douglas Chevalier

NI's fourth anniversary party, June 1962. In the center of the picture is Robert Good, NI's second president; beside him is Marvin Caplan, and to his right Naomi Caplan. Bob Good went on to become the first U.S. ambassador to Zambia.

Photo by Douglas Chevalier

Many of NI's successful anti-block-busting campaigns were planned in informal home meetings such as this. Naomi Caplan is seated third from the right.
Photo by Douglas Chevalier

Leaders of the March on Washington, August 28, 1963, pose before the Lincoln Memorial.
Front row, from left: Whitney M. Young, Jr., Cleveland Robinson, A. Philip Randolph,
Martin Luther King, Jr.; *back row, from left:* Arnold Aronson, Mathew Ahmann, Rabbi
Joachim Prinz, Joseph L. Rauh, Jr., John Lewis, Floyd S. McKissick, Rev. Eugene Carson
Blake, and Walter P. Reuther.
Courtesy Bernard Aronson

Marvin Caplan, director of the Leadership Conference on Civil Rights, and President
Lyndon B. Johnson shake hands at a bill-signing ceremony in the White House, 1968.
Official White House photograph, courtesy author

Old friends and colleagues confer at the LCCR annual dinner, 1973. *Left to right:* Roy Wilkins, chairman; Arnold Aronson, secretary; Sen. Jacob Javits (Rep.—N.Y.); Joseph L. Rauh, Jr., general counsel. Marvin Caplan is behind Rauh.

Photo by Del Ankers, courtesy Leadership Conference on Civil Rights

A delegation from the LCCR meets with President Gerald Ford at the White House, January 27, 1975.
Official White House photograph, courtesy author

A. Philip Randolph, one of the great heroes of the civil
rights movement and a founder of the Leadership Conference, is greeted by Sen. Edward Brooke (Rep.—Mass.)
at an LCCR affair in the late 1970s. Arnold Aronson,
LCCR secretary, looks on.
*Photo from National Education Association Publishing, Joe
Di Dio, courtesy Leadership Conference on Civil Rights*

Marvin Caplan, director of the LCCR, helps hold a conference banner in a demonstration
against apartheid outside the South African embassy in Washington in the early 1980s.
Courtesy Leadership Conference on Civil Rights

17

A Grim Time: 1972

A ceremonial event in 1972 became for me a landmark in assessing the complex and daunting problems that confronted the civil rights movement after the resounding triumphs of the sixties. The occasion was the opening of the Civil Rights Division of the LBJ Library in Austin in December of that year.

Summoned by Lyndon Johnson, some thirty of us gathered at the Braniff counter in Dulles International Airport for the flight down to Texas. Stirred for the moment out of the gloom we felt in those dismal Nixon years, the mood among us was exuberant.

"My God!" one of Hubert Humphrey's former aides exclaimed as he looked around at all the old familiar faces. "It's the last hurrah!"

There was more than a touch of that in the situation. Hubert Horatio Humphrey himself, old "Triple H," was in the check-in line, along with other notable comrades-in-arms: former assistant attorney general Burke Marshall for one; and Harry McPherson, LBJ's Special White House Counsel from 1964 to 1969, someone we in the Leadership Conference on Civil Rights felt was sympathetic to our endeavors. (Former chief justice of the U.S. Supreme Court Earl Warren and his wife were ushered through without a wait.) All around us in the terminal were others less well known—a representative but not a definitive selection of the men and women who had been active in the civil rights movement of the past decade.

What impelled so many to go from Washington to Austin on a Sunday afternoon in mid-December? Respect for LBJ and perhaps an inclination to seek respite from the northern winter in a warmer climate; nostalgia for a time when our civil rights objectives and our villains were a good deal clearer. We may also have hoped that in the course of reviewing the past we would find auguries for the future. For as part of the dedication ceremonies, there was to be a two-day symposium entitled "Equal Opportunity in the United States."

The program looked like a promising mix of the old and the new. In addition to Humphrey and Warren and Burke Marshall, other movement elders were going to speak: Roy Wilkins ("a living monument," the woman professor who introduced him had the poor taste to say); Clarence Mitchell; Vernon Jordan, director of the National Urban League. Among the newcomers scheduled to address us were harbingers of black success and influence in politics: Julian Bond, recently elected state senator in Georgia and one of Martin Luther King's close comrades-in-arms; Richard G. Hatcher, mayor of Gary, Indiana; and two newly elected women representatives to the U.S. Congress, Barbara Jordan of Texas and Yvonne Brathwaite Burke of Los Angeles.

Appropriately, it was left to Earl Warren and Roy Wilkins to summarize the past when the symposium got under way. Between them they recalled the origins in slavery of our current racial predicament and the hopes raised by a bloody civil war; the Supreme Court's affirmation of racial equality in the *Brown* decision of 1954; and then the marches, sit-ins, and Freedom Rides of the sixties that spurred enactment of the major civil rights laws of that decade. Mighty battles, noble moments that vibrated in our memories even as our speakers reduced them to line items.

For Roy Wilkins, the Voting Rights Act of 1965 was the major legislative accomplishment of this time. The evidence of that law's effectiveness was on the platform with him in the persons of Bond and Hatcher, Jordan and Burke.

Vernon Jordan and Hubert Humphrey sought to move beyond reminiscence and prescribe a course of action. For Jordan, our challenge at this time of "moral exhaustion" was "to keep the spirit of change and reform alive." What compounded the difficulty of that task was the need, at the same time, to try to hold on to the gains already made. One had to fight rearguard actions against old issues in new disguises. The opposition to busing and affirmative action and "goals and timetables" to open more jobs to minorities, he felt, masked the old resistance to giving blacks their equal rights. He hoped President Nixon would call black leaders together and learn firsthand of the "aspirations and needs of black Americans." What he wanted, plainly, was a return to those happier times when the White House door was open to civil rights leaders; when the government was on the side of the movement instead of filing joint suits with our enemies.

If President Nixon maintained his indifference, if the nation failed to meet its challenge, then our second Reconstruction period would end as ingloriously as the first. Only this time the nation would be left "enveloped in grief and in possible tragic eruptions." Whether we survived depended on our realization that our lives, white and black, are intertwined, and that though we came here in different ships, "we're all in the same boat now."

Humphrey, whose rousing speech reminded many of us of the time he led the Senate in the fight for the 1964 Civil Rights Act, took mild exception to Vernon Jordan. He felt that the civil rights movement had to go beyond its concern with black aspirations. He thought the falling off of broad public support for the unattained goals of the sixties was based on a faulty perception: more and more people, he said, had come to see, even if wrongly so, that the civil rights movement was an effort "to give blacks a special break that was afforded no other group in American society." He, too, called upon President Nixon to consider his place in history and take the lead in the fight for racial justice. "We should be devising political strategy for compelling Nixon to make this move."

He believed our conception of civil rights had to be broadened to include rights and opportunities for all disadvantaged groups. Who could deny him when he said: "We must identify civil rights with the civil right of every American" to adequate health care, to freedom from poverty, to productive and gainful employment, to privacy—in short, to every benefit of our society. He would enlist in the fight not only racial and ethnic minorities but the physically handicapped, the mentally retarded, the elderly. During his speech, the Humphrey magic worked; all goals seemed within our grasp. Only on reflection, considering the diverse forces he meant to call together for the struggle, did old nagging doubts come back upon us like a chill.

It was cold in Austin those two days. Texas was in the grip of an unprecedented sleet storm. The Austin runway was so icy that when our group from Washington arrived, it had to be flown farther south, to San Antonio, then driven back to Austin on buses, prompting many jokes about "forced busing." The broad marble pavements that surround the LBJ Library were strewn with muddy sand paths. It was worth your neck to stray from one of them. The weather suited the occasion. It recalled a line from the poem Robert Lowell wrote on Eisenhower's inauguration in 1953: "Ice, ice. Our wheels no longer move."

If one looked for signs of hope, they could be found among the younger participants in the symposium. More for what they signified than what they said. They did not lack self-confidence. "Texas," Barbara Jordan declared, "has done a lot for this country. We gave you Lyndon Johnson and now we give you Barbara Jordan." And Julian Bond defined himself as "a politician. A statesman is a politician who cannot get elected." Both grew more modest when they were urged to define their aims. Like their elders, they called for a coalition of the disadvantaged and for new approaches to the president.

For those who had participated in the civil rights movement over the last ten years, the celebration in which we were taking part bore a strong resemblance to a series of events in the Johnson Era: the gala ceremonies LBJ organized for signing into law the major civil rights and social welfare laws of his administration. To those affairs, too, hundreds of people were invited by a mysterious process that left out many who worked hard for the legislation and included many others for whom the moment could be no more than a prestigious social gathering. In Austin, the national labor leaders who worked for civil rights were conspicuous by their absence.

Lyndon Johnson himself was very much in evidence. For most of the two days, he and Lady Bird sat in the first row of the library auditorium. He was unnaturally subdued, his face ashen. Every now and then he turned and looked back at the crowded rows with a mild, paternal smile.

But if Johnson was there, so, in a sense, was Richard Nixon. In the explicit appeals and condemnations, but also in oblique references to one of the famous phrases of his first term. Chief Justice Warren in his speech said that enactment of the first major civil rights law of this century, the weak and modest law Johnson, as Senate majority leader, piloted to passage in 1957, "reversed almost a century of 'benign neglect.'" Vernon Jordan recalled that "we have seen the benign activism of the sixties replaced by the 'benign neglect' of black people." And yet another speaker, on introducing Julian Bond, spoke of our present time as one of "'benign neglect' if not of total disregard."

On Monday night the Johnsons hosted a reception in the Great Hall of the library, a room reminiscent in its vastness of the library in *Citizen Kane*. Hundreds of well-wishers moved in slow procession from the ground floor up a flight of huge stone steps to where the former president and his wife stood waiting to greet them on the landing. Towering above their heads were the glassed-in stacks, four floors of Johnson papers in red manuscript boxes with gold pulls. Thirty-one million of them; nearly one million concerned with civil rights. It was a display of such awesome symmetry it was hard to imagine anyone bold enough to disarrange it by calling for documents.

For that one evening the company drank and ate and talked, convivial among the displays of artifacts and photographs of the Johnson years. To my delight I found myself at a table with Ralph Ellison, author of one of this century's most highly regarded novels, *Invisible Man.* I told him that not only did I admire the book, which is something he might have expected, but that my daughter Anne, a high school junior, had been very moved by it. That, I could see, pleased him.

Johnson sat at one of the little supper tables, engaged in informal talk with anyone who happened by. The general opinion murmured among us was that he did not look well. On the following day he spoke at the very end of the program.

His appearance had been heralded in the accolades of earlier speakers. Whatever errors of judgment and arrogance he may have committed in the past were forgiven him. Even Julian Bond, who in 1966 was denied his seat in the Georgia legislature for signing a statement against the Vietnam War, deplored the "four lost years" of Nixon's first term. He recalled the advances under Johnson and cried, "a human-hearted man had his hands on the levers of power. . . . And O, my God, how I wish he were there now!"

When Johnson rose to speak, against his doctor's advice, a reverential hush fell upon us. To those who felt that the last four years under Nixon had been a time of intolerable regression he had words of comfort. "All is not lost, all has not been in vain. All we have to do is reorganize. We can't overcome all injustices or make this a perfect world overnight. But we are going to do just that before it's over." He confessed he had not always seen the plight of the nation's minorities as clearly as he did now. Yet no one doubted him when he said that of all the records in the library "it is the record of this work [civil rights] that holds most of myself within it."

For him, as for Wilkins, the salvation of black people—and by black he meant all who suffered discrimination because of their color or national heritage—lay in exercising the right to vote. Too few voted now. He speculated on the need to make voting compulsory. So much still needed doing! "I don't want this symposium to spend two days talking about what we have done. . . . I want to report I'm *ashamed* of myself that I had six years and couldn't do more than I did."

He addressed himself, as he had in earlier speeches, to the continuing inequality between the races and the need for compensatory treatment. "Whites stand on history's mountain; blacks stand in history's hollow." It was a ruminative and moving speech, all the more moving for being given on the hostile soil of his native state. He ended with a declaration that had become one of his trademarks: "I am confident we shall overcome." Yet what had once been a stirring, even startling, statement coming from his lips, now sounded familiar, even a little mechanical.

Johnson left the lectern, but circumstances brought him back quickly. Earlier in the day Roy Innis, national president of CORE, who made his career in those days out of black separatism, succeeded in getting five minutes to address the gathering by threatening to disrupt it if he were denied a chance to speak. Now, as Johnson came down the shallow steps from the stage, one of Innis's aides, the Reverend A. Kendall Smith, came running forward and after a brief exchange with Johnson was given leave to speak. Noting that the symposium had begun and was about to end without prayer, he then proceeded to harangue the audience with demands for some rectifying religious action.

His insistence seemed about to provoke the kind of confrontation that Innis likes, for Clarence Mitchell jumped up and, after upbraiding Innis, who sat in the audience smirking, shouted, "If Lyndon Johnson has the courage in Texas to speak out against white demagoguery, wherever I am, I'm going to speak out against black demagoguery."

Johnson averted a dispute by taking the stage again. Yes, he had been told there would be a disruption, but he was used to disruption. Threats had not made him agree to let Smith and Innis speak; it was rather a wish to include "everyone with a spark of interest." He spoke now with an ill old man's humility, a sense, perhaps, of coming to the end of things. He found, he said, in the poverty of his early life, in the pain of the bonus marchers and the Depression poor, the beginning of his own sensitivity to suffering.

All presidents, he said, have "left office wiser than when they entered it." Even President Nixon, he felt, "wants to do what's right. However, *knowing* what's right is important. I look back on things I did and wish I'd known a little bit more." He admonished everyone to try to organize a meeting with the president. "Don't start off by saying he's terrible." What he was saying to that audience, perhaps, was that he, Johnson, had proved to be not so terrible as many of us in the civil rights movement feared he would be when he took office.

The group rose in a standing ovation when he finished speaking. Our accolade was as much an expression of a presentiment among us that we might be seeing him for the last time as for his accomplishments. His subdued manner was so uncharacteristic. It was no surprise to those of us who saw him then that he died within the year.

The symposium over, we quickly dispersed, dozens of us scurrying up the aisles to catch planes. Outside the library the sun shone. The day was suddenly warm and mild.

What was accomplished in Austin in those two days? A review of our common history, ours and Johnson's, but not much more. Directions but no map.

Hubert Humphrey and Clarence Mitchell, two unquenchable optimists, felt that in the Nixon years, confronted by many disappointments, we were becoming in Humphrey's phrase "fascinated with failures."

There were many calls then, as there are today, to revive the coalition of the sixties. Yet in all that time one coalition continued to exist: the Leadership Conference on Civil Rights. Because its agenda was essentially a narrow one—the enactment and enforcement of civil rights legislation—it was and is still able to do effective work in spite of rivalries and tensions among various minority groups.

Looking back on Austin today, we can derive the hope that in spite of disappointments and disillusionments and setbacks we can still count on the unexpected. The weather is not always what you think it's going to be. Johnson, that weekend, was the brightest ray. For he had emerged from the undistinguished ranks of reactionary southern politicians to make his own unique commitment to equality. History repeats itself, not only in its failures but in its triumphs, too. Lyndon Johnson, in the area of civil rights, was one of the triumphs. Those of us who kept that in mind were sustained during the rest of the gloomy Nixon years and during the setbacks we suffered in the dozen years of the Reagan-Bush administrations.

Part V

Back to Old Stamping Grounds
1981–

18

I Become an Unpaid
Volunteer Again

In 1980, that gratifying life I had made for myself, based largely on my work for the Leadership Conference, began to fall apart. The disrupting forces came from two directions. At the Industrial Union Department a new president arrived, who had his own ideas of what I should be doing for the division. At home we had begun to realize that the stomach cramps Naomi complained of were symptoms of something far more serious than a seasonal flu.

The presidency of the IUD had changed several times during the eighteen years that I was there, the first time with dramatic, jolting effect. That was back in 1968, only five years after I had joined the staff, when the long-smoldering rivalry between Walter Reuther and George Meany finally exploded and Reuther pulled out of the federation, taking Jack Conway along with him.

The change, to my relief, had little effect on my situation. Those who succeeded Reuther and Conway as heads of the department respected the original arrangement between the Leadership Conference and the IUD. So I continued to wear two hats—as the IUD's senior lobbyist and as the director of the LCCR's Washington office.

But then Jacob Clayman, who was Conway's administrative director when I first came to the IUD, and who had moved up into the presidency in 1973, decided after seven years in office that it was time to retire. I saw his approaching departure with foreboding, for Jake was a good-natured, easygoing sort and we had had a warm relationship. His successor, Howard Samuel, an energetic, ambitious man, undertook an extensive redecoration of department headquarters and a thorough reorganization of the staff. In the course of his changes he created a new position for me: legislative director. Since the IUD had only two Capitol Hill lobbyists, a chap named Phil Daugherty and me, I thought this formal rearrangement somewhat unnecessary, even though Samuel intended to give me additional responsibilities. But since I was being elevated from rank and file to management, with an accompanying boost in pay, who was I to question the wisdom of Samuel's decision?

Unfortunately, Howard Samuel also decided I could not hold two directorships. So he decreed that the Leadership Conference would have to find a new director. He recognized, however, that the IUD had obligations as a pivotal member of the Conference, and assured everyone involved that his department would make substantial contributions to the new director's salary.

Uneasy at what Samuel seemed to have in store for me, I was ready to consider an alternative to staying on at the IUD. In less than a year, I would be sixty-two—eligible for early retirement. All at once that became an attractive prospect. What drew me to it was realizing that much as I enjoyed lobbying for causes I believed in, the Leadership Conference was the essential component of my work; I would be deprived of much of an impelling drive if I no longer represented it. Then, too, for a personal reason I felt I would welcome the distraction that would come from reordering the way I lived. Naomi and I now knew the worst: my dear wife of more than thirty years was in the terminal stages of ovarian cancer. How, I wondered, could I go on without her?

Naomi died in January 1981. In July of that year, two weeks after my sixty-second birthday, I left the IUD.

The search for my successor at the Leadership Conference was already under way. Joe and Arnold approached me and suggested I become my own successor, in other words, return to the LCCR as its new director, independent of the IUD. But perversely perhaps, or maybe because I just felt weary, I turned the offer down. I wanted to strike off in a new direction, even though I had no clear idea of what direction I would take.

Luckily I could afford to be indecisive. It was a cruel irony that just as Naomi's life was drawing to an end, she and I had come to realize that after years of scrimping, we were pretty well off financially. The job at the IUD I had taken so hesitantly paid me a higher wage than I could have ever hoped to get at Fairchild. And my earnings were supplemented by Naomi's. At least fifteen years before she died she had resumed her interrupted career as a psychologist, working full-time for the state mental health center in Alexandria and even engaging in a bit of private practice. On top of that, her father died sometime in the late sixties and left her several lucrative stock investments as an inheritance.

Carried upward on a wave of affluence, we moved from our modest cedar-shingle bungalow to a much grander place, a large brick house in Shepherd Park, an upper-middle-class neighborhood that had become the hub of Neighbors, Inc., activity. Our whole family benefited from the change, for Freya, Anne, and Bennett now each had rooms of their own.

By 1981, the costs of moving and redecorating were behind us. So, too, were most of our children's college tuition expenses. My retirement pension and health plan were quite generous. So though I was a saddened, single man, from any reasonable perspective I was a fairly solvent one.

Even as I undertook to fashion a new life for myself, I still maintained connections with the Federation and the Leadership Conference. Indeed, I was barely into retirement when the AFL-CIO called me out again.

In less than two years, the Ronald Reagan presidency had aroused consternation in both the labor and the civil rights movements. It was evident that under Mr. Reagan's amiable direction, the federal government was out to dismantle many social programs that my associates and I considered essential. The final straw for the labor movement was Reagan's peremptory firing of 11,400 federal air-traffic controllers who struck the Federal Aviation Administration because of their wretched working conditions.

AFL-CIO president Lane Kirkland reacted by issuing a call to unions and their sympathizers to join him in a protest demonstration. "Solidarity Day" was to be the name of the event, and it was scheduled to be held within three months of his summons, on September 19, 1981. Eighteen years after Phil Randolph's March on Washington, the AFL-CIO was ready to have us march again, under several slogans, including "For Jobs and Justice," which for some of us had a strong resemblance to the slogan under which we marched on that memorable day in August 1963: "For Jobs and Freedom."

I was temporarily rehired as an associate coordinator, and it was my assignment to enlist as marchers sympathetic nonlabor groups—essentially the Leadership Conference constituency. I took on the job with great enthusiasm, noting as I did so that the AFL-CIO had probably committed a gaffe by holding the event on a Saturday. That, as I feared, aroused dismay and grumbling from some of the Jewish organizations. Lane Kirkland sought to mollify them—and did, I feel, to a considerable extent—by sending them a letter explaining that since "the vast majority of the participants will be working people, who will be paying their own fares and expenses to come to Washington, the loss of a day's pay would be an additional burden."

It was a plausible excuse, plausible enough so that Solidarity Day attracted a large Jewish contingent. Still, I couldn't help reflecting that the 1963 march took place on a Wednesday and was an enormous success, even though for thousands it meant going without a working day's compensation.

Once again, I had a desk and phone in the AFL-CIO headquarters on Sixteenth Street. I had to admit: it felt good to be back. And as I got under way, I was joined by an invaluable co-worker, Arnold Aronson, who offered his services free of charge.

Arnie had retired in 1976, five years before I did. He and his wife, Annette, an artist, chose to leave Rye, New York, and move down to Washington, where Arnold, at least, could be in the thick of things that mattered most to him. Naomi and I applauded their decision to relocate because we gained two great friends. And now I had the benefit of Arnold's advice as I undertook the non-labor mobilization for Solidarity Day.

Since Washington seems to judge these events by the numbers, Solidarity Day can be counted a success. At least 260,000 of us marched down Constitution Avenue, from the Ellipse outside the White House to the Mall below the Capitol. Nothing as memorable as Martin Luther King's speech was said. And we marched not at a time of hope, as we had in 1963, but in a bleak time, when labor's fortunes were in decline. But we all drew comfort from the large turnout, even though I do not believe it had much impact on Reagan or on our Capitol Hill opponents.

Reactivated, I was ready for more work after the signs and banners of the march were put away. I volunteered for assignments at the LCCR. But it was soon evident to me that they didn't have all that much need of my services over there. Changed circumstances had phased me out.

During my months of absence, while I was engaged in new legislative duties at the IUD, and afterward, during my involvement with Solidarity Day, Arnold pinch-hit as director of the Conference. He and my former executive assistant, a very capable black woman, Yvonne Price, ran the office. (Geraldine Boykin had left some time earlier for an administrative position with the American Federation of State, County, and Municipal Employees.) By the time I was ready to proffer my help for free, the Conference had engaged a new director.

My successor was Ralph G. Neas. The Conference could not have made a better choice. Ralph was, to my mind at least, an anomaly: a Republican, yet passionately committed to all the causes I had worked for. He was a dynamic young lawyer whom many of us in the labor and civil rights movement had come to know and respect while he was still engaged in his previous job. Before he came to the Conference, he had been chief legislative assistant to Senator Edward W. Brooke, Republican of Massachusetts, the Senate's first black member since Reconstruction. Ralph's new concerns were not so different from his old ones as he moved from Capitol Hill to the LCCR offices near Dupont Circle, in the basement of Reform Judaism's Religious Action Center. Under his exuberant direction, the Conference pursued its customary goals: the enactment and enforcement of civil rights and progressive social legislation. In the wake of legislative successes, the Conference expanded. Today it has a staff of eight persons. Its legislative work is supplemented by the research of an education fund. And it has a membership, as I write, of 180 national organizations.

I played an attenuating role in these developments. I did some lobbying for a while. And in 1990, when the LCCR organized a celebration of its fortieth anniversary, I wrote a brief comprehensive history of the coalition for inclusion in the program. For a short time I was on call whenever help was needed at a mailing and stuffing party. And I was of some use at first as a supplementary staff person when the LCCR staged its annual event, the Hubert H. Humphrey Civil Rights Award Dinner, a convocation that regularly brings more than five hundred supporters together and has become LCCR's principal fundraiser. But as the staff grew, the kind of routine services I could offer were no longer necessary.

Today I rarely visit the LCCR office. I attend executive committee meetings whenever one is called. Once a year a place is reserved for me on the dais at the annual awards dinner. And I have acquired a new title, an impressive one even if it is nonfunctional: honorary chairperson.

Do I mind this superannuation? No. These days my energies are devoted to other causes, in consonance, I believe, with basic tenets of the Leadership Conference. If I've been shelved, I like to think I have a pretty good shelf-life still.

Nowadays, whenever I'm asked to state my occupation—usually on a medical form—I put down "writer."

Measured by what I get into print, that may seem presumptuous. But I do spend a good part of every working day at my typewriter or word processor. I write, but publish less than I would like to. Yet isn't that most writers' fate?

Personal essays occupy much of my time, and it may be some evidence of their quality that the *Washington Post* has run several of them. The Historical

Society of Washington has included in its quarterly my reminiscences of life in such haunts as Trenton Terrace and Shepherd Park. And the editor has let me know she'd welcome more of my Washington recollections.

I am also one of a group of about ten writers whose members meet almost every Monday night to read their work aloud for critical analysis. The group has published three books of short stories and essays. I have work in two of them.

But writing is only one thing I do. I would not put down "neighborhood activist" when I am asked my trade, and yet I am still involved in neighborhood work. I continue to serve on the board of Neighbors, Inc. I have, on occasion, put on an "orange hat" and patrolled the avenue near the house, searching for evidence of drug-dealing activity. And I chair a "neighborhood watch," a group that snoops around the three or four blocks near the house for zoning violations and evidence of urban decay.

If I'm to tell all that I do these days, I must mention my newest preoccupations—preoccupations of a Jewish sort. What am I saying? How can this be new, when I was once an editor of the *Southern Jewish Outlook*?

Let's say, rather, that I've resumed activities that appeal to the Jewish side of my nature.

One involvement was, I think, a natural extension of my labor movement activities. I was still working for the IUD when I was invited to join a recently organized group, the Washington Area Friends of Histadrut—WAFOH. Histadrut is Israel's General Federation of Labor. Like our AFL-CIO, it is a federation of unions. But that resemblance does not begin to convey the extent of Histadrut's activities or its importance in its country's development. Histadrut came into existence in the early twenties, before Israel was a nation. From the outset, it was almost a de facto government: it ran banks and factories and schools; it organized Kupat Holim, Israel's health service.

WAFOH was formed by a group of local Jewish trade unionists who, after Israel's Yom Kippur War in 1973, came together to consider what they could do to help the beleaguered country. By the time I joined, support for Histadrut's schools had become WAFOH's main area of concentration. Money was raised for technical equipment—computers, for instance—and for scholarships. Since my inclination whenever I join a group is to become more than a dues-paying member, I was soon taking part in various WAFOH projects and even served as its president for several years.

Upon my retirement from the IUD, I took on assignments in WAFOH's ambitious "sister-school" program. We paired a vocational school in Tiberias with one in Washington, D.C. The Washington school—Burdick Career Development Center—had a largely black student body and faculty. It trained its students for careers in restaurant and hotel management and in kindergarten education.

WAFOH ran fund-raisers and split the proceeds between the two schools. Since my days were relatively open, I undertook a project that had a strong appeal for me: taking Burdick students on field trips. By unintentional coincidence, I found myself traveling down Memory Lane.

I gave the students guided tours of Capitol Hill, where I had once worked as a reporter and lobbyist, introducing them to such arcane and useful lobbying tools as the one phone on the House side from which you can make free outside calls.

Through my AFL-CIO connections, I got the Hotel and Restaurant Workers interested in taking my charges behind the scenes in some of D.C.'s major hostelries and even treating them to free lunches.

I arranged visits to the U.S. Supreme Court, which I had once covered for Fairchild, and took them on a trip to the D.C. courthouse where my old friend Spott Robinson was presiding as chief judge of the U.S. Court of Appeals. It was a thrilling moment—for me, anyway—when Spott invited our party into his chambers and gave us an eyewitness account of the legal battles that had helped end racial discrimination in many aspects of American public life.

By way of adding a cultural dimension to our trips I took the students to several of the capital's magnificent museums, paying particular attention to the new Museum of African Art. I even managed to get them into the Kennedy Center to watch a rehearsal of the Alvin Ailey Dance Theater.

I enjoyed our excursions—more, I think, than the students did. Participation in the field trips was optional, and except when we visited the hotels or the Kennedy Center, student turnout was meager. The faculty members, with only two exceptions—a woman homeroom teacher and a male instructor in computer technology—gave more lip-service than active support to our "sister school." So eventually WAFOH dropped the project. Shortly after that, in 1995, those of us who served on WAFOH's board concluded that the organization no longer served a useful purpose. So we phased it out.

My second connection—or reconnection—with Jewish experience, led me into an exploration of the rich realms of the Yiddish language. And here I feel I must provide a setting if I am to describe how that came about.

Shepherd Park, a longtime resident once told me, was "everyone's 'second home' neighborhood." By that she meant its handsome houses attracted members of an upwardly mobile middle class who felt they had outgrown more modest dwellings as their incomes improved. Surely that was the impulse that led Naomi and me to move there.

The neighborhood originated in the early 1920s as an enclave reserved for WASPs only, an exclusionary right that was written into almost every deed. In the late 1940s and early '50s, after the Supreme Court ruled these restrictive covenants unenforceable, Jews started moving into Shepherd Park. By 1960, the pastor of the area's largest Presbyterian church estimated (ruefully, no doubt) that the neighborhood was at least 80 percent Jewish.

Evidence of this development was unmistakable. The Jewish newcomers built three handsome synagogues in the area, two Orthodox and one Conservative.

It was the Conservative temple, Tifereth Israel—TI, as most of its congregants call it—that gained Naomi and me as members. It gained us after it had begun to lose members at a fairly unsettling rate.

As black families began moving into Shepherd Park in the late fifties and early sixties, even as the Presbyterian minister spoke, Jewish residents in growing numbers fled along with the other whites into the neighboring suburbs. Some of Tifereth Israel's old-timers, founding members among them, became alarmed. They advocated selling the synagogue to a black congregation and using the proceeds to reestablish TI in some racially exclusive section of Maryland.

Their proposal was defeated. And it was defeated largely because of Neighbors, Inc. NI had attracted a sizable number of young Jewish professionals who wanted to raise their families in a racially integrated environment. Many of them, to my surprise, were observant Jews. They joined Tifereth Israel and, in their high-spirited, aggressive style, took an active role in its operations. One of them became president; others joined the executive committee and soon aligned themselves with older members who were committed to keeping TI in the District. When the formal motion to sell and move came up, the votes of the Neighbors, Inc., newcomers were crucial in getting it rejected. They had the full support of TI's new rabbi, A. Nathan "Buddy" Abramowitz, who had accepted his pulpit in 1960.

Quite early in his residency, Abramowitz revealed his idealistic temperament by siding with the resistance in the fight to move, and by accepting a nomination to the board of Neighbors, Inc.

By the time Naomi and I moved into Shepherd Park, in 1966, the fight to sell TI was over. The temple's membership had momentarily stabilized, having shrunk from an initial roster of four hundred families to about three hundred. Some of the new synagogue leaders, who were also co-workers of ours in

Neighbors, approached Naomi and me and urged us to become members. We
were needed, they said, to keep TI from going under. Given our inclinations—
our almost reflexive impulse to side with the underdog—Naomi and I
promptly signed an application.

We joined just as the synagogue braced itself for a new altercation, one even
more brutal than the battle to stay in Shepherd Park. The same Neighbors,
Inc., activists who had led that fight now undertook a campaign to make fundamental changes in the synagogue's services. They proposed that women in
the congregation be given "equal honors" with men. For members of an older
generation, this was nothing less than heresy. It meant that women would no
longer have to remain passive in their seats throughout the services, a condition
seemingly imposed upon them by centuries of tradition. Instead, they would be
allowed the same religious rights that men enjoyed.

Under this radical proposal a woman would be permitted to mount the
steps to the bimah—the platform that lies across the front of our sanctuary and
gives access to the Ark. It would be a woman's newfound right to draw aside
the curtains of the Ark and reveal the Torah, to take the Torah from its cabinet, and to hold it cradled in her arms while the congregation saluted the Holy
Presence. And just like any male member of TI, a woman would be entitled to
uncover and untie the sacred scroll, spread it across the lectern, and daven—
lead the congregation in prayer.

For many veteran members of TI, women as well as men, this was too
much. Presented with what many considered a desecration, the congregation
practically split in two. For months, every membership meeting was riven by
argument. Naomi, daughter and granddaughter of Talmudic scholars, much
better versed in prayer and Hebrew than I, made a change in services her
cause. Many an evening when the congregation met in the social hall to debate
the issue, I sat and winced as my irrepressible mate jumped to her feet and argued, in joyful, militant spirit, for full equality.

To his credit, Buddy Abramowitz did not try to duck the issue. He sided
with the rebels, saying, in reasonable tones, that he found nothing in his re-
searches into Jewish law that would consign his women members to what I,
with my civil rights orientation, would choose to call "second-class citizenship."

The innovators won the vote.

To my surprise, our victory did not, as I had feared, cause another exodus of
the more conservative members. Instead, most of them took the basic reforma-
tion with good grace. Buddy Abramowitz deserves full credit for their acceptance. During that fevered time, when we struggled with the issue of "equal

honors," he made it his personal assignment to seek out the older, tradition-oriented congregants and reassure them—often soothingly in Yiddish—that allowing women full participation in temple rites would in no way affect our liturgy. Not a word of our services and prayers, he promised them, would change. Nor would the service be shortened. So most of these members were mollified. Few if any left.

It was another consolation to the hidebound among us that the new allocation of honors took place slowly. For many weeks our women members did no more than climb the steps to the bimah and pull the cords that opened and closed the curtains on the Ark. Then, one memorable Sabbath, a woman with a marvelous gift for davening took a significant part in prayer. She chanted the Haftorah portion, one of the selections from the Prophets, that is read—often by a Bar Mitzvah boy—at the conclusion of the main service.

When she came down to the aisles again, old Mr. Reamer, a founding member of TI and one of the most outspoken opponents of "full honors" for women, came over to congratulate her. Close to tears, he took her hand in both of his and murmured the traditional compliment, "Yasher Koakh! ["May you go from strength to strength!"] Beautiful. Beautiful."

Word of the new freedom our women congregants enjoyed soon got around. Throughout the Washington area's Jewish community, Tifereth Israel acquired a reputation for openness to innovation, and our membership grew as we began to attract progressive young Jewish couples into our fold.

I like to think I helped contribute to the community's view of us as a lively, innovative congregation by picking up on one of Buddy Abramowitz's bright ideas. This proposal aroused no controversy whatsoever, even though it had an air of novelty about it.

At an education committee meeting, which I had not attended, he expressed the view that a whole dimension of Jewish culture was missing from TI's activities in that we ignored Yiddish. To remedy the situation, he suggested that at least once a month TI ought to offer a Yiddish program. He even had a name for it: "Yiddish ahf Shabbes" ("Yiddish on the Sabbath").

When a committee member wondered who among us could conduct such a program, Buddy said, "Let's ask Marvin. Marvin knows a lot about Yiddish."

I didn't. Oh, it's true I grew up with the sound of Yiddish in my ears. My parents often spoke in Yiddish to each other. After our midday Sunday dinner, my father would often entertain my mother by reading aloud to her from the "Bintel Brif" ("Bundle of Letters")—the letters-to-the-editor column in his favorite Yiddish daily, *Der Forverts* (*Forward!*). These were intriguing, sometimes spicy appeals for help from immigrants seeking advice on how to handle problems of work and finance and the heart. (It is a tradition carried on today, I feel, by Ann Landers and her sister Abby, both Jews.)

In our butcher store, Yiddish was the language my parents and their customers used to converse and bargain. I had learned to read Yiddish a little back in those days, enough to stumble through a paragraph in *Der Forverts*. It was a feat that would prompt a customer to exclaim, in approbation, "Oy! Ah lebn oyf zayn keppele!" ("May long life crown his little head!")

I discovered an unexpected asset when I took up Yiddish again in later years. Since Yiddish is about 70 percent German, I came to it with useful recollections from my German literature studies in college. But since Yiddish is written in Hebrew characters, at the outset I read it haltingly.

My *Outlook* experiences were of little use. When Harry Bernstein and I were editing the magazine, we ran English translations of Yiddish literature—of Sholem Aleichem, for instance. It never occurred to me, though, to try to read such works in the original. I had had trouble enough in my futile struggle to master Hebrew.

Yet when the woman who chaired the TI Education Committee called and relayed Buddy's suggestion that I conduct a monthly Yiddish program, for some unfathomable reason I was taken with the idea and agreed to do it.

In hindsight, now, I can fathom a reason. At bottom, I believe, it was my inclination to be attracted by the challenge of a seemingly lost cause. Yiddish, at the time I enlisted among its champions, was considered by many Jews to be a dying tongue. Many still consider it so today. Hitler, among his other crimes, virtually destroyed the source of Yiddish culture by murdering at least 75 percent of the European Jews who spoke the language. Here in America, Yiddish was being done in by assimilation.

Many second-generation Jews, the American-born sons and daughters of the 2 million or so immigrants who came here around the beginning of the century, would have little to do with Yiddish. It was the greenhorn's badge. They wanted to rid themselves of it as they strived to become Americans.

Rejection by Jews aspiring for a place in the mainstream of whatever country they found themselves in was hardly a new phenomenon in the thousand-year history of the language. In the early nineteenth century, in the time of the *Haskalah,* the Enlightenment, when the ghettos were opened and Jews were allowed to involve themselves in the cultural life of Germany or anywhere in Russia and the rest of Europe, Yiddish was often regarded with contempt.

One of the earliest founders of Yiddish literature, Sholom Jacob Abramovitz (1836–1917), who wrote under the pen name of "Mendele the Itinerant

Bookseller," tells in a memoir the struggle he went through before deciding to write in Yiddish in order to reach a broad audience. Friends warned him, he said, that "I would cover my reputation with shame" by writing in Yiddish. But in the end, he said, "I conquered my empty vanity and I resolved: come what may, I will take pity on Yiddish the rejected daughter and write for my people."

As recently as 1978, when he was awarded the Nobel Prize for Literature, Isaac Bashevis Singer, one of the great Yiddish artists of all time, still felt he had to say something in defense of the language he wrote in. At the ceremony in Stockholm he declared: "The high honor bestowed on me by the Swedish Academy is also a recognition of the Yiddish language—a language of exile, without a land, without frontiers, not supported by any government . . . a language that was despised by both gentiles and Jews."

A few years earlier, Singer spoke at the University of Maryland, and I, a recent convert to the Yiddish cause, was in the audience. In the question period I asked, "Isn't Yiddish dying? Where are the new young Yiddish writers? Who comes after you?"

With great patience Singer answered, as he must have answered numerous times: "No. Yiddish is not dead. It is sick. And among us Jews, between being sick and being dead is a long, long way."

A response like that encouraged me to go on with the monthly series at TI. I had, as I say, only the skimpiest knowledge of Yiddish when I began. I was fortunate, however, to find among TI's congregants three or four members with strong Yiddish backgrounds who readily joined me in presentations. Naomi, with less Yiddish than I, became an eager participant. And by happy coincidence, we discovered in our next-door neighbor someone with talent enough to become one of our star performers.

This was Clara Fram, an elderly widow, who earned her living by tutoring young boys in preparation for their Bar Mitzvahs. Clara had spoken Yiddish since birth, and she had a true dramatic flair. As a Hebrew scholar, she tended to deprecate the *Mame-Loshn* (Mother Tongue), as Yiddish is known among Jews. Even so, she responded to our newfound enthusiasm. Although she belonged to one of the Orthodox congregations in the neighborhood, she came readily to ours at least one Saturday afternoon a month, to read and act in Yiddish, to the enjoyment of a faithful audience of about thirty or forty of our members.

From the start, I recognized my shortcomings well enough to realize I had to do something about them. I took a Yiddish course, with Naomi steadfastly beside me, at the Rockville Jewish Community Center. I continued a family tradition by becoming, like my father, a subscriber to *Der Forverts,* which by then had dropped from daily to weekly publication and had a dwindling subscription list of only a few thousand readers.

"Yiddish ahf Shabbes" was a feature at TI for about twelve years. Then we discontinued the series. But I have continued to be one of the language's passionate adherents. I spend many hours, many days, studying Yiddish, speaking it, writing about it and in support of it. I serve on the board of Yiddish of Greater Washington, a valiant little organization that originates and promotes Yiddish programs throughout the metropolitan Washington area. I am a member of the planning committee for the biennial Yiddish Culture Festival, a notable event in the life of the Washington Jewish community.

Yes, I am smitten. I love the full-throated sound of Yiddish, its sly, pungent humor. Singer speaks for me when he says, as he did in Stockholm, "In a figurative way, Yiddish is the wise and humble language of us all, the idiom of the frightened and hopeful humanity."

About two years after Naomi died, I remarried. It was what she would have wished for me.

On one of Naomi's last days, as we sat side by side in a hospital corridor, holding hands, waiting for an attendant to come and take her somewhere for another X-ray, she suddenly turned to me and asked, "Will you marry again?"

"What a question!"

"I want you to!" she exclaimed. "I *want* you to marry again! I don't want you to become a dried-out old bachelor!"

Bereft and lonely after she was gone, I reached back into my past and took as my wife someone I had first known thirty-five years earlier.

It was Betty Goren—Betty Schiff when I first met her, that tall, vivacious, black-haired woman who was married then to Moe Schiff, a co-founder of the Richmond Chapter of the American Veterans Committee.

After she and Moe broke up, Betty resumed her maiden name and moved back to Philadelphia—her hometown, as well as mine. Both Naomi and I were fond of Betty, and so over the years we always kept in touch with her, wherever she was living.

After a brief stint in Philadelphia as a bookkeeper, Betty, resourceful as ever, moved on to Manhattan, where she reentered college and acquired a graduate degree. Eventually she made a successful career for herself as a professor of early childhood education.

Her personal life was less successful. She got married again. Her husband was an Australian Jew, Wilfred Heiman, an economist who taught in a small college in Hartford, Connecticut. Betty found a place for herself on the faculty too, and realized an ardent dream of hers when she gave birth to a baby girl. Eventually, though, this second marriage ended in divorce.

Like many of our old friends, Betty was soon aware of Naomi's illness. And when Naomi died, Betty was among the first I called with the tragic news.

By then she had moved out to California to be near her daughter, Delisa, who had settled in San Francisco. There she operated a small art gallery and gift shop and had begun to establish herself as a collage artist.

Betty came east not long after Naomi's funeral, and so we met again. As a young man, I had been attracted to Betty. As a much older man, I rediscovered her attraction for me.

In January 1983, we had a small, joyful wedding at the house. The prospects for a happy marriage seemed auspicious. We had been co-workers in good causes, warm friends for over thirty years. I was certain we could share our lives as man and wife. Circumstances proved I was mistaken.

Our first few years were happy ones, or so they seemed to me. But then differences arose between us: a continent divided us; so, too, did our temperaments.

The geographic division is easier to understand. I was tied to the East Coast by years of association and work and by physical proximity to my three children and their families—to Annique in Boston, to Freya in Manhattan, to Bennett, a twenty-minute drive away in Rockville, Maryland. Betty had equally close connections to California. Her dearest friends were out there; she had created a demand for her services as a lecturer and counselor; most important of all, she was near Delisa.

We tried reciprocal visits, of several months at a time. But in Betty's condo, in The Pines of La Jolla, I yearned for Shepherd Park. And in the winter gloom of my old house, Betty longed for the unchanging sunlight of her patio.

The distance between Washington, D.C., and San Diego is a measurable one. Immeasurable was the distance between us when we sat opposite each other at the breakfast table. I believe she found me remote, evasive, preoccupied with my own affairs. I was put off by her sudden outbursts of temper, set off no doubt by my self-absorption.

Betty, a counselor of women in unhappy marriages, found counselors for us. But after many strenuous sessions with therapists, it was apparent that the one thing we shared was our disappointment in each other.

After eleven years of trying to make a go of it, we were forced to recognize how mismatched we were. And so we parted.

19

Here and Now

So once again I live alone.

And yet I'm not unhappy. For one thing, I love this house. A doctor had it custom-built in 1936. He was a major at Walter Reed Army Medical Center, the national institution two blocks south of here, hospital to generals and presidents. He was also, our next-door neighbor told us, a very short man and very vain. I consider the spacious living room, with its second-floor balcony and magnificent cathedral ceiling, testament to his high opinion of himself. And the showers in two of our three bathrooms are probable evidence of his physical size. The heads are set so low I can't get under them; when I turn one of these showers on, the jet of water hits my belly button.

The breakfast room is a pleasurable nook: in warm seasons and in good weather it is full of sun and offers vistas of my own and my neighbors' green and flower-flecked backyards. No. I'll never move. Even though I'm in my seventies and chafe at the housekeeping chores I must perform, it is my intention to stay here until I'm carried out.

The neighborhood is still racially integrated. It has "stabilized," to use the technical term current when Naomi and I took part in the founding of Neighbors, Inc. The national census figures confirm this: in 1980, Shepherd Park was 66 percent black; in 1990, 67 percent.

Neighbors, Inc., still exists, but after forty years it has lost considerable significance. Its dedication to a racially integrated society may strike many African Americans and even many white liberals as somewhat passé. "You have shown the way," Robert Kennedy declared when he spoke at NI's first art and book festival in 1963. Today, a lot of people would say we have *lost* our way; or that we are irrelevant.

The evidence of NI's diminished role is clear. NI no longer has an office or a paid staff. Membership has dropped from 1,400 to around 350. And our big events are usually social ones—an annual Valentine's Day cabaret or Spring Fling in the basement ballroom of Tifereth Israel synagogue; and an occasional Neighbors, Inc., open house in some hospitable member's home.

But NI is still engaged in dealing with the problems of our Northwest corner of Washington. And it has allies: at least five other neighborhood groups, including local chapters of the Citizens' Association, which dropped "whites only" from its membership clause a good many years ago. Our monthly newsletter, under the resourceful editorship of Jo Ann Scott, has become a valuable guide to community activities.

The informal coalition NI has formed with the other local groups continues to prove its worth. Our combined campaign against seven crack houses was so effective that the *Washington Post* devoted a page-one feature story to it in August 1996. And in that same year the Historical Society of Washington created a traveling exhibit of nine "Washington success stories" and heralded Neighbors, Inc., as one of them.

NI, I stubbornly insist, did much to create an atmosphere that makes black and white residents more tolerant of each other here in Shepherd Park. It is not uncommon in our area for neighbors of both races to share such family events as marriages and graduations and the ceremonies of births and deaths.

However, I cannot ignore our limitations. Shepherd Elementary School, which Anne and Bennett attended, is 95 percent black. If it doesn't reflect the area's racial mix (67 percent black), that's because many white and quite a few black parents choose to send their children to private schools rather than consign them to racially segregated institutions. And we are a staunchly well-to-do, middle-class neighborhood. We are always ready, I am sorry to say, to band together, no matter what our race, in firm and effective opposition whenever the ill or poor or wayward try to set up group homes among us.

We enjoy the luxury of spacious dwellings, custom-built of brick and stone, of seasoned woodframe and stucco; situated on broad sweeps of lawns, meticulously kept. And we have quiet, tree-lined streets to walk and drive on and lilacs and azaleas to savor in the springtime. Appropriately, we find ourselves in what Washingtonians call "the flower alphabet." Our cross streets are named, in alphabetical order, after trees and flowers. My house is on Geranium Street.

But we live in the city, after all. And we are aware of urban peril. At least half of the fifteen houses on my block have suffered break-ins. Locking the doors of our houses and cars is a reflexive habit with us. It is gross exaggeration to call Washington, D.C., the Murder Capital of the U.S.A. But I must admit that evidence of theft and criminal violence is not all that far from our doorsteps.

A block and a half from my house is one of the capital's major traffic arteries: Georgia Avenue. It is a broad thoroughfare—six lanes wide. Herds of cars and buses go surging by at almost all times of day or night, back and forth between the central city and suburban Maryland.

The commuters rarely stop. Why should they? Some of them are afraid to. And anyhow, there is little along the way to make you want to linger. In the old Works Projects Administration Guidebook, *Washington City and Capital,* an anonymous writer observed, "From Walter Reed Hospital on to the District Line and beyond to Silver Spring, Georgia Avenue ceases to hold any interest, being simply an area of businesses and occasional homes." The writer was describing the five or six blocks that constitute a boundary of Shepherd Park. And he wrote that in 1937. Georgia Avenue has not changed much since then.

Low banks of faded red and yellow brick buildings are ranged along both sides of the avenue—rows of small porch houses and little apartment houses, two or three stories high. Interspersed is an occasional commercial strip—a row of little retail businesses, usually in buildings two stories tall so that the merchants and their families can live above the stores.

Wherever they occur, these enclaves of private enterprise give Georgia Avenue a small-town Main Street look. And yet something unexpected or upsetting is too often happening to remind us that we are connected to the rest of Washington. One of my earliest recollections of the avenue is of a day shortly after Martin Luther King, Jr., was assassinated. We knew from radio and TV broadcasts that Georgia Avenue had been a riot corridor. Even so, I was unprepared for what I found the next morning when I left the house and strolled up our street of peaceful, tree-girt homes.

It must have been around 10 A.M. on a sunny Saturday when I arrived at the corner of Georgia and Geranium. Every shop was shut. And on both sides of the street, along the curbs as far as I could see in both directions, lines of soldiers in olive-drab battle dress and helmets stood at parade rest, their rifle butts on the pavement, their left arms behind their backs. The street was empty. Not a bus or passenger car went by. Every now and then a police car or an official-looking army vehicle came cruising past. I did not dare speak to anyone. I stood and stared, arrested by the grim tableau. Then I turned and, heavy-hearted, went on home.

By Monday morning things were back to normal. But Georgia Avenue, even at its normal temperature, isn't all that inviting, particularly these days. Few of its stores are meant to browse in. They are there for our convenience—auto supplies, upholsterers, laundromats, beauty parlors, dry cleaners, liquor. Little groceries, for those times you're out of milk or bread and have no inclination to drive over to a supermarket.

In the thirty years I've lived here the nature of the businesses on Georgia Avenue, as places to go to when you run short or need services, has remained virtually unchanged. The small-town aspect has even survived the appearance on the street of several national fast-food chain outlets—McDonald's, Kentucky Fried Chicken, Pizza Hut. But noticeable and substantial changes have occurred in the ethnic and racial composition of the independent businessmen. The Geranium Market, our corner grocery, was run by Jews when we arrived. After six or seven years a black couple took it over. Not long ago ownership passed to three Koreans.

A Korean couple now runs Rex Cleaners. The little Jewish bakery is gone, and in its place is a grocery by the name of Montego Bay. Phil's Italian Restaurant is gone, a good family-style eating-house that Naomi and I, in our broad-minded way, continued to go to with the kids even after we discovered the owner was a Reagan Republican. Today it's called Charlie's, and it's a bar and serves Jamaican food. Hard by Charlie's, another newcomer to the strip is a Chinese fast-food carryout. The corner opposite the Geranium Market has been pleasantly upgraded. Instead of a raucous all-night beer joint we now have El Tamarindo, a restaurant serving tasty Mexican and Salvadoran food.

The new storekeepers keep the same relentless, round-the-clock hours that their largely Jewish and Italian predecessors did. However, our stretch of avenue has suffered a qualitative change, one over which the honest businessmen have no control. We have always had intermingled among the little family stores a few neighborhood nuisances that Neighbors, Inc., and the other citizens groups fought against: two go-go dens, a massage parlor, and the all-night bar that spewed loud drunks and quarrels out onto.our quiet residential streets. Now, though, our nuisances have become uglier.

Drugs and crime and joblessness have moved slowly up Georgia Avenue into our neighborhood. Idle men sometimes loiter on the corner outside the Geranium Market, taking swigs out of bottles in brown paper bags and panhandling us when we wait at the bus stop. Another old restaurant location, two doors below Charlie's, became a nightclub, the Hummingbird. The police soon spotted it as a drug dealers' hangout, and the neighbors who live behind it were awakened not by shouts or screams or curses, but by gunshots.

Up Georgia Avenue, near the District line, a little jewelry store run by a Vietnamese family was robbed in broad daylight. The young man behind the counter took a bullet in the knee, and his aunt was pistol-whipped. Three doors down from the Geranium Market, a young Jewish couple, a rarity nowadays among store owners, bought the Mayfair Liquor Store. But after they were held up three times, and when the gunmen, the last time, forced them and a couple of customers to lie down on the floor and threatened to shoot them, they rolled down the metal guards over their glass front and moved away.

By now a number of my friends and at least two of my children wonder why I don't move, too. To say I love the house and Shepherd Park and enjoy the cultural resources of this city (where would I be without the Library of Congress?) may sound like insufficient reasons for staying on.

Yet if I'm staying, I suppose I should address the broader picture—the future of the nation's capital as a place to live and work. The future is not bright. The widespread impression of Washington as a dysfunctional metropolis is pretty accurate. Much of the blame for our problems is leveled against Marion Barry, four times our mayor in the twenty years from 1978 to 1998. I believe there is substantial basis for the charges against him. Barry never impressed me. I never voted for him, and the subsequent evidence of his arrogance and fiscal mismanagement has not surprised me. But I must say in his defense that you can't put all the blame on him.

Many of the problems we face here are inherent in the governmental structure our Founding Fathers inflicted on the District of Columbia. An often hostile Congress controls the District's budget and its fundamental operations. Congress can exert ultimate veto power on almost any program or project our local officials seek to undertake. And we rarely have recourse. That bitter epithet for the District, "The Last Colony," rings true to me. The odds, I fear, are heavily against the efforts to remake this city into a well-functioning municipality.

But when I am confronted with the suggestion that I ought to go, I consider the alternatives. Go? Where to? I've visited leisure villages, those immaculate, synthetic communities for the elderly. I've seen their cute, identical bungalows in neighborhoods whose history began a couple of hours ago. No thanks. I don't want to devote my final years to golf or bridge or folk dancing in the

project social hall. I'd rather stay here and work, as I do, in the citizen campaigns to revoke the Hummingbird's liquor license and to shut down the crack
houses in our section of Washington. And oh yes, to agitate—when the rare occasion presents itself—for genuine home rule.

Who will live here when I'm gone?

Neither Freya nor Bennett would dream of taking up residence in their old
home. Freya lives in a mid-town Manhattan apartment with her husband,
Richard, and two young sons, Mark and Joshua. Bennett and his wife, Ann,
and their daughter Allison and son Nathaniel, live just outside of Washington
in a suburban "townhouse" in Rockville, Maryland.

Bennett, who was born and raised in the District and got an education good
enough to win him acceptance at first-rank colleges and become an attorney
specializing in international trade, has nothing but contempt for D.C. and the
D.C. schools.

As far as he's concerned, his dad is daft. I believe Freya questions the useful-
ness of my commitment, too.

"I couldn't give a rat's ass for all you think you've done for integration," Bennett told me rudely once. Freya is less vituperative than he. But she remembers her days here with no pleasure. She, as the eldest, experienced the full
trauma of white flight that snatched more and more white schoolmates away
from her with each semester. When in the course of writing these recollections
I asked Freya if she would like to offer me a paragraph or two of reminiscence,
she simply couldn't bring herself to do it.

Only Anne sat down and tried to recall for me what living here meant and
means to her. She was always the most unconventional of our three children;
the one readiest to spring surprises on us. Even her profession was a surprise.
When time came in college to choose a career, Naomi, who was still living,
urged her daughters to become social workers. Social work, Naomi felt, would
offer them more varied and more lucrative job opportunities than her field,
psychology. Freya took her mother's advice. Today she directs the social work
department of a prominent Manhattan hospital. Anne chose, instead—will-
fully and bravely—to become a psychology major. With incredible persistence
she won the doctorate her mother was unable to achieve and today conducts a
private practice in Cambridge. About fifteen years ago, for reasons I have
never grasped, Anne legally changed her name. She calls herself "Annique."
The name has more than a passing resemblance to "unique," and I suspect the
likeness is not entirely a coincidence.

Annique wrote:

My experience growing up and attending schools in the Black community presented a collage of wonderful richness and challenge as well as a frightening, confusing scenario. In looking back, I think the most important information that I culled from the experience was to view prevailing ideas with skepticism. Because the information which was disseminated about the Black community did not fit my experience with that community, I had to think creatively about people, their experiences, the myths about them and how they cope. I learned this quite simply and starkly. The things that I was told about the Black community by some Whites, particularly those who fled from our neighborhood when Blacks moved in, were just not true. And I knew this because I *lived* in that community.

In sixth grade, when most White children were going to private schools or moving to the suburbs rather than attend Paul Junior High, a virtually all Black public school, no one said, "I'm not going because it's all Black." They told terrible stories about the school and the children who went there. I learned about hypocrisy in the most intimate of ways.

I also came to understand the incredible damage that racism wreaks, because I experienced it from the inside. I developed a strong identification with the Black community and I felt the pain and anguish of Black people as White people moved away from our neighborhood. I felt it as a personal rejection. I felt that there was something wrong with *me*.

I had to spend many years sorting out my identity, claiming myself as a Jew, claiming an identity outside the Black community and then reclaiming my identification with that community. I was spared what would have been an incredibly painful experience for me of feeling complicit with a mainstream society which has spurned a group of people for the flimsiest of reasons. I've had little guilt to expiate. I also think that some of my courage in life has come from living intimately in a community seen by others as "dangerous." What I found in that community was tremendous vitality, warmth and humor. I experienced many of the dynamics which get set up in a community under siege—sometimes cohesiveness, sometimes rage. My time in the Black community was my window into the soul of America.

Two more important experiences I had, which most Whites lack, were intimacy with the Blacks and the experience of having them in positions of power over me. The intimacy removed fears. Having them in

power over me gave me respect. Respect, lack of fear and intimacy are
crucial components lacking in most Black/White interactions. To me,
these qualities are intrinsic to my interactions with African Americans
because I came of age in that community and they gave me all they had
to offer—the best and the worst with no stinting because of my race or
religion.

I draw some solace from Annique's generally positive experience in the
community she was forced to live in because of her father's convictions. But I
will not say it balances the pain and anguish Freya and Bennett suffered because of their father's single-mindedness. Have they forgiven me? I hope so.
Freya calls at least once a week to see how I'm doing. And when on one occasion I expressed regret for some parental shortcoming he had pointed out to
me, Bennett laughed. "There are tons of dads worse than you," he said.

To live here, in a neighborhood still racially integrated, has become an article
of faith with me.

Alone, I have plenty of time to reflect upon some of my old obsessions, three
for instance: Socialism. Trade Unionism. Integration. Bad times have befallen
all of them. Yet I am not discouraged or disillusioned. Nor am I ready to dismiss these old causes as failed causes.

There is no Socialist Party of any consequence in America anymore. As a
political philosophy, it no longer holds for young truth-seekers the spellbinding
attraction it once held for many young idealists of my generation. But the Socialist notion that the federal government is responsible for the welfare of all its
citizens seems to me—in spite of disappointments and setbacks and stringent
"downsizing"—to have an unshakable grip on our legislative process; it is a
tenet both Democrats and Republicans feel they must subscribe to, even if their
allegiance is often mere lip service.

The labor movement may be in decline, but its purposes are not. I believe—
and how this dates me!—that Joe Hill is not dead. "What they forgot to kill,"
the old ballad about him reminds us, "went on to organize!"

Brave words, even empty ones perhaps, when measured against the precipi-
tous drop in union membership in my time. As recently as 1975, unions represented almost 30 percent of the nonagricultural working population; today as I
write they represent around 16 percent. Union membership has declined from
an all-time high of 22 million in 1975 to somewhere around 17 million. Almost
85 million workers remain unorganized.[1] And yet organized labor, under new

1. *New York Times*, February 17, 1997.

leadership, displayed an impressive militancy in the 1996 federal elections. And once again, the labor movement seems to be attracting into its ranks an appreciable number of young people in search of socially significant careers.

Thanks to at least a century of union effort, I believe the right to organize is firmly established and remains an abiding principle for working men and women.

Finally, I am not persuaded that the shining goal of a racially integrated society is unattainable, no matter how many times it is renounced.

Former Harvard law professor Derrick Bell speaks today for many blacks of his education and well-established middle-class background when he declares that he has given up on integration, convinced it is a fraud perpetrated by the white majority, and that "racism is an integral, permanent and indestructible component of this society."

Stephen Carter has written a book strongly attacking affirmative action, even though he himself benefited from a program that many of us are still convinced is an essential component of the effort to advance racial equality.

The Reverend Louis Farrakhan and his associates, if we can believe the poll-takers, have found receptive audiences among middle-class blacks and black college students for their vituperative and anti-Semitic attacks; if so, then perhaps the old ties between Jews and blacks, forged in decades of common struggle, are broken. Indeed, I sometimes wonder if even in the sixties those ties were as strong as they are often made out to be.

I can ignore Farrakhan and his ilk. Their wild assertions—Jews as "bloodsuckers," Jews as the predominant slave owners of the Old South—may not find much credence among thoughtful members of the black community. But Bell and Carter strike at my basic convictions. In my mind I argue with them all the time.

I believe I comprehend their exasperation and disenchantment. The great social convulsions of the sixties and the subsequent federal laws they inspired did much to open the mainstream of American society to minorities—to those with the talent and energy to enter it. The laws did much to advance the growth, income, and political power of a black middle class. Those laws, however, have done little to help the black underclass. Indeed, some blacks would say they have inflicted unanticipated injury on that class.

The black journalist Nathan McCall, on an Oprah Winfrey program, maintained that one result of the federal fair-housing laws has been to change the composition of urban black communities in a fundamental way. When metropolitan housing was rigidly segregated, he said, the poorest and worst-off blacks could always look down the street and see someone who was doing better—teachers, Pullman porters, postal workers, and the like. But once housing segregation was broken by law, those blacks who could afford to moved out of the ghettos. Today, if I understand McCall correctly, inner-city black kids have no role models, no one to instruct them by example, or offer them hope that they can escape a bleak fate through hard work and application to their studies. But even if that is so, would Nathan McCall have it otherwise? Would he prefer that fair housing and other basic civil rights laws had *not* been enacted?

Given the wretched lot of millions of African Americans today, it is not hard to see why some black leaders succumb to hopelessness. At a recent civil rights symposium marking the enactment of the Civil Rights Act of 1964, William Walker, executive director of the Martin Luther King, Jr., Center for Non-Violent Social Change in Atlanta exclaimed: "How can anyone say we're better off today? We're *worse* off today than we were thirty years ago."

He offered statistics to support that cry of pain: the disproportionate rate of death by violence for young blacks between the ages of fifteen and twenty-four, the 50 percent jobless rate for young black males, the soaring numbers of unwed mothers and victims of AIDS and crack.

It is easy to understand the provocation for Mr. Walker's outburst. But I think it was unworthy of him; particularly unworthy since it was, in a sense, a repudiation of Dr. King's legacy and example.

To dismiss the gains of the past thirty years as many blacks besides Mr. Walker do, and to proclaim as frauds the programs that have opened better lives for millions of African Americans, suggests to me a woeful readiness to let emotion distort perspective.

I cannot, by accident of skin, ever know what it is like to be black in America. And yet I shall not deny the evidence of my own experience. When the vicious, debasing racial segregation I remember is gone from Virginia, and when that state has made advances toward racial reconciliation incredible in my time of residency there, you cannot expect me to believe things are worse than they were thirty years ago.

And when I see blacks enjoying the restaurants and cultural resources of the District of Columbia, and when I see blacks in eminent positions in the federal government, you cannot convince me that our postwar desegregation campaign brought no improvement. And when I see blacks able to live where they please in our metropolitan area, protected by law when they encounter discrimination, I find it hard to accept the argument that the success of our efforts to equalize housing opportunities is of little consequence.

Granted, these gains seem modest when we measure them against the indignities and life-threatening dangers that are still endured by blacks and other minorities trapped in our inner cities. But the civil rights laws we have enacted and programs we have instituted were not intended to redress those wrongs. We must have new laws and new programs, and we can win them only if we revive the cooperative spirit of those old crusades. What must be done cannot be done by African Americans acting alone. The monstrous injustices that confront us still can be overcome only through the kind of concerted agitation by blacks *and* whites together that won the civil rights victories of the past three decades.

Frederick Douglass's counsel for dealing with the social evils of 1890 is still relevant today. "It is not a Negro problem," he said. "It is a great national problem."

Joe Rauh used to say of Clarence Mitchell that he was "an incorrigible optimist."

"He had to be," Joe said. "It was the only way he could survive."

I'm that kind of blinkered optimist, too. I grasp at straws. I look for reaffirmation of my unstylish beliefs in single instances:

I think of Clarence Mitchell, my comrade-in-arms in the days we worked together in the Leadership Conference on Civil Rights for the enactment of the basic federal civil rights laws of this century. In 1975, he took a leave of absence from the NAACP to become a member of the U.S. delegation to the United Nations, headed by Daniel Patrick Moynihan, a much reviled figure in the American black community. Clarence himself became an object of black opprobrium. He incensed legions of blacks at home by defending Moynihan for calling Uganda's president Idi Amin "a racist murderer" when Amin denounced Zionism and called for the extinction of Israel. Clarence won few black friends when on his own he spoke out against the infamous U.N. resolution that equated Zionism with racism. But Clarence justified my trust in him.

I think of one of the first blacks I met in my early days in Richmond, the geneticist Dr. Percy H. Baker, "Bunny" to his friends. I recall that in 1979 he was invited to a meeting here in Washington, convened by the Black Leadership Forum, to protest the forced resignation of Andrew Young as U.S. representative to the U.N. Contrary to American policy, Young had held unauthorized conferences with agents of the Palestine Liberation Organization (PLO). The D.C. protest meeting, Bunny's wife Helen told Naomi and me afterwards, soon took a nasty turn. Speaker after speaker accused the Jews of pressuring President Carter into firing Young (although Young himself had denied that Jews forced his resignation). So it went, Helen said, until Bunny gained the floor. "I would be disloyal to good friends of mine," he told the gathering, which sat in sullen silence as he spoke, "if I did not reply to some of the accusations I have heard here today." He then proceeded, in the quiet, elegant manner of the native-born Virginia gentleman he was, to upbraid those who had indulged, he felt, in blatant bigotry and anti-Semitism.

And when I recall the Los Angeles riots of April 1992 that followed the acquittal by an all-white jury of the four white policemen who mercilessly clubbed black motorist Rodney King, what remains with me is a kernel of consolation: that when black street toughs attacked and robbed and almost killed the white truck driver Reginald Denny, four African Americans came to his rescue and carried him off to the hospital and away from almost certain death.

I remember, with great affection, Bayard Rustin. Bon vivant. Raconteur. Noble, eloquent spirit. He is best remembered, and rightly so, for the major role he played in organizing the 1963 March on Washington. But in my own mind I celebrate him for a more modest accomplishment. On his own he demonstrated his commitment to a democratic society in the Middle East by establishing an organization he called the Black Americans to Support Israel Committee. BASIC. The acronym has a resonance for me beyond its literal meaning. It asserts, once more, the need for a fundamental connection between blacks and Jews.

And in the course of these meditations I consider the situation that confronts Annique. Undeterred by my warnings of the terrible social problems she would face, deaf to my expressed concern for the difficult life she would make for herself, she married Greg Williams, a young African American intellectual, born Catholic, who found his spiritual home in a Quaker meetinghouse. For fourteen years she shared his sometimes bitter lot—the slights and rejections he encountered because of race. Then their marriage ended. To what extent it was undone by racism, I cannot say and do not want to speculate. Today they live apart and share the parenting of two beautiful, spirited, endearing children, Isaac Martin and Marya Naomi. I worry for those two, and yet, if I'm not deluded, I think the society they're entering is readier than mine or their parents' to consider them in terms of personal worth.

It is March as I write, almost spring. I wander through the house, reflecting. From my louvered porch, as I look out at Geranium Street on a tranquil afternoon, I see a neighbor of mine, Ralph Blessing, that young, white father of the appropriate name. He is hard at work on the tree box, the curbside strip of lawn in front of the house of Annie Thomas, a recently widowed black neighbor of ours. He is digging a hole and planting a tree for her.

As I continue pondering answers to the critics of integration, I think of black Americans with whom I share allegiance to that much maligned ideal.

I believe I would have found an ally in Frederick Douglass. It is true that in the anti-slavery speech he presented on the Fourth of July, 1852, he declared, "What to the American slave is your Fourth of July? I answer: a day that reveals to him, more than all other days in the year, the gross injustice and cruelty to which he is the constant victim." Yet when it was proposed in the years before the Civil War, even by well-intentioned whites, that black slaves be encouraged to return to Africa, he came out resoundingly against the idea. In his newspaper, *North Star,* in November 1858, he wrote: "We deem it a settled point that the destiny of the colored man is bound up with that of white people in this country. . . . *We are here,* and here we are likely to be. To imagine that we shall ever be eradicated is absurd and ridiculous."

Today I am allied with the sociologist Shelby Steele as he comes to the realization that "being 'black' in no way spared me the necessity of being myself." And I am allied with the novelist Ralph Ellison, who, in response to his critics, said, "I'm not a separatist. The imagination is integrative. That's how you make the new—by putting something else with what you've got. And so I am unashamedly an American integrationist."

I make a rash prediction. We shall come full circle. Integration will emerge again as an American societal goal. Not, as its critics fear, an assimilation of the black experience and the experiences of other racial and ethnic groups until they disappear into some inchoate mass defined by our white Anglo-Saxon forebears, but a vibrant mingling of our distinct and different strands of history, our different ancestral connections.

I doubt that I shall live to see the day. And my children may not live to see the day. But, farther along, in my grandchildren's time, I do believe that day will come.

Index

Abernathy, Rev. Ralph, 187

Abramovitz, Sholom Jacob, 255–56

Abramowitz, Rabbi A. Nathan "Buddy," 252–55

Affirmative action, 2, 27, 173, 237, 267

AFL-CIO, 193, 201, 205, 215, 221, 234, 247–48. *See also* American Federation of Labor (AFL); Congress of Industrial Organizations (CIO)

Africa, 170, 172, 178, 269

African Americans: and segregation in Washington, D.C., 3, 72–73, 98–99, 111–12, 114; in army, 15–16, 60; and segregation generally, 15–18, 25–28; job discrimination against, 38, 71–72; as Republicans, 44, 95; voter registration of, 56, 66, 81–82; political campaigns of, 65–66, 81–83; police brutality against, 71, 270; voting behavior of, 72; as Democrats, 95; voting rights for, 95–96, 189, 232, 233, 237; and labor unions, 120; in Manor Park, 145–78; racism against, 173, 267, 270; and Kennedy, 203; stereotypes of, 204n1; Johnson's meeting with leaders, 220–21; and Jews, 267, 270. *See also* Civil rights; Integration; Segregation

Agriculture Department, 131, 169

Aleichem, Sholem, 47, 255

Alexandria, Va., 50, 51

Allott, Gordon, 223–24

Almond, J. Lindsay, 145, 150

Alvin Ailey Dance Theater, 251

Amalgamated Clothing Workers, 90n1, 217

American Civil Liberties Union, 189, 216

American Council for Judaism, 86

American Council of the Blind, 234

American Federation of Labor (AFL), 35, 36, 72, 193. *See also* AFL-CIO

American Federation of State, County, and Municipal Employees, 248

American Friends Service Committee, 157, 164, 172

American Jewish Committee, 183

American Jewish Congress, 183

American Legion, 34, 52, 88, 97–99

American Veterans Committee (AVC): Richmond chapter of, 33–34, 257; Communists in, 45, 67–68; members of, 47, 51–52, 60, 61, 62, 108, 168; and Bolte's visit to Richmond, 52–55; Caplan as chairman of, 52, 89; and Hill's political campaigns, 65; second national convention of, 67–70; size of, 67; and Truman civil rights report, 70, 71; in Washington, D.C., 117

Americans for Democratic Action (ADA), 67–69, 126, 168, 181–82, 189, 199

Amin, Idi, 269

Anderson, Marian, 73

Anderson, Sherwood, 78

Ansley, Mildred, 96–97

Anti-Communism: and integration, 35–36; and Southern Conference for Human Welfare, 46;